MIND OR BODY

MIND OR BODY

Distinguishing Psychological from Organic Disorders

ROBERT L. TAYLOR, M.D.

McGRAW-HILL BOOK COMPANY

New York St. Louis San Francisco
Auckland Bogotá Hamburg Johannesburg London Madrid
Mexico Montreal New Delhi Panama Paris São Paulo
Singapore Sydney Tokyo Toronto

Thomas H. Quinn, Michael Hennelly, and Karen Seriguchi were the editors of this book. Christine Aulicino was the designer. Paul Malchow supervised the production. It was set in Compano by Haddon Craftsmen, Inc.

Printed and bound by R. R. Donnelley and Sons, Inc.

Library of Congress Cataloging in Publication Data

Taylor, Robert L.
Mind or body.

Includes bibliographies and index.
1. Psychological manifestations of general diseases. 2. Mental illness—Diagnosis.
I. Title.
RC454.4.T38 616.89'075 81-19312
ISBN 0-07-062963-3 AACR2
1 2 3 4 5 6 7 8 9 DODO 8 9 8 7 6 5 4 3 2

ISBN 0-07-062963-3

To

Lester and Mary Lou Taylor

AND TO

Vanessa and Abbott

CONTENTS

PREFACE

THE PERSONAL encounters we have in our everyday lives can create striking changes in the way we think, feel, and act. But mental and emotional changes are not invariably related to external events; sometimes, they are the unrecognized product of underlying physical disease. In these instances, despite a "psychological" appearance, the symptoms reflect a breakdown in the body itself, a breakdown that is usually beyond the corrective influence of psychological therapies.

Distinguishing "organic masqueraders" from psychological problems is an ongoing challenge to all human service practitioners, and the stakes are considerable. Errors in this *critical assessment* lead to frustration, inappropriate therapy, and, in more tragic cases, residual disability and even death. Few moments are more distressing than to find that a client for whose symptoms one has constructed an elaborate psychological explanation is, in fact, suffering from a brain tumor, seizure disorder, or other organic condition.

This book is a practical guide to the clinical recognition of organic mental disorders. Illustrative case histories, drawn primarily from published accounts, are interwoven with general principles. Instead of an encyclopedic detailing of every medical disease known to cause psychiatric symptoms, the book provides the reader with a basic approach that if applied consistently reduces the chances of mistaking organic for psychological problems.

I want to express special thanks to Larry Koran who several years ago set me to seriously thinking about the subject of this book and who thoughtfully reviewed early draft chapters.

I am grateful to Barbara Arons and the staff of the inpatient psychiatric service at Santa Clara Valley Medical Center (San Jose, California) from whom I learned invaluable lessons with respect to distinguishing psychological problems from organic mental disorders.

For their published accounts of masquerading organic conditions I am also indebted to various authors—most of whom I have never met.

Finally, the book has been improved considerably in response to comments from Frank Benson, Pat Jordon, Bev Abbott, David Lam, Linda Olvera-Perales, Lenore Morrell, and Merna McMillan.

Robert L. Taylor, M.D.
Woodside, California

CHAPTER 1

THE PROBLEM BEFORE US

"Difficulties lie in our habits of thought rather than in the nature of things."

André Tardieu

PSYCHIATRIC SYMPTOMS are not always best explained psychologically. Mental and emotional changes commonly associated with various problems in living can also result from dysfunctions within the body itself. This creates a problem in critical assessment for the human service professional. Is the client depressed because of a job failure or loss of a lover; or is the depression a manifestation of hormonal imbalance, brain tumor, or epilepsy?

Certain organic disorders have an uncanny potential for producing symptoms easily misconstrued as nonmedical conditions. In a sense these disorders masquerade, and by doing so they often complicate the lives of clients as well as of professionals who struggle to detect their true nature. The need for critical assessment cannot be dismissed by the nonmedically trained professional as a "medical task." Individuals who come for help are often at a loss for words to describe what is bothering them. To further complicate matters, people do not automatically find their way to the most appropriate service facility or professional. Individuals experiencing problems in living may inappropriately seek the care of physicians, and persons with brain disease sometimes look for a cure in psychotherapy. Like it or not, all professionals engaged in providing human services are confronted with the problem of *critical assessment:* the task of clinically differentiating psychological reactions to problems in living from organic mental disorders.

Critical assessment cannot be avoided; it can be *bungled,* but it cannot be avoided. Clear distinctions between medical and nonmedical responsibility occur only on organizational charts and in the pages of job descriptions and textbooks. In the everyday world, the boundaries are blurred. Mastering the clinical skills and knowledge necessary to minimize the chances of misinterpreting organic mental disorders is the responsibility of all human service professionals. We owe this to ourselves as professionals and, more importantly, to our clients.

This does not imply that human service professionals should plunge into an intensive study of neurology. A familiarization with certain basic principles *is* necessary, principles that when applied clinically significantly reduce the likelihood of errors in critical assessment. True, there are those cases that despite the most sophisticated medical testing procedures remain undetected as organic masqueraders until it is too late for corrective intervention. This is regrettable but unavoidable given our present state of knowledge. In many other cases, however, alert observation and a working familiarity with certain tell-tale clues of organic disease can lead to clinical suspicion and, ultimately, a correct diagnosis. For the nonmedically trained professional, critical assessment does not require the diagnosis of specific organic diseases; this is the role of medical specialists. *The objective of critical assessment is appropriately to suspect organicity in cases that on the surface appear psychological, so that referral for further medical evaluation can be made.*

STORY OF TWO LANGUAGES

Throughout this book we shall contrast psychological reactions with organic mental disorders. At times the discussion may seem to portray them as entirely different from each other, suggesting that human problems are either organic or psychological in nature. Actually, human problems are neither organic nor psychological. It is the language we choose to explain a given problem that is "organic" or "psychological." If our knowledge of human behavior were complete, one all-encompassing language would suffice. As it is, various partial languages or systems are used to explain different problems. Among the disciplines primarily concerned with explaining human behavior, two languages are commonly used. For convenience we can call them Language I and Language II.

Language I is mechanistic and precise in character. It is utilized in the physical and biological sciences because of its capacity for communicating with considerable specificity. In contrast, Language II is much more subjective and metaphorical. It is widely utilized in the arts and social sciences due to its considerable potential for expressing motivation, meaning, and feeling.

Psychological reactions to problems in living are much more readily described in Language II than in Language I. Consequently, explanations for these reactions are characteristically framed as psychological hypotheses. The man is depressed because he did not get the position at work that he desired. The loss is a blow to his self-esteem that leads to a sense of despondency. This explanation suggests such nonbiological remedies as acquiring another job or exploring his self-image in psychotherapy.

Language II is not nearly as useful with respect to other kinds of problems, however. For example, it is quite inefficient in describing and understanding abdominal pain associated with appendicitis or peptic ulcer. In contrast, physiological explanations stated in Language I lead to effective treatments like surgical intervention or the use of histamine-blocking medication. This is not to say that Language II could not describe abdominal pain; it is just that the forthcoming solutions would not be as effective as those stemming from Language I. The opposite would be true with respect to other types of problems. An explanation of human grief stated in biochemical terms using Language I is rather limited in the insights and productive solutions that can be derived from them; not so with Language II.

This is all to say that any human problem can be explained in organic (Language I) or psychological (Language II) terms. *The choice of one language over the other should depend on which will provide the more useful basis for productive solutions.* This book is concerned with those symptoms that are generally more appropriately described in psychological terms but that on occasion require organic conceptualization. Errors in this aspect of clinical judgment set the stage for treating brain tumor as a personality disturbance, thyroid disease as anxiety, or a brain seizure as psychosis. It is for this reason I have labeled the clinical activity aimed at avoiding such mistakes *critical* assessment.

Failure to identify organic mental disorders causes unnecessary expense, inappropriate treatment, frustration of both client and clinician, and, in some cases, even death.

> A college senior began to experience a sensation of pressure in her head. Following graduation, she found herself becoming easily upset about minor problems arising in her new job as a school teacher. In a short time she had lost 15 pounds and had no appetite for food. She sought the help of a psychiatrist, who diagnosed her condition as schizophrenia.
>
> Subsequently, she underwent a complete medical evaluation after suffering fainting episodes, vomiting, and unexplained fever. No physical basis for these symptoms could be found.
>
> Although the symptoms gradually disappeared without treatment, the woman began to act peculiar. She was treated with electroshock therapy, but became increasingly delusional and was admitted to a psychiatric hospital for further observation. She was described as "silly," with alternating periods of euphoric excitement and withdrawn depression. On occasion she expressed concern over what she feared was her impending death. Her admitting psychiatric diagnosis was hebephrenic schizophrenia.[1]

Later, this diagnosis was questioned. On the basis of certain neurological findings, surgery was conducted and revealed a large frontal lobe brain tumor. Even though the tumor was not malignant, it could not be successfully removed due to its size. The patient died.

This failure at critical assessment resulted in death, a death that could have been avoided had the organic condition been suspected earlier.

ORGANIC MASQUERADERS: HOW COMMON ARE THEY?

Over the years several studies have been conducted to determine the frequency of organic masqueraders—cases of organic mental disorder that are initially mistaken for psychological reactions.

In a recent, well-designed research investigation, an evaluation for "medical disorders productive of psychiatric symptoms" was made on 658 *consecutive* psychiatric outpatients. All these individuals had sought help for psychiatric symptoms. The results showed that approximately one out of every two patients (46%) suffered from medical diseases that were contributing to their symptoms. Furthermore, in 9% of the cases the person was actually experiencing a specific organic disorder that fully accounted for the presenting problem. The researchers concluded: "Psychiatric symptoms are nonspecific and commonly occur in medical as well as psychiatric disease."[2]

Another, somewhat larger study conducted on 2,090 patients receiving outpatient psychiatric services showed an even higher incidence of medical problems manifesting as psychiatric symptoms: 18% of the patients were experiencing symptoms directly attributable to organic disease. The author of the report emphasized the importance of persistent vigilance by clinicians: "The examiner must continually entertain the question: What other than the obvious might be the cause of or a contributing factor to the presenting symptom."[3]

A review of "100 patients of lower socioeconomic class" admitted to a state hospital showed that 46% of the patients had medical illnesses that "directly caused or greatly exacerbated their symptoms." This determination was made on the basis of an extensive diagnostic evaluation, which included physical, psychiatric, and neurological examinations along with a 34-panel, automated blood analysis and complete blood count, urinalysis, EKG, and sleep-deprived EEG. An additional 34% were found to have previously unrecognized physical illnesses, which—although not causative of psychiatric symptoms—"would have routinely been treated by a general physician if its presence were known."[4]

Taking a reverse approach, researchers focused on 395 neurology patients, all of whom had well-documented organic diseases.[5] The question was asked: How many of these cases were initially thought to have been psychological reactions? The researchers conducted an extensive review of the medical records, which showed that 53 (13%) of these patients' symptoms had been originally diagnosed as psychological reactions. The erroneous psychiatric diagnoses included hysteria, schizophrenia, hypochondriasis, psychopathic personality, obsessive compulsive neurosis, anxiety, and somatization. On the average these mistaken clinical diagnoses had been maintained for 4 years. At one time or another over the course of their illnesses, all of these patients had received psychotherapy for symptoms that eventually were fully accounted for on a neurological basis.

Some startling findings were unearthed through an investigation of male sexual impotence—a symptom considered "psychological" in the vast majority of cases.[6] Roughly 75% of the 105 men studied were found to have such physical diseases as diabetes mellitus or specific sex-hormone imbalance, or to use drugs that were likely causes of their impotence. Of those 34 men with hormonal problems who received treatment, 33 had a return of sexual potency. Fourteen of these men had undergone psychotherapy unsuccessfully in an attempt to correct the problem. Undoubtedly, a frustrating experience!

Finally, one investigation followed 85 persons who under the examining eyes of physicians were presumed to have hysteria, a condition characterized by somatic complaints without demonstrable organic disease and thought to be the manifestation of psychological conflict.[7] These patients were followed for periods ranging from 7 to 11 years. During this time more than one-third proved to have organic diseases causing their initial complaints.

These selected studies will alert the reader to the fact that mistakes in critical assessment are by no means rare. From these studies one can conclude conservatively that in outpatient psychiatric settings roughly *10%* of persons seen for psychological symptoms, if adequately evaluated, will be found to suffer from a causative organic disease. These problems are often completely resolved by treatment of the organic disease. The figure of 10% for organic masqueraders increases as we move from outpatient to inpatient settings. This is particularly true of emergency treatment or crisis intervention units. Similarly, the 10% figure is increased if certain higher risk populations, such as the elderly, or diagnostic categories such as hysteria are targeted.

These findings do not minimize the fact that the majority of cases involving psychiatric symptoms are appropriately explained psychologically. They do indicate, however, that any human service professional actively engaged in seeing clients can expect to see a significant number of organic masqueraders over the course of a clinical career.

A KEY TO CRITICAL ASSESSMENT

A sound approach to critical assessment requires a sensitivity to the possibility of organic masquerade and a recognition that organic mental disorders and psychological reactions *are not primarily distinguishable* by the characteristics of the mental and emotional symptoms themselves.

It is the broader clinical context—the patient's history as well as other clinical observations—that provides the most reliable basis for critical assessment.

Consider the following case:

> A 42-year-old man—the proprietor of a small grocery store in a rural area—was brought in for treatment, somewhat unwillingly, by his wife and brother. They stated that he had become highly irresponsible, engaging in impulsive and extravagant business deals.
>
> Further history revealed that the man had been a respected member of his community for many years. Although described as having his particular faults, such as boasting and ostentatious spending of money from time to time, he had been a responsible husband-provider with no history of mental illness. Over the past year, however, his wife had noticed several striking changes. He had become extremely forgetful and prone to spells of unexplained anger. At other times his mood would shift abruptly to one of inappropriate euphoria. During these periods the man would indulge in wild spending sprees and became preoccupied with fantastic schemes. In recent months he had neglected his grocery store business; instead, he spent most of his time driving about the countryside looking for new places to build bigger stores.
>
> The man's wife was finally convinced of his need for professional help when he impulsively purchased an automobile and the following day solicited a large loan from the town banker at the conclusion of church services. He had gotten quite excited as he tried convincing the banker of the merits of his proposal, to the point of becoming incoherent.
>
> A clinical evaluation confirmed the man's inappropriate euphoria. He also showed a notable inability to perform simple mathematical calculations and to understand commonly used proverbs.[8]

The changes in this man could have been explained psychologically. Nothing in his presenting symptoms per se was incompatible with a psychological reaction. Here was a man in his mid-forties, possibly confronting the meaning of his life, unable to avoid the inevitability of aging and eventual death. Construing this man's problem as a mid-life crisis would not have been unreasonable. Irrational, manic behavior does occur as a reaction to stress. In this case, however, a psychological characterization was not the most appropriate explanation, as was suggested by the clinical findings of serious difficulty in performing simple calculations, particularly unexpected in a man who owned his own grocery store, and the absence of any previous history of manic behavior.

When this man was medically examined, his pupils were found to be abnormal; they were quite constricted and barely reactive to light. A blood test for syphilis was strongly positive, leading to a diagnosis of syphilitic brain disease. Additional history confirmed an untreated chancre sore during adolescence.

He was treated with high doses of intramuscular penicillin and after 6 weeks showed virtually complete recovery, a fortunate but somewhat unusual therapeutic response for advanced (tertiary) syphilis.

WE SEE WHAT WE LOOK FOR

Distinguishing between organic mental disorders and psychological reactions is complicated by our fixed patterns of perception—our mental set. While words and concepts help to organize the world around us, they powerfully influence what we perceive. For example, people who live most of their lives surrounded by snow learn to distinguish many different kinds, whereas a visitor may have difficulty discerning more than a single variety. This phenomenon is also at work as we evaluate human problems clinically. All of us develop favorite explanations for various kinds of behavior. We become attached to these concepts, sometimes to the extent that they adversely affect the clinical observations we make. Evidence that supports our predisposed position may be selectively recorded while contradictory findings are ignored, both forms of distortion occurring outside our conscious awareness. If this tendency becomes exaggerated, it is not long before we are viewing every new case as another instance of "repressed anger" or "primary narcissism" or "neurotransmitter imbalance." Although clinical hypotheses provide a valuable function by allowing us to organize our clinical observations, they also create blind spots.[9]

In G. K. Chesterton's *The Invisible Man,* one of the characters, sensing that murder is intended, sends four men to keep vigilance over the home of the intended victim.[10] Despite these precautions the murderer manages to enter the house unseen and carries out his homicidal plan. Each of the four men sent to guard the house denies seeing the murderer come and go At the conclusion of the story, it becomes clear that the killer had been "invisible" to these men because he was the *postman.* This story illustrates how the same mental set that helps conveniently to arrange our world of experience can also create blindness to an unanticipated finding.

The clinical setting in which we practice, our typical clientele, the consensus of viewpoint often adopted by clinicians who work together—all these factors fashion a context that can distort our clinical observations. This effect was dramatically illustrated in a now-famous research study involving eight "pseudo-patients" admitted to one of twelve different mental treatment facilities.[11] The eight individuals who volunteered for this study included a graduate student, a housewife, a painter, three psychologists, a psychiatrist, and a pediatrician, none of whom had any history of psychiatric problems. Individually, they presented themselves to treatment facilities with a standard complaint: "I have been hearing voices. They go empty, hollow, thud." Real names and occupations were not given; the pseudo-patients were otherwise completely truthful in reporting their lives. All of them were admitted for treatment, and all but one received an admitting diagnosis of schizophrenia.

The research protocol prohibited these individuals from giving fictitious complaints subsequent to their hospital admission; in fact, they were required to speak of their admitting problem as though it were a thing of the past. Despite these restrictions they were retained for periods ranging from 7 to 52 days, with an overall average of 19 days. During the course of these various hospitalizations, collectively they received a total of 2100 pills, which in most instances they managed to dispose of without detection. Upon discharge all were diagnosed as schizophrenia in remission.

The most telling feature of this study came out during follow-up interviews. Professional staff and patients were questioned with reference to suspicions they might have had about the real identities of the pseudo-patients. Whereas none of the professionals indicated any suspicion, several patients related how they had guessed that these were not actual patients. The designer of this study commented on his findings: "The hospital itself imposes a special environment in which the meanings of behavior can easily be misunderstood."[11]

Our clinical orientation must be "porous" enough to allow the registering of unexpected clues suggestive of masquerading organic disorders. Critical assessment requires that we sift through what is apparent in order to view the hidden. This clinical task requires, on one hand, more than a passive recording of every word that is spoken, every fact that is given, every behavior that is performed; and, on the other, a struggle against attending only to those items of information that conform to our favorite psychological explanations. Given that psychiatric symptoms are frequently best explained psychologically, we continually run the risk in human service work of being lulled into an insensitivity to organic mental disorders. The objective of critical assessment is to prevent this from happening.

BRIEF PREVIEW

In the following chapter we shall consider the design of the nervous system, with emphasis on the structural basis of common organic mental disorders.

Chapter 3 presents several clinical misconceptions that create blind spots for the clinician and predispose one to errors in critical assessment.

Chapters 4 and 5 discuss basic elements of critical assessment. The approach takes as a starting point the clinical recognition of brain syndrome and adds other clues frequently associated with organic mental disorders.

In Chapter 6 a practical method for integrating critical assessment into the clinical interview is outlined.

Three masqueraders are reviewed in Chapter 7, three kinds of organic disorders frequently misconstrued as psychological reactions: brain tumors, epilepsy, and endocrine disorders.

Chapter 8 considers organic mental disorders induced by drugs, including medications and alcohol. Chemical substances taken into the body are the number one cause of organic mental disorders.

The topic of somatization is taken up in Chapter 9 as a means of alerting the reader to findings that are inconsistent with a psychosomatic explanation of physical symptoms. The important recognition that physical symptoms can be manifestations of psychological conflicts can be loosely applied as a clinical hypothesis, sometimes with tragic results.

Chapter 10 focuses on critical assessment relative to children and to the elderly.

A brief summary of the major points of the book is provided in Chapter 11, as well as a self-test section containing ten cases for the reader's consideration.

Finally an annotated bibliography, containing 23 selected references relevant to critical assessment, appears at the end of the book.

CHAPTER 2

DESIGN OF THE NERVOUS SYSTEM

"Man seems to be a rickety poor sort of thing. . . . A machine that was as unreliable as he is would have no market."

Mark Twain

THE HUMAN NERVOUS SYSTEM is a complex communication network. Messages from the outside world are picked up by specialized sensory detectors in the form of light (vision), chemical reactions (taste, smell) and mechanical stimulation (touch, vibration, sound), and then transmitted over peripheral channels into a central processing area where incoming information is analyzed and interpreted with respect to other information, past and present. Outgoing messages are generated and, in turn, translated into various responses: muscle action, speech, emotional response, glandular activity, contemplation, and many others. Through this arrangement the nervous system is able to maintain contact with the outside world as well as with the other systems of the human body on which it is vitally dependent. This communication network enables the nervous system to plan and direct the essential human activities of protection, maintenance, growth, and creation.

Skill in critical assessment is enhanced by a working knowledge of the general design of the nervous system. This does not necessitate a detailed, technical understanding of neurophysiology or neuroanatomy, but a basic grasp of the common "breakpoints" or sources of potential problems with their characteristic manifestations. This chapter highlights those aspects of the nervous system that carry the greatest potential for going amiss in a manner that produces organic mental disorder.

THE BRAIN AND ITS HOUSING

Brain substance is not hard; it resembles a firm gelatin, which, with its extension, the spinal cord, requires protection from injury. A rigid, bony covering—the skull and spinal vertebrae—and three layers of coverings that separate the brain from its stonelike housing provide this protective function. In addition the brain and spinal cord are further insulated by a watery cerebrospinal fluid contained within the surrounding membranous layers.

This arrangement, however, is not invincible. While protecting against external trauma to the brain, this rigid casing, by being incapable of expansion, predisposes the brain to other problems. If fluid collects within the brain—as sometimes occurs with infection or bleeding—or if tumorous growth develops, there is no "give" in the brain's rigid covering. The result: inward encroachment on adjoining brain substance and neurological dysfunction, often with prominent psychiatric symptoms.

Another potential problem stems from the fluid in which the brain is suspended. This cerebrospinal fluid not only surrounds the brain and spinal cord, it also flows through the brain by way of a series of small canals known as ventricles. These passageways are relatively narrow and can be obstructed by the growth of tumor as well as other forms of encroachment from surrounding brain tissue. The destructive consequence is similar to the effect of damming a river: increased pressure builds behind the obstruction and cannot be dissipated outward because of the rigid housing. Instead, the brain substance is "pressured" into dysfunction or even death. In newborn infants—because the skull has not yet ossified into bone—blockage of one of the fluid channels in the brain produces an outward enlargement of the cartilaginous skull, resulting in the enormous head size seen in hydrocephalus. Eventually, however, the limits of accommodation are reached, and the rising intracranial pressure is transmitted inward, resulting in severe mental retardation.

The soft coverings (meninges) of the brain can become infected, a condition known as meningitis. Although typically manifested by stiff neck and headache, meningitis may also cause confusion, bizarre behavior, or even changes in personality. In certain cases the invading infectious agents—particularly viruses—attack the brain substance itself, resulting in an infection called encephalitis. In effect, billions of nerve cells are invaded by an outside force that begins to consume the brain's nutrients and interferes with its functioning. The resulting clinical picture ranges from subtle discomfort in the form of a headache or symptoms of a cold to gross aberrations in thinking, sensing, moving, and behaving. Sometimes behavioral changes are the most prominent manifestation.

MESSAGE TRANSMISSION

The fundamental unit of the human nervous system is the neuron. Approximately 10 billion of these microscopic cells are intricately woven into a vast communication network. Each neuron is composed of three elements: a cell body, an axon, and dendrites. Through a chemical language, messages are conveyed from one neuron to another.

Since neurons do not make actual physical contact, but instead are microscopically separated by spaces known as synapses, a means for transmitting the messages from one neuron to another is required. This is provided in the form of chemical vehicles called neurotransmitters.[1] These chemical messengers are released at the end of one neuron into the synaptic space. Through chemical diffusion, the substance reaches the other side and communicates its message, which can be either positive or negative (excitatory or inhibitory) to the adjacent neuron. The state of the nervous system is the ongoing summation of these positive and negative messages across billions of neurons. Out of this basic chemical process emerges human experience.

Several different chemical messengers convey similar messages to different parts of the brain. Some are highly concentrated in certain brain sites, while others are found throughout the nervous system. A common problem shared by these neurotransmitters, however, is that of saturation. Once a transmitter substance has been released from one neuron and has communicated its message to the receptor site on an adjacent neuron, the chemical messenger must be destroyed to free the communication system. In other words, the signal that has been given must be turned off before a new message can be sent. This message-erasing is also accomplished chemically. Communication within the nervous system is completely dependent on neurotransmitters, the chemicals that erase them, and the relative proportions of neurotransmitters to one another and to the erasing chemicals.

What is the clinical significance of this chemical brain language? Neurotransmitters and their erasers are similar to a variety of drugs, both medicinal and nonmedicinal. This fact sets the stage for the striking behavioral changes that drugs are capable of inducing. Drugs can send messages inappropriate to the situation as a result of chemical "jamming." Drugs, including medications, are increasingly the cause of mental disturbances, because the chemical nature of brain communication is easily distorted by other chemicals. We will consider this problem at some length in a later chapter on drug-induced organic mental disorders.

BRAIN SPECIALIZATION

Highly specialized areas are scattered throughout the brain. Certain of these areas coordinate brain activities which when disturbed create readily identifiable neurological problems. Other areas, however, do not directly affect movement or sensation; rather, they are essential to interpretation, integration, and subjective response. Deficits are manifested as behavioral changes or emotional aberrations rather than paralysis or loss of sensation. A general familiarity with these areas—how they function and sometimes go wrong—gives the clinician a greater sensitivity to organic brain disease masquerading as psychological reactions. The following brief descriptions focus on specialized areas which when disordered produce the greatest challenges for critical assessment.

Frontal Lobes

The frontal lobes are the most recently evolved part of the human brain. As the name implies, this area is located in the most anterior portion of the skull, bilaterally, and represents approximately 50% of the total surface area of the brain. Much of the frontal lobes is not involved with motor movement and sensory experience—thus its characterization as a relatively "silent area." It is quite possible for frontal lobe disease to progress for an extended period of time without the emergence of obvious neurological symptoms. The earliest signs are frequently changes in mood, behavior, and personality.[2]

This area plays a crucial role in abstract thinking and logical problem-solving; it underlies the ability to grasp the meaning of a symbol and to see the commonality shared by several objects. For example, a plum, an orange, and an apple may not be recognized as three different kinds of fruit; rather, the person with frontal disease may be locked into the *shape* they share: they are all round. It is easy to see how the capacity for applying common sense is often compromised in frontal lobe disease. In a clinical situation, the person may be unable to satisfactorily answer such simple hypothetical questions as, what should be done if the person happened to lose the key to the house or discovered an addressed, stamped letter lying on the street. Simple mathematical calculations may prove highly problematic.

Impulse control is another important frontal lobe activity. Here, among other places in the brain, is the basis for delaying gratification, for social behavior, and for considering the welfare and feelings of others. It is as though this part of the brain watches over primitive urges arising from other areas, ensuring that they are translated into more acceptable expression. When this role is compromised, personal hygiene practices often deteriorate and sexual and aggressive behavior emerges that conflicts with accepted social mores. Along with these socially unacceptable practices, there is sometimes also a pervasive childlike quality and a proclivity for silly puns and pranks.

Changes in impulse control affect motivation. Depending on the location of the disease, frontal lobe disorders can produce a loss of motivation to the point of apathy, or a shift toward hyperactive, impulsive, manic-like behavior. The apathetic, unmotivated person withdraws from normal activities and loses the capacity for pleasure and humor. This condition can be mistaken for psychological depression. On occasion, this frontal lobe deficit becomes so severe that the person is immobilized, unable to even initiate speech, a condition which can be mistaken for catatonic schizophrenia. The opposite clinical picture involving loss of impulse control can be falsely construed as manic-depressive disorder. The person appears driven, frenetic, unable to concentrate on one thing before being taken with something else. He may relate to others, even close friends, in a sociopathic manner without regard for their feelings or welfare.

Despite the relatively "silent" nature of the frontal lobes, certain changes in motor control and sensory experience can result from frontal disease particularly in advanced stages. Due to the connections between the frontal lobes and other parts of the brain, disturbances in walking characterized by a gradual decrease in the size of steps and a simultaneous deterioration in balance can be an early harbinger of frontal disease. Disturbances in bladder function, starting with a recurrent sense of urgency and progressing to complete loss of control, is also sometimes observed. *Urinary incontinence should never be ignored in persons with mental problems.*

Finally, as a result of the anatomical juxtaposition of the optic and olfactory nerves to the underside of the frontal lobes, disturbances in vision and diminution in the sense of smell may accompany progressive frontal disease long before other changes are apparent.

Temporal Lobes

The way we perceive the world as it is communicated to us by our senses is critically dependent on the temporal lobes. This bilateral, middle portion of the brain works to integrate the tremendous variety of sensations received by the brain. Thus, it is not surprising that temporal lobe dysfunction is frequently characterized by gross perceptual distortions.[3] Hallucinations, such as the smell of unpleasant odors, the sight of strange visual images, or even the sound of distant music may result. Distortions of an illusionary nature are experienced: everything suddenly appearing quite gigantic or minuscule in size; new surroundings abruptly seeming inexplicably familiar or well-known settings defying recognition. Such dramatic perceptual distortions can be mistaken as schizophrenic or hysterical.

On the dominant side of the brain (the left side in the vast majority of persons), a language area is located at the margin of the temporal and parietal lobes. This area is essential to the understanding and use of spoken and written language. When disordered, bizarre patterns of language emerge, patterns suggestive of the rambling, incoherent verbal productions seen in psychosis. They are the product of an organic deficit known as aphasia.

At their medial margins, the temporal lobes merge into the rest of the limbic system and have extensive connections with this ancient brain, which, as we shall discuss in a moment, is the seat of primitive emotions. Consequently, temporal lobe disorders are sometimes associated with the unprovoked release of powerful emotions, such as fear, rage, and sexual aggression.

Associative Cortical Areas

Coursing through the brain are associative areas essential to the recognition of objects and to the proper understanding of how to execute specific movements of the body. Disruptions in these associative areas produce a variety of bewildering deficits. Failure to grasp the significance of a stimulus in the absence of any disturbance in the sensory pathways themselves is called agnosia. The person so affected may be unable to recognize familiar objects through looking, hearing, or touching. To an outside observer, such bewildering deficits in recognition often appear hysterical in character. One rare form of agnosia leaves the person unaware of one side of the body, so that when the person is shown his own leg or arm, he will vehemently deny this fact.

Apraxia is the inability to carry out a desired action despite the absence of any difficulty with actual muscle movement. Although aware of the desired outcome, the person cannot translate this awareness into action. Common tasks like dressing oneself become perplexing if not impossible.

Difficulty reproducing simple geometric figures is another expression of apraxia. When the person attempts to copy triangles, squares, or rectangles, the angles and lines are distorted. This constructional deficit results from a disturbance in the appreciation for spatial relationships and provides the basis for two clinical screening tests later described as the Draw-a-Clock and Copy-a-Three-Dimensional-Figure Tests.

Limbic System

From an evolutionary perspective, the limbic system is a much older brain than the cerebral cortex. It is the center of activities on which individual and species survival depend.[4] One researcher has summarized these functions as the "four F's of the limbic system": feeding, fighting, fleeing, and the undertaking of mating activity.[5] Given the vital nature of these activities, it is not surprising that this area is the initiator of powerful and primitive emotions like rage and terror. These feelings, as well as sexual urges, have been experimentally elicited by electrical brain stimulation. Dramatic mood changes, sometimes of psychotic proportion and persisting for hours, have followed this form of surgical arousal.

In a famous research study on monkeys, two investigators demonstrated that the bilateral removal of portions of the limbic brain led to a bizarre constellation of behavioral alterations.[6] The animals became extremely docile; they no longer experienced a sense of fear, as demonstrated by their playing casually with snakes that had previously terrified them. In addition they engaged in frenetic and indiscriminate sexual behavior and were observed to compulsively repeat stereotypical oral movements—chewing, licking, sucking, and swallowing.

Such studies convincingly demonstrate the unusual behavior that can arise from the limbic system. It is little wonder that destructive or irritative diseases affecting this area of the brain are frequently mistaken for psychological reactions. One virus—herpes simplex—preferentially attacks the limbic brain when it invades the nervous system, resulting in an encephalitis characterized by striking emotional and behavioral changes. The following case history illustrates how easily this condition can be mistaken for a psychological reaction, particularly when stressful interpersonal events occur in association with the emergence of psychiatric symptoms.

A 30-year-old divorced woman was accompanied by her mother to the hospital. Unable to relate a coherent history, she was able to state: "I'm crazy—maybe I have been crazy all my life." She managed to express the feeling that she had been "living in a dream" and that things had seemed "unreal" for the past several weeks. The woman's mother described her as despondent and agitated, with a poor appetite and difficulty falling asleep. In a 2-week period she had lost 10 pounds and had become progressively more disorganized and confused.

Further history revealed that she had engaged in a serious love affair with her employer, whom she had fully expected to marry after he was free from his wife. Shortly before her symptoms appeared, the man had taken his wife and family on an expensive vacation to the "island paradise" where the patient had anticipated moving with him when they were married. "She acted like her dreams were shattered."

In the hospital the woman appeared frightened and upset. Many of her answers to questions, particularly those regarding where she was and the time of day, were flippant, circumstantial, or inappropriate. Her speech was incoherent at times, but no obvious hallucinations or instances of delusional thinking were observed. A neurological examination was normal, as were her vital signs, with the exception of a slightly elevated pulse rate of 104. All admission laboratory work was normal. The provisional diagnosis was acute schizophrenic episode, precipitated by the stress in her personal life. Despite treatment with tranquilizer medication, her condition worsened. She became mute and suffered obvious neurological deficits. A diagnosis of herpes simplex encephalitis was made on the basis of a striking rise in antibodies to the herpes virus.[7]

Autonomic Nervous System (ANS)

This part of the nervous system carries out automatic functions essential to body maintenance and response to stress. Arising deep within the brain, in an area known as the hypothalamus, the ANS divides into two divisions: the sympathetic and the parasympathetic. Generally, the parasympathetic division initiates physiological changes conducive to body maintenance and repair, producing a calming effect. The heart rate slows and the blood pressure diminishes. Blood is diverted from the muscles to the gastrointestinal tract as a means of promoting the absorption of nutrients. The pupils are constricted; the body temperature is slightly lowered; energy is conserved.

In contrast the sympathetic division readies the body for emergency: a stimulating effect. Heart rate increases and the blood pressure rises. Blood is selectively directed to the muscles in preparation for action. The pupils are dilated; body temperature rises, and sweating ensues. Energy is expended in preparation for action.

These two divisions of the ANS utilize different chemical communicators (neurotransmitters), which various drugs can enhance or block. ANS manifestations, easily observed by the alert clinician, often provide valuable clues to the presence of drugs. For example, widely dilated pupils result when a person has used a stimulant such as amphetamine. A similar finding is seen when the parasympathetic division is suppressed through the action of an anticholinergic drug.

Basal Ganglia

Located deep in the mid-brain, the basal ganglia are a complex of neurons crucial to smooth, coordinated movement. As with the ANS, the functions of the basal ganglia depend on a proper balance between two different neurotransmitter substances. When there is an excess of acetylcholine, a pervasive stiffness and rigidity of movement results; an excess of dopamine leads to twitching, jerking forms of movement. A balance between these two substances and the receptors they stimulate is essential to normal movements.

This same neurotransmitter balance is essential to functioning at higher levels of the brain, areas having to do with consciousness and other complex human behavior. Treatment with psychoactive medications favorably alters the disturbed ratio of these brain substances; but, whereas a proper balance may be restored at higher cortical levels, thereby ameliorating the symptoms of psychosis, simultaneously an imbalance may be precipitated within the basal ganglia, creating such disturbances of movement as parkinsonian symptoms—stiffness, muscle spasms and tremor—common side effects of many neuroleptic medications.

Several neurological disorders of movement characteristically include striking psychiatric symptoms that are sometimes the initial manifestation of what will eventually develop into a full-blown neurological disorder. Huntington's chorea is a severe degenerative neurological disease primarily affecting the basal ganglia in combination with the cerebral cortex. This condition is characterized by explosive, involuntary writhing with muscle jerks and twitches and declining mental ability. Antisocial behavior, poor impulse control, and frank psychosis is also frequently found in this genetic condition experienced by approximately 50% of the children of an affected parent. These psychological changes sometimes overshadow the abnormalities of movement and in certain cases are the initial manifestations, emerging sometimes years before other neurological deficits become apparent.

After a period of adolescent delinquency involving theft and drunkenness with actual assault on several occasions, a young man, age 22, experienced the gradual onset of an unexplained awkwardness in walking. In a short while he also began to have strange facial grimacing and jerky movements in his arms that had a threatening air about them.

At 24 he married. Later, his wife would relate how he was extremely demanding, particularly sexually, insisting on intercourse frequently at inconvenient times and in inappropriate situations. If denied, he would become vindictive, if not actually violent.

Three years after the marriage the man was forcefully committed to a criminal asylum after a vicious attack on his wife. By this time there was also an extensive history of brutality toward his children. His condition was diagnosed as psychopathic personality.

Further investigation, however, revealed that the patient's mother had died at age 42 of Huntington's chorea. A thorough neurological evaluation confirmed that the patient was suffering the same fate. He had severe unsteadiness in walking, and his arms and legs flung wildly about. His speech was slurred, and he had a serious memory deficit.

The man's condition relentlessly progressed until at the age of 32 he died of a complicating bout of bronchopneumonia.[8]

The reader should become sensitive to the connection between organic mental disorder and abnormalities of movement. The integrity of the basal ganglia and psychological well-being are closely tied.

THE SUPPORTING CAST

As highly evolved organisms far from our ancient beginnings, we are confronted with the complex task of maintaining an internal environment reminiscent of the primordial sea.[9] Slight variations in body temperature, oxygen availability, or salt concentration become life-threatening. Levels of various chemicals in the body must remain within a narrow range of values lest vital processes fail to function properly. Waste products created from life-sustaining energy consumption must be eliminated regularly if death secondary to internal pollution is to be avoided. Unlike simple life forms that carry out all life activities within a single cell, the human animal is highly specialized and requires the integrated performance of many different organ systems to conduct its routine, day-to-day business of living.

The brain directs this complicated array of life-support processes; but in the end, it is the adequate performance of each of the contributing organ systems on which continuing brain functioning and life itself depend. Like most bosses, the brain is dependent on the activities of its subordinates. When members of this supporting cast fail, problems in the brain as well as the rest of the nervous system are not far behind. The emergence of psychiatric symptoms in a person with known medical disease should always alert the clinician to the possibility of brain disturbance secondary to a failing body support system, adversely affected by chronic disease. Secondary brain problems are often more subtle in their presentations than are primary diseases of the nervous system; *secondary brain failure* is an important concept for the clinician to keep in mind.

Heart, Lungs, and Blood

The nervous system is vitally dependent on an uninterrupted supply of oxygen; sudden cessation of this resource produces coma in less than 60 seconds and death within a matter of 5–10 minutes. For oxygen to reach the nervous system, the lungs must remove it from the air and transport it into the circulatory system. In turn the heart must maintain a continuous stream of oxygen-laden blood by its systematic pumping action. Certain alterations in the rhythm of the heart can significantly compromise its pumping effectiveness and can rapidly lead to brain dysfunction with loss of consciousness and death unless the problem is immediately corrected. Other arrhythmias do not cause such drastic reductions in heart functioning; they are sometimes expressed as subtle behavioral changes or unusual subjective complaints. Consider the following case:

> A widowed woman, age 54, became extremely anxious and seemingly guilt-ridden following the death of her husband. At times her heart would seem to beat rapidly, and she would become tense and fearful. The woman's children attributed these changes to her having "taken up" with a former associate of her husband. She resisted this interpretation but eventually, with considerable reluctance, agreed to see a psychiatrist.

When the woman entered the physician's office, he noticed that she appeared unsteady on her feet and that her ankles were swollen. These observations, plus the patient's story of episodic palpitations associated with a pervasive sense of anxiety and dread, led to the diagnosis of paroxysmal atrial tachycardia, a heart condition characterized by sudden, explosive episodes of rapid heart action.

Further investigation confirmed this diagnosis and also established the precise cause: a defective heart valve (mitral stenosis). Corrective surgery was performed, and the woman subsequently had no further attacks of anxiety or guilt, despite the continuation of her new relationship.[10]

In addition to an adequate pumping action by the heart, the transporting of nutrient-rich blood to the brain requires that the "pipelines" be unobstructed. These arterial vessels running from the heart to the nervous system can become obstructed by clot formation, bleeding, or tumor encroachment. The resulting blockage of blood flow produces what is commonly known as a stroke. The specific disability emanating from a stroke depends on the precise location of the obstruction. If, for example, the interruption occurs in an artery supplying the motor cortex on the left side of the brain, the person will likely experience a weakness or complete paralysis of his arm or leg or both on the right side of the body. But not all strokes have such obvious physical consequences; in fact, there may be no physical disability or loss of sensation, but only mental or emotional changes.

Suddenly, without warning, a 61-year-old banker failed to go to work one morning. Despite his wife's puzzled questioning, he provided no explanation; furthermore, he never again returned to work or even so much as mentioned the bank where he had worked for years.

The man was examined by several physicians who could find "nothing wrong."

His wife, however, described a variety of other changes that emerged after her husband's sudden refusal to go to work. She said that much of his charm and wit seemed to fade away. Overnight, this once capable and dynamic man was transformed into an apathetic, dull, and sexless person. He no longer assumed responsibilities, made decisions, or did any reading. On one occasion his wife watched him walk into a wall, as though he did not see it. Another time he suddenly fell to the floor and lost consciousness. Although he quickly recovered, for a time he was unable to speak clearly. Increasingly, he became confused and began to experience considerable difficulty shaving and dressing himself.

Several years later another medical appraisal led to the diagnosis of stroke. It was felt that this man had suffered a series of small strokes that accounted for these striking changes in his personality and decline in his overall competence.[11]

Acute problems that lead to a complete deprivation of oxygen are easily recognized as organic emergencies, but the clinician is often faced with more subtle findings. A diversity of psychiatric symptoms may be observed, alone or in various combinations: irritability, confusion, apathy, depression, suspiciousness, and bizarre behavior. Through scarring that occurs at the interface between the lungs and capillaries, chronic lung disease can reduce the amount of oxygen diffusing into the bloodstream. Likewise, cancer of the lung can produce a similar problem. Cancer of the lung is the most common cancer in American males, and its incidence among women is rapidly rising. Before lung cancer is medically detectable, mental disorder sometimes results as an organic consequence of this malignant condition. In some cases this is a reflection of the early spread of the disease to the brain; in others, the mental manifestations stem from a compromise in vital lung function due to the invading tumor cells. The lungs become unable to breathe properly, creating a relative deprivation of oxygen for brain functioning. The clinical result may appear quite unlike that anticipated from lung disease.

The man was strong of body and mind, a bricklayer, 53 years of age. Although rarely given to drink, he was a heavy smoker, consuming 40 cigarettes a day. He was described by friends as full of nervous energy, restless, often worried over things, sometimes depressed, but never bad-tempered.

But over a 6-month period, he changed: his appetite failed and he slept poorly; he appeared vacant at times. Gradually, he became less outgoing, and when he was with others, he was frequently quarrelsome.

On a holiday, he suddenly became excited, burst out of his house and ran across the field in the early morning hours, shouting that he had to go to work. He was calmed down by his family, and there were no further occurrences for several months. He then began to act bizarre, making strange demands on his wife to meet him in distant places. When she would arrive, he might not be there, or, if he did appear, he might wander off suddenly without explanation.

He became religiously preoccupied and eventually violent. On one occasion he locked his wife and one of his children in a room with himself, then proceeded to read loudly from the Bible. Periodically, he called out to "Lord Jesus" and scribbled incoherencies on the walls of the room. When the police arrived, he threw the Bible on the fire, and then in front of the onlooking officers suddenly grabbed burning coals from the fireplace and rubbed them across his own face, sustaining burns about his forehead.

The man was taken to the local hospital and admitted to the mental ward, where he was diagnosed as having paranoid schizophrenia. He spontaneously improved enough to be discharged and returned to work. Shortly thereafter he suffered a severe vacant attack, and was readmitted to the hospital completely irrational, walking up and down, and talking nonsense.

Over the next 12 days his condition rapidly deteriorated and he died. At autopsy the cause for his paranoid schizophrenia was found: cancer of the lung.[12]

Stomach, Intestines, and the Endocrine System

The energy source for the nervous system is glucose; continuous availability is essential. Unlike other parts of the body, the nervous system cannot readily utilize other forms of caloric energy. Since it has no direct supply of glucose, the nervous system must depend on other organs of the body to secure its vital energy. After being ingested, the glucose must first be absorbed into the body. This occurs in the gastrointestinal tract and can be seriously impaired by diseases of this part of the body.

Because the nervous system is dependent on external sources of glucose, a storage reservoir is necessary to ensure a steady level of glucose even at times when glucose is not being ingested. The liver is an important warehouse in which glucose is stacked for future use in the form of glycogen, long chains of glucose. When blood glucose decreases, glycogen is broken down, diffused into the blood, and made available to the rest of the body, the nervous system taking a disproportionately large share. Conditions that impair the liver—like cirrhosis secondary to chronic alcohol consumption—predispose an individual to periods of low blood sugar (hypoglycemia), which can produce dramatic debilitating changes in brain functioning.

Another important factor in regulating blood sugar is insulin, a hormone manufactured in the pancreas. The pancreas is a small endocrine gland attached to the intestinal tract just below the stomach. It is essential to normal digestion because of its production of several digestive enzymes. Destructive processes such as inflammation, tumors, and trauma can seriously impair the ability of the pancreas to produce and secrete insulin; consequently, the blood sugar level may become quite erratic: too low at times, too high at others.

Diabetes mellitus is a deficiency disease resulting from failure of the pancreas to produce adequate amounts of insulin. In its most severe form, diabetes develops early in a person's life and requires daily injections of insulin, without which death occurs. Some individuals with this condition have considerable difficulty in achieving a stable level of blood sugar; consequently, despite taking regular insulin injections, they may experience tremendous swings in their blood sugar levels, swings that can produce dramatic behavioral changes. If the clinician observing such a person has no knowledge of the diabetic condition, these manifestations can be misconstrued as psychological reactions.

In less severe cases of diabetes, the most prominent manifestations can be emotional and mental changes. On the basis of an extensive investigation, one researcher has identified a significant incidence of diabetic problems in psychiatric clinic populations.[13] One account included in his report described a couple who seemed on the verge of divorce. They reported a pattern of almost nightly quarreling at bedtime. Marital therapy had been tried without any improvement in their rapidly deteriorating relationship. Eventually, a test that measures the body's reaction to a standard quantity of ingested sugar (5-hour Glucose Tolerance Test) was given. The results showed that approximately 3 hours after a meal both the husband and wife experienced a significant drop in blood sugar, presumably due to an excessive release of insulin from the pancreas. This after-dinner hypoglycemia was giving rise to the irritable, anxious, subjective feelings experienced by this quarreling couple. In Chapter 7 we will further explore the amazing gamut of psychiatric symptoms associated with hypoglycemia as well as other endocrine disorders, particularly those involving the thyroid gland.

Liver and Kidneys: The Body's Garbage Disposal System

As the human body consumes energy, it generates waste products that must be eliminated. Under normal conditions, this task is ably handled by special pollution-control systems within the body, of which the liver and kidneys are key elements. Although both of these organs have tremendous reserve potential, their limits can be reached, leading to the accumulation of waste products to toxic levels. In a polluted internal environment, the nervous system begins to fail. Initially, if the disease is slow in developing, there may be only subtle changes. The person becomes irritable, apathetic, or mildly confused. As the condition progresses, more serious alterations are likely to develop: a loss of the correct sense of time and place, failing memory for recent events, and the inability to solve simple problems. It is as though the pollutants deprive the brain of its essential nutrients without which it can no longer conduct routine tasks. In this situation, it is not unusual for a person to completely lose contact with reality. Such a psychotic episode is difficult to distinguish from such so-called functional psychoses as schizophrenia and manic-depressive disorder.

In this chapter we have reviewed some of the structural aspects of the nervous system that underlie the development of organic mental disorders. Now we are ready to consider certain clinical errors that hamper the proper distinguishing between psychological and organic disturbances.

CHAPTER 3

CLINICAL DECEPTIONS

"Even brute beasts and wandering birds do not fall into the same traps or nets twice."

St. Jerome

A RELATIVELY SMALL NUMBER of misleading clinical assumptions and practices account for a disproportionately large percentage of errors in critical assessment. In this chapter we will review these clinical traps under four categories.

- Mistaking symptoms for their causes
- Listening without fully considering
- Equating psychosis with schizophrenia
- Relying on a single information source

MISTAKING SYMPTOMS FOR THEIR CAUSES

Labeling has a certain magical quality about it. As clinicians we sometimes lull ourselves into a false sense of certainty by applying a familiar clinical term to a particular symptom. It is as though by naming the symptom, we understand it. One author has called this proclivity the "Rumpelstiltskin Complex," after the wonderful fairy tale about a lady who, in order to save herself from the power of an evil, ugly little man, must correctly guess his name, Rumpelstiltskin.[1] At one level this fairy tale describes our magical belief in the process of naming: name it, understand it, control it!

But such magic is not always productive; sometimes labeling leads us astray. This is particularly true of certain commonly used behavioral descriptors that have come incorrectly to imply psychological etiology—terms like anxious, depressed, paranoid, catatonic, and manic. Such clinical adjectives signify nothing with respect to specific causation. Both organic and psychological problems give rise to these reactions. As symptoms they cannot be trusted to differentiate organic mental disorders from psychological reactions. *Descriptive labeling does not provide causative understanding.*

Paranoia

Our psychosocial development depends on the resolution of a series of fundamental life crises. The degree of success with respect to each powerfully influences the handling of subsequent crises. According to this perspective, the first and most important of these centers on the question of trust versus mistrust.[2] Although this issue may be more favorably resolved by some than others, for all of us it remains somewhat of an open question throughout our lives; thus, it is not surprising that instances of irrational suspiciousness are experienced from time to time by a majority of people. Paranoia emerges in a variety of situations, often under conditions of increased stress or incomplete information, almost as though the question of basic trust is quick to reassert itself given the smallest opportunity. Being paranoid is characterized by a constellation of symptoms centering around unwarranted suspicion. While contradictory evidence is ignored, other findings, even the most insignificant, are selectively collected to prove the person's suspicions. Feelings associated with paranoia are predictably those of fear and anxiety, as well as an obsessive concern with the objects of suspicion.

As paranoia intensifies, a distinct belief frequently emerges that there is a plot afoot to harm the individual, which may, more rarely, become associated with a growing conviction in one's supernatural powers or cosmic importance. When paranoia reaches this stage, it becomes totally absorbing, capable of distorting all evidence and fashioning supportive proof out of the most irrelevant facts and observations. It reaches psychotic intensity. The severely paranoid person is extremely cautious, reluctant to give information, often speaking in guarded fashion so as not to be overheard. Despite such precautions, the feeling of being "closed in on" periodically surfaces; panic may erupt and on occasion lead to acts of violence in presumed self-defense.

Clinicians sometimes make the mistake of equating severe paranoia with schizophrenia, but paranoia also occurs as a manifestation of numerous organic disorders.

A young soldier, 26 years of age, abruptly became apprehensive and suspicious. He was obsessed with the idea that "the Nationals" were trying to kill him.

The soldier appeared extremely anxious. He was disoriented and exhibited a striking paranoid fear that fluctuated markedly over short periods. At its height, this fear was clearly delusional. The soldier's thinking was disjointed. His body coordination was impaired and his eyes were notably reddened.

Eventually, he was able to relate that, just prior to the onset of this frightening experience, he had smoked marijuana. Over the next few hours, the soldier's condition rapidly improved; 2 days later he returned to duty. There was no recurrence of paranoid behavior during a 3-month follow-up period.[3]

The reader should note that the clinical clues to the toxic, organic nature of the problem came not from observing the paranoid behavior, but rather from taking note of its sudden onset, body incoordination, and tell-tale reddening of the eyes. Nothing about the paranoia itself suggested the presence of an organic problem.

The officials at a local airport anxiously requested the state police when a man in his late forties, a married schoolteacher, created a noisy scene. He became combative and began to scream about "doctors trying to kill him" by giving him poison pills that would lead to "death by dehydration." The man frantically claimed it was important he make contact with the CIA and the Food and Drug Administration to prevent this crime against himself.

Following his admission to the psychiatric service of a general hospital, he was confused, unable to give the correct month or day, and paranoid to the point of being delusional.

A routine laboratory study showed that he was suffering from a severe water and chemical imbalance, a condition referred to as water intoxication. With adequate restriction of fluids, the confusional state promptly cleared; and, although the psychotic behavior persisted for a brief time, it completely resolved after treatment with an antipsychotic medication.[4]

Numerous cases of water intoxication leading to dramatic behavioral changes have been reported. In some instances this strange condition has been traced to the inappropriate production of a hormone in the body known as ADH (antidiuretic hormone). An excess of this hormone prevents the appropriate excretion of water and leads to a flooding of the body. Other cases result from the overconsumption of water, usually in persons who are already psychotic.

Paranoid reactions are frequently encountered by the clinician. Their causative basis can be organic as well as psychological; in fact, virtually any significant physical disease can be associated with paranoid symptomatology.

Depression

This disturbance in mood is by far the most prevalent condition for which mental health services are sought. At one time or another approximately 50% of North Americans and Western Europeans experience a significant depression.[5] The term, however, is applied quite loosely to disturbances ranging from "the blues" to suicidal and psychotic depression. It describes a wide spectrum of behavior that can result from different causes.

Despite the highly popular clinical notion that depression is the product of failure to express anger or resentment, usually in relation to some form of personal loss, this is not the only causative explanation. Certain organic problems are heralded by depressive changes prior to the emergence of any physical symptoms. This is often true of internal cancers, certain endocrine diseases, degenerative diseases, and subclinical infections. Increasingly, medications are a cause of depression in patients being treated for other problems.

Clinicians should be careful in searching for personal loss as an explanation for depression. Few persons go for extended periods without experiencing some form of personal loss—economic, occupational, romantic, symbolic. Such losses are not invariably the causative factor. Furthermore, individuals who become depressed as the result of an organic illness may also have a notable personal loss that is of no etiological consequence. This can become a misleading clinical finding in organic masqueraders presenting as psychological reactive depression.

Regardless of underlying cause, the defining characteristics of depression are a diminished sense of self-worth with a decrease in productive motivation and the capacity for pleasure. Changes in appetite and sleeping habits may occur. For some, food no longer seems desirable and weight loss ensues; for others, depression leads to voracious eating with weight gain. Similarly, a person may find it difficult to fall asleep; and, even when sleep finally comes, it may not last for long. The opposite pattern is also experienced: excessive sleep that seems to provide an escape from the painful depressive mood.

Usually, depression is accompanied by a decrease in level of activity and slowed movement. The person cannot seem to get going; a sense of tiredness pervades his life. In its extreme form, this psychomotor retardation immobilizes the person, leading to an inability for self-care. In other cases of depression agitation is seen rather than passive apathy. The depressed individual appears anxious, irritable, and is easily provoked to outbursts. Even in these cases of agitated depression, however, the more characteristic manifestations of depression periodically emerge.

Severe depression is a frequent precursor of serious thoughts of suicide and delusional thinking consistent with this mood: "rotting insides," "possession by the devil," or "personal guilt for all that is evil."

The clinical identification of depression does not resolve the question of etiology. As the following cases illustrate, the overall context of the depression, including other symptoms, must be considered for causative clues.

A 29-year-old woman, a college graduate, was seen at a psychiatric clinic for what she described as depression. For several months she had felt "down" to the extent of considering that living might be an unnecessary burden. She would awaken early in the morning, unable to fall back to sleep, and then would feel lethargic throughout the day. Even more disturbing to her, she experienced a growing resentment and alienation from her children and husband.

Depression ran in the woman's family; her father had committed suicide and her mother had suffered from an involutional depressive psychosis. The woman herself had been significantly depressed on two previous occasions: once shortly after starting on birth control pills and again immediately following the birth of her second child.

Given this history of hormonal-connected depressive episodes, she was advised to stop taking the "pill," and, simultaneously, was enrolled in outpatient psychotherapy as treatment for her current symptoms. Over the next several weeks, she showed considerable improvement as her depression lifted and her relationship with her family became more satisfying.

Six months later the woman discussed the question of contraception with her psychiatrist, who encouraged her to return to her gynecologist for an alternative birth control method. Instead, as a means of economizing, she resumed taking the birth control pills that she still had at home. Within one week she became severely agitated and depressed and was admitted to a state mental hospital for increasingly bizarre behavior. A schizoaffective reaction was diagnosed. Shortly after her release, she suffered yet another episode of severe depression complicated by hallucinations and strong impulses to kill her children. This occurred when she was started on an alternative birth control pill!

On cessation of the pill, the symptoms promptly disappeared. The woman was thoroughly instructed about the relationship between her mental episodes and the taking of oral contraceptives. At a follow-up visit, she reported no recurrent symptoms.[6]

Hormonal-related depression is not an uncommon condition, particularly in women who have a family history for affective disturbances (manic or depressive). As in the preceding case, this form of depression can be precipitated by the use of birth control pills, but also may be brought on by pregnancy or its termination. In some instances depression occurs monthly in association with a woman's menstrual period. Presumably, this cyclical pattern is related to the prominent shift in hormonal levels at these times.

Although people who experience psychological depression often exaggerate minor somatic aches and pains, persistent physical complaints should never be ignored. They should always raise the possibility of an underlying, organic disorder.

A 60-year-old lawyer became obviously depressed. Upon falling asleep at night, he would promptly awaken. His energy and initiative steadily declined. He had an extensive past history of depressive episodes; some had been rather severe, requiring electroconvulsive therapy.

With the advent of his current depression, he also experienced an unexplained bout of diarrhea, which persisted without notable improvement. It was this troublesome physical symptom which brought the man to a physician who, upon reviewing the case, concluded that the diarrhea was simply a manifestation of a functional agitated depression. He was referred for treatment to a consulting psychiatrist who felt that further investigations were indicated. The results showed the patient suffered from ulcerative colitis. He responded favorably to steroid medications with a simultaneous resolution of the depression.[7]

Mania

In contrast to the lowered self-esteem, absence of pleasure, and slowed-down feeling associated with depression, the person exhibiting manic behavior is euphoric—unreasonably so—with a falsely inflated self-image and a tendency to be flighty and overactive. The person becomes obsessed with his own importance; fun and pleasure are pursued at any cost; and, sometimes, delusional beliefs of omnipotence and grandiosity emerge as the condition builds.

The euphoric and heightened activity does not result in improved performance; occupational and family commitments are usually severely curtailed during these episodes. The sense of responsibility is lost. Characteristically, the manic person sleeps rarely and his appetite is diminished. If the episode continues for a prolonged period, significant weight loss can result.

Encountering someone with mania is an experience. It is difficult to get a word into the conversation, and keeping up with the one-sided conversation is next to impossible as the person flits from one topic to another with only a tenuous thread of coherence. He is easily distracted by surrounding events, and at the slightest hint of being ignored or resisted, the nonstop joking and laughter quickly converts into irritation and even outright belligerence. But the manic can be quite entertaining; the humor is infectious, and the interviewer may find himself laughing despite considerable effort at maintaining composure.

Although manic episodes are associated with the condition

known as manic-depressive disorder—a cyclical mood disorder that tends to run in families—this is not invariably the cause. The clinical literature is full of examples of mania resulting from a variety of organic disorders.

> A 69-year-old, retired drawbridge operator without any similar history abruptly developed an inappropriate, sustained euphoria that progressed over a 5-week period into flagrant manic behavior. Having become intolerable to his exhausted family, he was admitted to a hospital.
>
> When initially interviewed, the man aggressively accused his physician of plotting against him; he demanded to call his lawyer so that he might bring suit against the hospital. The family described an exaggerated self-confidence, hyperactive behavior, and diminished natural inhibitions, all appearing simultaneously over the past 5 weeks.
>
> An important piece of additional history strongly suggested this case of manic behavior was not a reflection of problems in living. For 8 years the patient had suffered from Parkinson's disease. Recently, he had started on a new medication, L-Dopa, without any notable improvement, until a dosage of 3 grams had been reached. At that point, 5 weeks prior to the man's hospitalization, his Parkinsonian tremor and rigidity suddenly disappeared and a profound shift in mood occurred.
>
> The patient was suffering from a drug-induced manic psychosis, secondary to the medication L-Dopa. With an adjustment in dosage, the symptoms of mania subsided, and the man was able to complete an enjoyable ocean cruise with his wife.[8]

L-Dopa has proven to be an effective agent in the treatment of Parkinson's disease. It is not, however, without side effects, manic behavior being a commonly encountered side-reaction.

Anxiety

Anxiety is a disquieting, uncomfortable emotional state: a pervasive sense of being threatened or of losing control. It may erupt episodically in the form of attacks or be sustained over long periods of time. Unlike fear, anxiety often stems from no clearly identifiable threat. The anxious person may become preoccupied with this threatening feeling, thereby producing further anxiety and a vicious cycle that leads to full-scale panic. Even in its milder versions, anxiety usually includes a foreboding sense of the future; here, anxiety and depression fuse as emotional experiences and are often difficult to distinguish clinically.

Physical expressions of anxiety are usually prominent: tremulousness, a worried look, increased perspiration, and muscle tension, particularly in the muscles of the face, neck, and jaw. The muscle tension of anxiety may extend along the muscles of the spine, resulting in a slightly rigid appearance. With this increased muscle tension, it is not surprising that anxiety is commonly associated with increased body aches and pains, particularly headache and back discomfort.

Anxiety is manifested behaviorally as increased restlessness. The person may fidget or pace. Tension-binding habits like smoking, drinking, and other drug use increase.

Organic conditions that stimulate the sympathetic nervous system can easily be mistaken for anxiety neurosis. Long before they are diagnosed, physical diseases are sometimes experienced by the person as a subjective sense of anxiety, a sense of impending doom. As discussed in Chapter 7, hyperthyroidism and hypoglycemia typically produce the outward appearance of anxiety.

In the following case prominent anxiety was incorrectly interpreted as a psychiatric problem.

An unmarried piano teacher, 39 years of age, was chronically nervous. Fifteen years earlier he had been accused by one of his pupils of sexual advances. The accusation led to a court case. The teacher was eventually acquitted, but the experience was such an emotional trauma that he was left extremely nervous.

Ten years later the man became noticeably more anxious and experienced daily bouts of diarrhea. He was evaluated by two physicians, both of whom concluded that he was obviously still nervous from his courtroom experience. During one of these examinations he was found to have an elevated blood pressure, but this finding was ignored.

The symptoms persisted, and finally—quite reluctantly—the man agreed to the requests of his family that he see a third physician. By this time, he had lost 25 pounds and had become virtually homebound. He was noted to be tremulous, apprehensive, and thin with clammy palms. A full-scale medical workup for persistent diarrhea was ordered; x-ray studies of the abdomen and kidneys revealed an abnormal mass over the right kidney. At surgery an adrenal tumor was removed and diagnosed as a pheochromocytoma.

Ten months later, the man had regained his normal weight. He had become outgoing again and his general well-being was vastly improved.[9]

Pheochromocytoma is an unusual tumor of that portion of the adrenal gland that secretes catecholamines, the body's natural stimulants. The tumor secretes excessive amounts of catecholamines, sometimes episodically but in other instances continuously, as was true in the previous case. As the hormones from this tumor course through the body, the individual feels a sense of anxiety. This subjective sensation is often accompanied by an elevated pulse rate, hypertension, excessive perspiration, and severe headache. Since this tumor is not usually malignant, surgical removal is curative.

Coffee and tea are extensively consumed by the American public. Both of these popular drinks contain caffeine, which acts as a stimulant. Individual sensitivity to caffeine is highly variable, but when a person has exceeded his particular limit, nervousness, irritability, agitation, tremulousness, headaches, and palpitations are apt to appear.

Caffeine is not restricted to coffee and tea; it is an ingredient in cola drinks, chocolate, and numerous over-the-counter preparations.

Unknowingly, persons can become hooked on caffeine; then, when consumption is stopped or sometimes simply reduced, feelings of apathy and depression develop and drive the person to resume using caffeine.

An ambitious, hard-driving lieutenant colonel in the Army was referred from a military medical clinic to an outpatient psychiatric service for the evaluation of chronic anxiety.

As a daily occurrence for almost 2 years, the man had experienced symptoms of dizziness, tremulousness, apprehension, and difficulty in falling and remaining asleep. Scores obtained on the Hamilton Anxiety Scale were significantly elevated, and complete medical workups on three occasions had been reported as normal.

Treatment with Librium for 10 months followed by a 4-month trial on Valium had proven fruitless. The man's comment regarding these medications was that he disliked them because they "impaired his occupational precision."

On close questioning it was discovered that the 37-year-old lieutenant colonel regularly consumed 8–14 cups of coffee each day. He stated: "My coffee pot is a permanent fixture on my desk." In addition, prior to going to bed he habitually drank hot cocoa as a way of relaxing. His soft drink preference was cola, which he managed to consume three or four of daily. His total estimated daily caffeine intake was 1200 mg. When confronted with the possibility that he was suffering from caffeine toxicity (caffeinism), he expressed considerable cynicism and was unwilling to alter his caffeine intake even on a trial basis. Shortly thereafter, however, he reluctantly reconsidered. Within 4 weeks of starting on a caffeine-restricted diet, he reported a distinct improvement in the tremulousness, insomnia, and other troublesome physical symptoms. To prove the causal relationship, caffeine was reintroduced, with a prompt return of the manifestations of chronic anxiety.

Several months later—having returned to a caffeine-restricted diet—the lieutenant scored considerably lower on the Hamilton Anxiety Scale. Subjectively, he was free of anxiety and had shown no deterioration in his job performance.[10]

Cases of anxiety involving persons who regularly conserve the daily equivalent of 800 mg of caffeine or more should be evaluated for the possibility of caffeinism.

The equating of mental symptoms with psychological causation is an unsound clinical practice. Paranoia, depression, mania, and anxiety as well as a host of other clinical manifestations are symptom patterns that can result from psychological and organic problems alike. As symptoms, they are indistinguishable relative to etiology. It is the overall context in which they appear—clinical history, related symptoms, risk factors—that must guide the clinician in making the critical assessment.

TABLE 3-1 CAFFEINE CHART

Substance	*Caffeine content in milligrams*
Coffee	
Brewed	100–150/cup
Instant	85–100/cup
Tea	60–75/cup
Cola	40–60/cup
OTC Drugs	Variable, but often 100 mg/tab[11]

LISTENING WITHOUT FULLY CONSIDERING

Various versions of this clinical trap stem from the same basic mistake: accepting the alleged story without considering the overall condition of the person with the problem.

Sometimes a previously established diagnosis of functional mental disorder can set the stage for this clinical mistake. The typical example goes something like this: A person presents with the classic manifestations of a well-established psychological condition. A review of the person's psychiatric chart shows several previous episodes of similar behavior. Conclusion: the person is reexperiencing the same psychological problem. Open and shut case! Right? Wrong!

The clinician must never forget that people can have and frequently do have more than one problem at a time. Clinicians are often encouraged to find a single, all-encompassing explanation, but this is not always appropriate. Psychological and organic problems can exist side by side; there is nothing to prevent the person who experiences a problem in living from becoming physically ill. Failure to respect this possibility is the source of serious mistakes in clinical assessment. Recall that in a study of psychiatric outpatients, researchers discovered that 46% suffered from medical illnesses previously undiagnosed.[12]

> A 38-year-old woman with a well-documented history of manic-depressive disorder complained of increasing fatigability and a strange sensitivity to cold weather, something she had not experienced previously. She also reported a recent weight gain of 13 pounds and stated that upon washing her hair in the mornings, the drain would become clogged with large amounts of hair.
>
> The woman had been maintained on lithium carbonate for 3 years with splendid results in controlling her mood swings; nevertheless, it was the clinician's impression that she was now experiencing the early breakthrough signs of a depressive episode.[13]

This turned out to be a false assumption. Fatigue, weight gain, sensitivity to cold, and thinning of the hair are characteristic of a deficient thyroid gland (hypothyroidism). In this case, the hypothyroid condition resulted from the prolonged use of lithium carbonate. The patient's troublesome symptoms disappeared once she was started on replacement thyroid hormone.

Sometimes as clinicians, we become so preoccupied with getting "the story" we fail to make critical observations with respect to the person's outward physical appearance. Such observations provide important clues to the existence of previously unsuspected organic disease. When found in combination with outward manifestations of physical disease, psychiatric symptoms should always be assessed for organic causes. Sometimes the two problems will have no connection, but this cannot be assumed. The clinician's best defense against overlooking these findings is to develop a routine approach to scanning for this information as a part of interviewing.

The following table lists some of the more readily observable external signs that, although not invariably associated with organic disease, should be interpreted by the nonmedically trained professional as strongly indicative of a physical problem. The listing is not comprehensive, but it does provide the clinician with a useful starting point for observing outward manifestations of physical disease.

Reading through the list of physical manifestations, the clinician may be slightly overwhelmed at the number of observations that should be made. Once a routine is established, however, these observations can be made unobtrusively in a relatively short period of time. Listening should not come at the expense of the observation. Failure to detect physical disorders masquerading as problems in living frequently stems from overlooking the obvious.

A special instance of listening without fully considering occurs around the issue of medical clearance. The clinician should never be blinded to findings suggestive of an organic problem simply because the person has previously been examined by a physician and "medically cleared." When a person is evaluated medically, the examination will only reveal what is detectable at that particular time. Physical diseases frequently have periods during which clinical detection is virtually impossible. Even highly sensitive laboratory tests may fail to detect the disease at an early stage. Often, after a person has been medically examined and referred for counseling or therapy, enough time has elapsed for the problem to become manifest. Trust your observational skills. If the signs of physical disease are present, they cannot be

TABLE 3-2 OUTWARD MANIFESTATIONS OF PHYSICAL DISEASE

Symptoms	*Disease*
OVERALL APPEARANCE	
Dishevelment, gross errors in dress	Various causes of brain syndrome
MOVEMENT	
Tremors, jerkiness, twitching, flinging motions, rigidity	Serious neurological conditions, such as Parkinson's disease, Huntington's chorea, tardive dyskinesia, etc.
Disturbances in gait (walking)	Intoxications, cerebellar disease, normal pressure hydrocephalus, other neurological diseases
HEAD	
Cuts, abrasions, lumps, dried blood about the ear	Head trauma
FACE	
Asymmetries in movements	Variety of neurological conditions
EYES	
Bulging	Hyperthyroidism; or if on one side only, tumors of the orbit behind the ear
Drooping eyelids	Myasthenia gravis (made famous by Aristotle Onassis); or if one side only, selective nerve dysfunction
Deviations in pupil size	
Widely dilated	Numerous drugs, particularly hallucinogens, stimulants, and anticholinergics
Markedly constricted	Opiate drugs (heroin, morphine)
Difference in pupil size	Neurologic conditions resulting from increased intracranial pressure
Non-alignment (eyes not parallel)	Dysfunction in one or more of the cranial nerves which innervate the muscles of the eye
NECK	
Protruding lumps	Thyroid enlargement, aneurysm of major arteries of the neck, cancerous growths
SKIN	
Color changes	
Pallor	Anemia, shock
"Yellowing" (jaundice)	Diseases of the liver and gallbladder, cancer of the pancreas, acute anemia

TABLE 3-2 OUTWARD MANIFESTATIONS OF PHYSICAL DISEASE (*continued*)

Symptoms	*Disease*
Blue lips	Inadequate oxygenation as may be seen in certain lung and heart diseases
"Butterfly" rash (nose and face area)	Autoimmune diseases
Black and blue marks	Trauma or certain blood disorders involving clotting deficiencies
Lines of discoloration	Needle tracks from mainlining drugs, often found along the inner aspect of the arms
Thickening	Hypothyroidism
Excessive perspiration	Certain drugs and hypermetabolic conditions such as hyperthyroidism
HAIR	
Extremely coarse and dry	Hypothyroidism
Extremely fine and silky	Hyperthyroidism

ignored simply because the person has been cleared previously. Medical clearance must always be viewed as tentative, subject to new evidence.

Unfortunately, sometimes medical evaluations are performed by incompetent physicians. The medical profession is not dissimilar to other professions; there are competent and incompetent practitioners, and on the surface, it may be difficult to distinguish between them. Failure to diagnose a physical disease may not be a function of the invisibility of the disease, but rather the result of an inadequate examination. In addition, even the most capable of physicians have bad days, when their minds may be preoccupied with other things. The signs of an organic disease may simply be missed, an honest error which, nevertheless, can be tragic if it is neglected because "the doctor said there was nothing wrong."

Finally, the shifting nature of organic brain syndromes as well as certain diseases creates the distinct possibility of symptoms not being present at the time of examination. Later, sometimes even after a very brief period, the manifestations return and are readily observable if only the clinician will look.

A young teacher, 26 years of age, complained of spells of confusion and anxiety. At the initial stage of the medical evaluation, it was discovered that the woman was in the midst of a divorce and had been disowned by her family for living with a man they felt was "beneath" her. The woman was medically cleared and referred for supportive psychiatric treatment.

After no improvement in her condition, a more thorough evaluation showed that the patient had difficulty in making simple calculations. She also had a noticeable problem in expressing herself verbally, and her visual acuity was impaired. Further studies led to a diagnosis of stroke, from which the woman fully recovered.[14]

What appeared to be an obvious psychological problem arising from a stressful life transition was in fact an organic disturbance stemming from circulatory blockage to the brain. The diagnosis was made only after the woman had initially been medically cleared and referred for supportive psychiatric treatment.

The moral for the clinician is this: look and believe what you see, even if the client has been previously evaluated medically without abnormal findings.

EQUATING PSYCHOSIS WITH SCHIZOPHRENIA (OR FUNCTIONAL PSYCHOSIS)

The equating of psychotic behavior with schizophrenia is a serious and all too common clinical misconception. Although the psychosis of schizophrenia is the most popularized form of psychotic behavior, it is by no means the only form of psychosis. Psychotic episodes frequently arise from organic disorders. *In the absence of a well-established history of functional psychosis, any case of psychotic behavior should be strongly suspected of organicity.*

Although there are several characteristic points of differentiation between schizophrenia and organic psychosis, none of them are consistently reliable. Of course, if any of the core manifestations of brain syndrome are present, the diagnosis of schizophrenia should be questioned. This is not to say that such symptoms are never part of the clinical picture of schizophrenia; sometimes confusion, disorientation, and recent memory deficits occur with schizophrenia, but, in such cases, examination should be undertaken to rule out a specific causative organic condition, particularly if the symptoms persist beyond a short period of time.

Although, as we shall discuss in Chapter 4, signs of brain syndrome are characteristically found in cases of organic psychosis, exceptions are numerous. Certainly, the absence of such findings cannot be construed as positive proof of schizophrenia or functional psychosis.

> A 31-year-old, fifth-year medical student was admitted to the hospital speaking freely of the fact that he could read other people's minds and could hear his own internal thoughts spoken aloud. He had heard it proclaimed publicly that he was the son of a professor of psychiatry whom he believed to be the Duke of Gloucester in disguise. He had the compulsion to look at men "below the waist" and feared people thought he was homosexual.
>
> The young man's symptoms had slowly emerged over a 4-month period and intensified shortly after his wife gave birth to a second child. He began to feel he was being hypnotized and psychoanalyzed against his will.
>
> During a mental status examination, the patient said he saw the face of a dead relative and it smiled at him. He was, however, fully oriented and without any signs of brain syndrome. There was no previous history of mental disorder.[15]

This patient might easily have been diagnosed schizophrenic, but further investigation documented an extended use of amphetamines. He was suffering from an organic psychosis—without symptoms of brain syndrome—caused by chronic stimulant usage.

In summary, psychosis with brain syndrome manifestations should always be considered organic until proven otherwise, but psychosis without brain syndrome may also be organic and should not be characterized as schizophrenia without an evaluation for other findings suggestive of organic disorder.

There are other points of distinction between functional and organic psychoses that may be of aid to the clinician in making the critical assessment. Persons experiencing schizophrenia for the first time are usually in their late teens or early twenties. In contrast, organic psychoses more often occur in older individuals. Once again, this is a general rule that has exceptions. Despite certain exceptions the clinician should be highly suspicious of organicity when a person over the age of 30 without a previous history of mental disorder becomes psychotic. Numerous errors in critical assessment arise out of failure to heed this basic principle.

Hallucinations are a commonly encountered symptom of psychosis. This distorted sensory experience can involve any of the primary senses: sight, sound, touch, smell, and taste. This is true of functional hallucinations as well as those which result from organic conditions. Visual hallucinations are particularly characteristic of organic psychoses; much less so of schizophrenia and other functional psychoses. All hallucinations—other than auditory—have a greater prevalence in organic problems compared to functional ones. For the clinician the implication is that hallucinatory symptoms—except for the hearing of voices, which is a typical expression of schizophrenia—suggest an organic mental disorder.

A difference in overall adaptive style has been mentioned as a differentiating feature of functional and organic psychosis.[16] In the former, the familiar tends to be perceived as unfamiliar. Organic psychosis is characterized by the opposite tendency: mistaking the unfamiliar for the familiar. The first adaptive style creates an impression of bizarreness, the second, confusion. The functional style might result in the person viewing an old and previously trusted friend as a spy or an agent of the FBI. In contrast the organic style might lead the person into mistaking a total stranger for a friend or relative. It is as though control of the situation is exerted in functional psychosis by attributing special meaning to common things; whereas in organic psychosis control is established by reducing the unknown or unrecognized to the familiar. Illusions—distorted perceptions—are frequently instances of making the unfamiliar familiar. They are characteristic of organic psychosis and rarely occur in schizophrenia.

The ability to get outside of oneself and to view one's experience objectively is frequently severely disrupted in psychosis, but the waxing and waning of consciousness which characterizes organic psychosis produces momentary returns of self-awareness.[17] The person may express great concern over his mental condition: "Something terrible is wrong with me. This is not like me." Much more rarely is this seen in association with functional psychosis.

Certain forms of behavior have come to be erroneously equated with schizophrenia. Take catatonia, for example. Catatonia—muscular rigidity with bizarre posturing, negativism, and mutism—is seen in numerous medical conditions that have nothing to do with schizophrenia.[18] A partial listing of organic problems that cause catatonia includes:

viral encephalitis (limbic system)
brain tumors (frontal lobe and third ventricle)
petit mal epilepsy
head injuries
Wernicke's encephalopathy
syphilitic brain disease
narcolepsy
diabetic ketoacidosis
hypercalcemia
pellagra
acute intermittent porphyria
drug intoxications

In recent years catatonia has even been established as a side effect of certain psychiatric medications, particularly the higher potency neuroleptic drugs. This finding is not particularly surprising; catatonic-like rigidity in treated laboratory animals is one of the major screening criteria used by pharmaceutical manufacturers in searching for substances with neuroleptic potential.

The clinical picture of catatonia is dramatically eye-catching. Characteristically, the person appears frozen in space, reminiscent of the ray-gun effect portrayed in science fiction movies. A fixed posture may be maintained for hours and is usually accompanied by the absence of speech. Extreme muscle tension is present, particularly about the face and in the muscles of the arms and legs. The heart rate and blood pressure are elevated and may be accompanied by excessive perspiration and fever. During periods when the person is not assuming a rigid posture, walking may appear stiff or labored. If the person speaks at all, the words tend to be sluggish and barely audible. Peculiar grimacing in the absence of any appropriate context occurs intermittently. Despite the overall passive appearance of catatonia, an underlying sense of hostility and obstinence ("negativism") is characteristic and may periodically break through as violent outbursts, followed by a resumption of the more characteristic catatonic picture.

The presentation of catatonic behavior signals the clinician that a serious disruption in normal behavior has occurred, but it says nothing *per se* about the cause of the disruption. Catatonia can be functional or organic. It does not automatically mean schizophrenia, as illustrated in the following case history.

> A graduate student in chemistry awakened complaining of hearing a strange ringing in his ears. Within 30 minutes, after an episode of nausea and vomiting, he became confused. Alarmed, his wife rushed him to a hospital emergency room.
>
> By the time he was examined, he had become belligerent, uncooperative, and even violent. Gradually, the clinical picture changed to one of incoherence and fearfulness. Upon admission to the hospital, he was described as mute and drowsy with a slightly elevated heart rate.
>
> Over the next few hours the patient was observed by three staff psychiatrists who happened to be making rounds at the time. They described a fluctuating clinical picture, cycling approximately every 20 minutes, from extreme agitated excitement to stuporous catatonia with mutism. A provisional diagnosis was made of schizophrenic reaction, catatonic type.
>
> The patient received a modest dose of a neuroleptic drug and promptly fell asleep. Twelve hours later he awakened fully coherent, cooperative, and speaking normally. He then reported being in excellent health until 3 days prior to admission. He had been working with a chemical—difluoronitroacetyl fluoride—in a poorly ventilated laboratory. After complaining of numbness in his fingers, he awakened on the day of admission with the symptoms that led to his hospitalization.
>
> He was discharged with a revised diagnosis of acute organic brain syndrome, secondary to poisoning with an organic fluoride compound. At a one-year follow-up visit, no residual symptoms or further episodes of catatonic behavior were reported.[19]

RELYING ON A SINGLE INFORMATION SOURCE

Necessarily, the assessment of personal problems is sometimes based on information from one source: the person coming for help. In such cases clinicians must proceed as best they can in arriving at some understanding of the problem. Frequently, however, the absence of other information or another perspective misleads the clinician into errors with respect to critical assessment. When information can be supplemented by another source, particularly in cases where the person is intoxicated, incoherent, or perhaps even comatose, it is essential to utilize this additional resource. The actual causative nature of a problem may become apparent only when supplementary information is obtained from other persons or clinical records.

Information from other sources protects the clinician from several potential errors. It allows for the possibility of uncovering aspects of the case that simply may not be known to the client or patient; or, if known, because of the person's present condition, cannot be recalled or accurately reported. It also protects the clinician against the personal blind spots of the client. The client who does not want to face the problem may push an awareness that something is wrong out of consciousness. Deficits that the person is actively attempting to hide or minimize may go undetected clinically. The obtaining of information from someone else who knows the person well provides a balancing perspective on the problem and often makes obvious what may have been concealed in a brief interview. Even if a clinician feels smug about his skill at seeing through deception in the interview situation, the shifting nature of brain syndrome should give him pause. It is quite possible that an interview may take place when a client has it together, that is, at a time when the person's capacities are relatively intact so that there is really nothing to detect during the interview. If a relative or friend, however, reports that the person has been getting lost periodically over the past month, the clinical perception of the patient's condition may change considerably.

Information obtained from other sources is particularly critical with respect to problems of alcohol and drug abuse. Persons with such problems are notorious for not admitting to them. Their families may be falling apart, their jobs slipping away from them; nevertheless, it is not uncommon for the clinician to be told that there is no problem.

Because people who abuse substances are at high risk for a variety of organic (as well as functional) problems, information from another perspective should be obtained if at all possible. In the following case this kind of supplementary material proved life-saving.

A 23-year-old man with a history of severe alcoholism was seen in an emergency room for drunkenness. His speech was slurred and he periodically fell asleep.

The man was accompanied by his wife, who assumed that he was probably "drinking again." On closer questioning, however, she reported that her husband's alcohol intake over the past 24 hours had actually been quite minimal. She also was able to recall that on the preceding day her husband, while intoxicated, had fallen down the stairs in their home and was unconscious for several minutes.

This history from the wife led to further neurological testing and a diagnosis of subdural hematoma. The clot was evacuated by surgery, and the patient fully recovered.[20]

We have considered four types of clinical deceptions—mistaking symptoms for their causes, listening without fully considering, equating psychosis with schizophrenia, and relying on a single information source. Avoiding these conceptual traps is an essential prerequisite to critical assessment.

CHAPTER 4

A FIRST STEP TOWARD CRITICAL ASSESSMENT: RECOGNITION OF BRAIN SYNDROME

"The harbingers are come. See, see their mark. . . ."

George Herbert

FROM THE OUTSET, it must be emphasized that brain syndrome is *not* a specific disease; rather, it is a clinical expression of widespread brain failure that results from many different conditions, including tumors, infections, hypertension, endocrine and nutritional deficiencies, as well as others.

Recognition of brain syndrome is probably the single most important aspect of a sound clinical approach to critical assessment, because it is highly correlated with underlying organic disorders. Once identified clinically, cases of brain syndrome must be medically evaluated to determine the precise cause; it is the causative disease that must be treated, not the symptomatic manifestations. Although psychological reactions, particularly depression in the elderly, sometimes assume characteristics of brain syndrome, this is a rare occurrence overall; in fact, brain syndrome is so typically a reflection of organic disease that its presence must be considered presumptive evidence until proven otherwise.

Brain syndrome is a common clinical presentation. In this country one out of every five patients admitted to a mental hospital has these symptoms. Studies of elderly persons *living in the community* have demonstrated a prevalence rate of 10–20%, and in mental hospitals 50% of the elderly population have brain syndrome.[1]

Despite the misleading stereotype of brain syndrome as reflecting hopeless senility, the underlying organic causes are frequently either partially or completely reversible. In one report of 222 patients with brain syndrome, accurate recognition and subsequent medical evaluation demonstrated treatable conditions in 35–40% of the cases.[2] Unfortunately, failure to recognize brain syndrome is a prevalent clinical error. In one study of moderate-to-severe brain syndrome, the family physician failed to identify this clinical picture in more than 80% of the cases.[3]

A word of caution. The reader should not fall into the trap of expecting to find symptoms of brain syndrome only among the aged. The rise of drug and alcohol use in a younger population has created a substantial basis for the increased incidence of brain syndrome in this group.

A confusing terminology has developed with reference to brain syndrome. Dementia, delirium, confusion, acute and chronic organic brain syndrome, toxic psychosis, senility, presenility—all these terms have been used. Instead of clarifying the concept, however, this string of terms has created semantic confusion. The DSM-III (Third Edition of the APA Diagnostic and Statistical Manual of Mental Disorders) has further compounded the problem by listing eight different organic brain syndromes. This presentation is misleading in that it implies that the multiple symptoms associated with brain syndrome are typically found in pure isolation. Dissatisfied with this approach, I have used the term *brain syndrome* to indicate *a clinical picture—resulting from a variety of causes—characterized by one or more of five core cognitive deficits* occurring in varying combinations. If the reader familiarizes himself with this conceptualization, he should have little difficulty translating it into DSM-III terminology for the purposes of recording or discussing official diagnostic categories. Essentially, this portrayal of brain syndrome cuts across the DSM-III classification, providing, one hopes, a more practical way of organizing clinical observations.

The remainder of this chapter will consider in detail five characteristic cognitive deficits and will discuss two prominent clinical variations of brain syndrome: rapid-onset brain syndrome (ROBS) and slow-onset brain syndrome (SOBS). Illustrative cases will be presented, and factors that obscure recognition will be considered. Scattered through this chapter, the reader will find selections from a moving account of a 49-year-old academic researcher who developed brain syndrome secondary to Parkinson's disease, a condition for which at the time there was no known treatment. It is taken from an article entitled, "Death of a Mind: A Study in Disintegration," written by the man's son. This personal account provides a graphic portrayal of brain syndrome.

> I first remember my father as a well-built, active man with a wide range of interests. His work required both intellectual and practical ability, and those who could judge his achievement spoke highly of it. I was more impressed at the time by the happy enthusiasm with which he would turn from weightier matters to entertain his small daughter. . . . Over the period that we worked together, sometime in the early 1930s, I became gradually aware that the fine edge of his intellect was becoming dulled. He was less clear in discussion and less quick to make a jump from a new piece of evidence to its possible significance. . . . He tended also to become portentous and solemn about his subject, as though one small corner of knowledge nearly filled his world, and the wider horizons were narrowing in.[4]

The clinical picture of brain syndrome is greatly influenced by the rate of onset. If the compromise in brain functioning occurs rapidly, the outward manifestations are typically dramatic and severely disruptive of normal mental activity. On the other hand, if the causative condition is slow in developing, a much more subtle clinical picture emerges, one which may remain hidden from observers. Although differing in overall clinical presentation, the variations of brain syndrome are characterized by deficits in one or more of five cognitive functions: *attention, orientation, recent memory, reasoning, and sensory discrimination.*

COGNITIVE DEFICITS

Inattention

The ability to attend to the matter at hand is a basic prerequisite for normal behavior. There are organic conditions that severely compromise this function, making it impossible to maintain one's attention for any sustained period. The result is a frequent shifting from one concern or stimulus to another. Thinking, looking, listening, performing—none of these are effective without the ability to attend; otherwise, moment to moment, one distraction after another makes it impossible to concentrate. Clinically, the person's face may dramatically communicate difficulty with focusing for even the briefest period. The eyes may dart about, the facial expression abruptly and repetitively change. There may be extreme restlessness and inability to maintain a fixed position. The person may be continuously turning, getting up, twisting, sitting down, listening, tuning out, talking about one thing, then another and another and another.

When a person is having more subtle difficulty attending, a brief test known as "digit span retention" can be utilized to assess this problem more objectively. The person is asked to listen to a five-digit number and immediately to repeat it. Five random digits, such as 9-4-1-6-3, are presented allowing approximately 1 second between each number. Most adults perform this test without error; if not, the test should be repeated, using a different set of digits. Failure on two attempts is strong evidence of a significant deficit in attention.

When an individual is having trouble attending, assessment of at least three other cognitive functions becomes highly problematic because the ability to attend is essential to orientation, recent memory, and basic reasoning.

Disorientation

Orientation is the positioning of oneself with respect to time, space, and person. Disorientation frequently serves as an early signal of brain syndrome. Sometimes without a disturbance in orientation, a person may not know the exact date; generally, however, there is no difficulty in stating the correct month, year, and whether it is night or day time. The inability to do so constitutes evidence that a person is truly disoriented.

Specifying the nature of one's location should normally present no real problem to a person, whether it is home, workplace, hospital, clinic, or jail. Disorientation to place is not knowing where you are. Brain syndrome often disrupts this basic sense of orientation. Disorientation to place is often best evidenced by the actions of the person. Is there a history of the person wandering, unable to find the way home? Or, if the person is being observed as a patient, does he lose his way on the ward or go into the wrong room to sleep?

It is often said that, unlike disorientation to time and place, disorientation to person is rarely encountered as an aspect of brain syndrome. If by disorientation to person one means that there is no recognition of oneself, then this is true. If, however, disorientation to person is used to imply a failure to recognize people who should be familiar—relatives, friends, family physician, long-term therapist—then we are talking about a problem commonly seen with brain syndrome, although not as frequently as disorientation to time and place.

Orientation is a cornerstone of human experience. When a person becomes disoriented, a significant deficit exists that strongly suggests the presence of a brain disturbance.

Recent Memory Impairment

Recent memory is the recall of an experience after a short period of time, say 5 to 10 minutes. Our memory system works by first registering (attending) an experience, then recording it (recent memory) and, finally, storing the information permanently for future retrieval (remote memory). If a person cannot register the immediate experience, there is no possibility of its going on to become a recorded and stored memory. Similarly, even if an experience is registered, if it is not recorded as a recent memory, it will never become permanently stored. In contrast, even when immediate and recent memory are faulty, old memories may be brought to mind, memories that were recorded years before. It is a disturbance in *recent memory* that is a hallmark of brain syndrome, whereas remote memory may be affected minimally.

Perhaps the easiest method for testing recent memory is to identify four unrelated items (key, stone, book, cup) and inform the person that you will ask him to repeat these four items in a few minutes. Five minutes later the person should be able to list the four words (not necessarily in the order originally presented). The examiner should be careful not to select four words that can be connected through association, since it is much less difficult to recall associated words. Failure correctly to recall four objects after 5 minutes on two separate occasions indicates a defect in recent memory. The clinician should also be alert to a history of increasing forgetfulness: missed appointments, repetition of stories or questions, leaving the stove on, and other oversights. Such a history indicates problem with recent memory:

> In 1935, after a period of absence, I looked forward with especial pleasure to my homecoming, but when we met I knew with immediate certainty that I had lost the companion of my earlier years. . . . To me it was as though a light had gone out, but no one else seemed to notice anything amiss. . . . We paused to consider a problem which had thwarted us, and I hit on a solution and outlined the idea. My father could not grasp the principle of it until I gave a demonstration. . . . I was profoundly shocked. . . . His ability was still well within normal limits; but I knew what it had been, and the difference was startling. . . . He tried to carry on with his work, but he did not make any headway and became more and more depressed about it. His character remained essentially the same except that he could no longer endure unorthodox views . . . if he chanced to overhear one of the eager iconoclastic arguments of youth, he became disturbed and petulant and it seemed as though his mental organization had become less secure even at its deeper levels.[4]

Diminished Reasoning

A person's capacity for solving problems may be significantly diminished as a reflection of brain syndrome. Friends or relatives will point out ridiculous mistakes made at home or on the job, mistakes never made prior to this time. The decline in basic reasoning can make the solving of even simple problems a difficult task. Making change or keeping a golf score becomes problematic. Common sense judgment may be adversely affected. When asked what to do if accidentally locked out of the house or if in a car which has run out of gas, the person may show considerable difficulty in arriving at a reasonable reply.

Simple calculations are a remarkably good screening test for detecting deficits in problem-solving.

- What remains if you subtract 7 from 22?
- How many eggs would you have if you had one-third of a dozen?
- If you have six books and you wish to divide them so that

twice the number of books are on one shelf as as on the other, how many books will be on each shelf?

Brain syndrome tends to make these simple mathematical problems difficult to grasp and solve. But one word of caution: the clinician should realize that memory and problem-solving are *relative* skills; that is, there is no single standard against which to measure them. Within the so-called normal range tremendous variation exists with respect to memory and reasoning. For the particularly gifted, the task of recalling four items after 5 minutes or solving simple problems may create little difficulty despite the presence of a mild brain syndrome. Prior to the development of brain syndrome, however, the individual may have been able to recall twelve items after 5 minutes as well as being able to solve complex problems. Thus, whereas failure at these simple screening questions is always strongly suggestive of brain syndrome, success cannot be construed as eliminating that possibility. For this reason, the clinician should obtain information from relatives and friends on the patient's prior level of functioning as a context in which to interpret individual performance. A history of deteriorating cognitive skills at home or work is highly significant regardless of the person's performance on clinical tests.

Sensory Indiscrimination

During the course of day-to-day existence, we are exposed to massive amounts of sensory input, from the external world as well as from within, in the form of physiological sensations and recollections. The brain has the task of sorting out this information, assigning priorities, and construing its meanings. Of all the sensations received, only a relatively small number can be actively considered; otherwise, we would become lost in a vast gulf of stimulation. Our world of meaning would disintegrate into noise and confusion. A diminished capacity for sensory discrimination is commonly found with brain syndrome. Selectivity relative to sensory input fails; sensory overload threatens, and the misinterpretation of sensations becomes a problem.

Early in the emergence of brain syndrome, sensory indiscrimination typically takes the form of illusions. An illusion is the misidentification of an external sensory stimulus, the mistaking of something for what it is not. The individual may look at dimly lit curtains across the room gently moved by the wind and mistake them for a person entering the room. A street sound may be misinterpreted as the voice of a friend. This kind of perceptual distortion can involve any of the five senses—sight, sound, touch, taste, and smell—but, most often, illusions are visual or auditory in nature. Illusions are rarely seen as psychological reactions; their presence indicates organicity.

Hallucination is a second form of sensory indiscrimination. In contrast to illusions, hallucinations are perceptual experiences that have *no* external referent. They seem to be projected from within onto the outside world. The person may hear a voice when no one is speaking, or see things—a face, spiders on the wall, snakes on the floor, a hooded demon—in the absence of any remotely related external object. As with illusions, hallucinations can occur in all sensory modes, but *visual* hallucinations most frequently characterize brain syndrome. Sometimes visual hallucinations are extremely terrifying to the individual; in other instances the hallucinated experience is a source of pleasure. One author has reported observing a person with brain syndrome who intently followed a 30-minute football game between two teams of miniature elephants![5]

Other forms of hallucinatory experience are seen with brain syndrome. Although not as prevalent as visual and auditory hallucinations, their presence is strongly suggestive of an organic factor. Tactile hallucinations, especially prevalent in drug withdrawal, may take the form of tiny creatures crawling over the skin. Olfactory hallucinations are a hallmark of the initial phase of temporal lobe epilepsy; typically the person smells an awful odor, variously described as "rotten eggs," "burning rubber," or "old cheese." Auditory hallucinations may occur with brain syndrome; when present, they are almost invariably threatening or derogatory.[6]

Since hallucinations are also a frequent occurrence in so-called functional psychoses (schizophrenia, manic-depressive disorder), they present the clinician with a problematic indicator. The question arises, should the clinician consider any form of hallucination as indicative of organic brain disease? As an approach to screening, the following rule can be used: *the presence of any hallucination, other than auditory, is to be considered presumptive evidence of an organic problem.* In the absence of other evidence, auditory hallucinations *alone* are not strongly suggestive of an organic problem. The one major exception to this rule is seen in association with chronic alcoholism: a condition known as hallucinosis, characterized solely by the hearing of voices that are almost always threatening in nature.

In this book I distinguish schizophrenia and manic-depressive psychosis from organic mental disorders. This is despite the fact that considerable evidence argues for an organic explanation of these conditions. From the perspective of critical assessment, however, these functional psychoses differ from organic mental disorders in their clinical manifestations. Many of the clues highly suggestive of organicity are not usually associated with these conditions. It is essential that specific organic mental disorders not be mistakenly labeled schizophrenia or manic-depressive psychosis, as this will deter the search for the causative condition. This differentiation is an important aspect of critical assessment.

> If my father glanced at a dark shape which was rather like a black cat, he did not instinctively look again to make sure what it was; he simply saw a cat. His mind fitted the sensory impression to the first rough approximation which suggested itself, and accepted it without further question, however unlikely it might be in the context. . . . My father discussed the problem with me in some detail, as he was naturally disturbed to find that he kept on seeing things which were not there.[4]

BRAIN SYNDROME IN CONTEXT

We have considered five cognitive deficits found in varying combinations in brain syndrome. Now we need to fill in the picture by considering the typical clinical presentations of brain syndrome.

There are two prominent versions of brain syndrome, and scattered along a continuum between them are a number of variations resembling one more than the other but usually incorporating elements from each.

Rapid-Onset Brain Syndrome (ROBS)

Request for an "emergency psychiatric consultation" was made a few days after the admission of a 35-year-old man to the

> medical service of a hospital for treatment of pneumonia. The consultation request was accompanied by a brief note stating that the patient had become "schizophrenic with hallucinations and delusions."
>
> When examined, the man appeared extremely agitated; he was restless, fidgeting with the bed coverings, and sometimes waving his arms inappropriately. Unable to attend to any task for more than a few moments, the man was highly distractable and appeared frightened. Although he gave his name correctly, he did not seem to know that he was in a hospital. When pressed on this matter, he stated he thought it was a bakery; later, he said it was a bank. He gave the year as 1964, rather than 1971, and was unable to identify the month and day of the week. At times he reacted as if he were seeing things. He said that there was an angel standing beside his bed prepared to care for him, but he also volunteered that he wondered if the angel might not have been sent to harm rather than to protect him.[7]

This man was not suffering from schizophrenia. He was manifesting brain syndrome secondary to the pneumonia in his lungs. Probably this infectious process was preventing an adequate oxygen supply from reaching the brain. The result: brain syndrome. As the pneumonia was brought under control through antibiotic treatment, the symptoms cleared completely.

The most common causes of ROBS are drug and alcohol intoxications and the associated withdrawal states that sometimes occur in cases of chronic addiction. But many acute medical diseases, either through direct impairment of the brain or compromise of its support system, can also lead to ROBS.

Typically, this form of brain syndrome manifests as a relatively sudden, dramatic change in behavior. The individual will likely be disoriented to time and place and will be distractable, unable to focus on anything for more than a few seconds. If the person's attention can be captured long enough to test for recent memory, a severe disruption can usually be demonstrated. The inability to concentrate also makes simple problem-solving difficult, if not impossible, for the individual with ROBS. Overall, the person will project an appearance of being confused.

Misinterpretations of the surrounding environment, although often prominent, can sometimes be quite subtle, requiring close clinical attention for detection. Hallucinatory experiences,

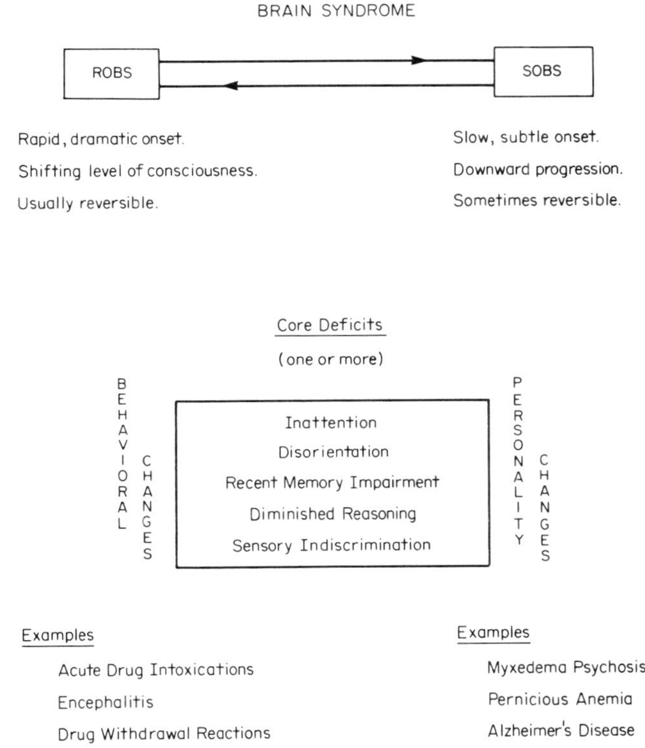

FIGURE 4-1

particularly visual, may be quite obvious as the person turns his head to listen or suddenly shouts back to an empty room; but, in other cases, these experiences may be carefully masked by the individual in the grip of paranoid thought who is afraid that others will know about these hallucinations.

Restlessness is one of the earliest behavioral indicators of impending ROBS. In a classic study of "delirium," investigators found that some degree of restlessness was "invariably present." Restlessness can present in several ways, including being easily startled, pacing the floor, continually fumbling with one's clothes or bed covers, and repetitively searching for things.[8]

Tremulousness—a fine, quivering movement of the muscles—may be seen with ROBS, particularly in cases involving drugs or alcohol, and can accentuate the clinical picture of restlessness.

A tendency toward insomnia, or a reversal of the sleep cycle so that what little sleep there is comes during the daylight hours, is also commonly found in ROBS.

The term *shifting level of consciousness* has been used to describe a striking characteristic of ROBS: one moment the person appears grossly confused, disoriented, and completely illogical; the next, calm, rational, and in control. During this so-called lucid interval, the deficits associated with brain syndrome, if detectable at all, may be much less noticeable. But this improvement is only momentary, after which the manifestations of brain syndrome return in full force. One well-known researcher has described an encounter with a patient experiencing a brain syndrome as he recovered in the hospital following back surgery.[9] The man, a minister, greeted the physician researcher shouting that he had lost his genitals in a car accident. In another moment he was screaming that a dog was biting his penis; then, suddenly, he shifted the conversation to a discussion of some tropical flowers that he appeared to hallucinate. After several more minutes of fragmented, one-way conversation, the man turned and said: "Am I sick? I seem to be hallucinating!" When told that this was true, he seemed relieved and remained quiet for a few minutes. Suddenly, he began to shout again: "Look, look, there's this dog again, biting me! Take the dog away!" This is an example of shifting level of consciousness, which to some degree characterizes most cases of ROBS.

ROBS can be influenced by environmental factors. The condition predictably worsens in the nighttime, presumably—at least in part—as a result of the loss of the orienting influence of light. Being left alone in a room, particularly one without windows, can also exacerbate ROBS, and individuals who have undergone surgery followed by convalescence in an intensive care unit develop ROBS with some degree of regularity, thought in part to result from sensory deprivation.

> The suggestion that he should then go for a trip abroad put me in a difficult position. He felt convinced that it would do him good, and his medical advisors encouraged this belief. . . . We left England at the end of the year. Our destination was an isolated resort in mountainous country about fifteen miles from the nearest small town. . . . It was soon evident, however, that unfamiliar faces and a foreign language were putting too heavy a strain on his fading

> facilities. . . . Now, listening every day to a background of foreign conversation which, even when fit, he could not easily have followed, he was bewildered. . . . His mind accepted the nearest English equivalent to the sounds he heard, and the task of keeping in touch with reality against such odds became impossible. Hearing what he thought was English spoken, he addressed other hotel residents in his own language to be met by uncomprehending stares. He naturally came to feel that they were hostile to him, and he began gradually to make order out of his mental chaos by systematizing, in a delusional way, what he heard and saw.[4]

Writers have described two contrasting versions of ROBS based primarily on the level of activity: one characterized by increased activity, the person appearing agitated, if not driven or frenzied; the other, by diminished activity, with an apathetic, withdrawn, or even drowsy appearance. This latter version of ROBS can be easily overlooked because the person is not disruptive. Regardless of its precise presentation, ROBS should be considered a medical emergency requiring immediate evaluation for the specific causative factor.

Slow-Onset Brain Syndrome (SOBS)

This form of brain syndrome emerges insidiously. Contrasted to the sudden, rapidly developing clinical picture of ROBS, there is characteristically a slow, progressive deterioration in orientation and recent memory combined with a decline in common judgment and problem-solving skills. The distinctive shifting level of consciousness associated with ROBS, however, is not a prominent aspect of SOBS.

A variety of organic conditions produces SOBS, some permanently. Others, as we shall discuss later, are completely or partially reversible with appropriate treatment. Although SOBS is more commonly seen among the elderly, it is by no means restricted to them.

Since SOBS has an insidious onset, the afflicted individual has time to adapt. Tasks that require intact recent memory and problem-solving skills are avoided. Eventually, however, the person becomes unaware of the extent of his cognitive deficits and his skill at evasion deteriorates. Judgment is compromised so that the person appears irresponsible and accident prone.

Difficulty in grasping abstract or symbolic meaning emerges.

Simple proverbs may no longer be understood; instead, they are interpreted literally or concretely. Thus, the saying, "The grass always seems greener on the other side," may lead the person with SOBS to comment on different kinds of grass or various shades of green rather than addressing the idea that things we do not have often appear more attractive than they are once we have them. This same difficulty with abstraction is observed when the person is asked to identify the one characteristic shared by several different things. For example, given a list of five colors, the person may be unable to perceive that blue, red, pink, purple, and green are similar in that they are all colors.

The ability to abstract is also compromised in cases of ROBS, but this deficit is often overshadowed by prominent behavioral changes. Although difficulty with abstraction is associated with schizophrenia as well, there is usually a bizarre twist to the literal interpretation not typically found in SOBS.

It should be kept in mind that the brief picture I am presenting of SOBS is a composite; not all cases will include each clinical element.

Let me encourage the reader to pause for a moment and fantasize the experience of SOBS. What would be your personal response to a slowly failing memory, disorientation, and a breakdown in reasoning—all of which have been dependable aspects of your life heretofore? At first you might try to deny what was occurring, but with time, denial would be impossible in the face of accumulating evidence to the contrary. Your self-confidence would diminish as the disturbing, if not terrifying, threat of losing control loomed. You would know that something dreadful was wrong, but you would not know precisely what. Even though you could no longer keep the truth from yourself, you might try to hide it from others. You would want to stop putting yourself on display; social engagements would be avoided, and you might even stop attending the card game you had enjoyed over the years because of an increasing number of foolish mistakes. But despite your best efforts, you fail to cover all your mistakes. Your checking account is reported as overdrawn—not once but repeatedly. You lose track of important engagements and fail to appear. Even at home, conversation with family and friends becomes stressful. Gradually, you say less and less, fading off into thinking about other things; then, when someone asks you a question, you are forced to make up something that leaves everyone with stares of bewilderment. As time goes on you find yourself more and more in situations that seem strange to you; you are not sure of what people are discussing or why they look at you and ask questions that make no sense. Things—familiar things—fleetingly appear different. Sometimes they almost seem to come alive, but when you refocus, nothing is there. You find it difficult to fall asleep; restlessly, you toss and turn in bed, almost afraid of what might happen if you do fall asleep. Your vitality leaves you; you find no humor in experiences that others find hilarious. You feel hopelessly confused and frightened, increasingly unaware of your failing faculties.

At the request of her family physician, a 78-year-old woman was seen in her home by a public health nurse. The woman had lived with her middle-aged daughter until recently, when the daughter required hospitalization for treatment of high blood pressure. The nurse observed that the house was messy and the woman unkempt. Throughout the conversation, the elderly woman kept insisting that her daughter had just stepped out briefly for a walk. She persisted in this story despite being told repeatedly that her daughter had been sent to the hospital. When queried about the date, she responded incorrectly by 2 years.

Three days later, the police escorted the woman to an emergency room, having found her wandering some distance from her home in her night clothes "looking for my daughter."

On examination she was unable to recall more than one of three objects after 5 minutes and failed to recognize the name of the current President. She insisted on referring to the examining physician as "Father," stating that she had not been to church enough lately. When asked the meaning of commonly used proverbs, she said they were "silly." In response to "a stitch in time saves nine," she replied that her eyes were too weak to sew. She was dignosed as suffering from senile dementia.[10]

Dramatic changes in personality are sometimes seen with SOBS and, in some instances, may be the initial manifestation. These changes fall roughly into four clinical patterns. The person may show an exaggeration of existing personality traits. An individual who has always been somewhat compulsive may become rigid and obstinate in dealing with others; the dependent individual may become demanding and infantile; and the previously anxious person may develop an obsessive concern with issues of minor importance. In short, the person comes to appear like a caricature of himself. In some cases of SOBS this pattern takes the form of excessive emotional displays, sometimes referred to as "lability of emotional expression." With the slightest provocation, the person will begin to laugh hysterically or, as is more often true, cry uncontrollably. These excessive emotional expressions are stereotypical in quality; particularly, the facial changes tend to be exactly the same each time the person experiences one of these exaggerated emotional outbursts. After a short time, the reaction subsides, only to return later at another inappropriate moment.

A second form of personality change involves restlessness, hyperactivity, loss of social discretion, and inappropriate bravado and euphoria which when restrained by others can quickly evolve into angry agitation. This pattern can be mistaken for the manic phase of manic-depressive disorder.

The opposite personality change is also seen with SOBS: apathy, social withdrawal, and depression. Many cases of SOBS are misinterpreted as instances of psychological reactive depression.

A fourth personality change is characterized by suspiciousness that can become frank paranoia. Often, irrational jealousy will be a major aspect of this paranoid personality.

When the personality changes precede or overshadow the cognitive deficits of SOBS, the stage is set for errors in critical assessment.

> He spent the days chasing non-existent spies in other people's bedrooms; while I chased after, explaining to the agitated guests and taking what steps I could to deal with the emergency . . . the situation forced me to restrain him. . . . In that moment of despair and disillusion the full force of his love for me was turned to bitter hatred. . . . When the crisis came we were alone in an upstairs gallery, and he turned on me with murder in his eyes . . . For a moment the issue hung in the balance. . . . but when my glance met his, he could not bring himself to do it. He relaxed at last with a gesture of sad acquiescence and let himself be quietly led away.[4]

THE QUESTION OF REVERSIBILITY

Although SOBS can reflect the underlying irreversible brain deterioration known as presenile and senile dementia (Alzheimer's disease), many cases are found to result from conditions that, when treated with the correct intervention, are partially or totally reversible.

A review of two sizable studies of patients with "progressive intellectual deterioration" found that approximately one out of every four cases had "an underlying disease potentially reversible by medical or surgical therapy"; nevertheless, persons with SOBS are all too frequently viewed as "crocks" or cases of "senility" for which nothing can be done. *SOBS must never be presumed irreversible until a thorough medical evaluation has been conducted.*[11]

A retired farm worker, age 67, with a history of sound physical and mental health, began to lose interest in activities which previously had given him considerable pleasure. His family found him distant and increasingly forgetful. One evening when he failed to return from his usual walk, a search of the surrounding area found him bizarrely covered with mud, soaking wet, and extremely confused. It was assumed he had either deliberately or accidentally fallen into the nearby river. After a night's sleep, the man seemed improved.

His family, however, remained concerned and insisted on a medical examination, which revealed "generalized rhonchi" in the chest. The man was admitted to the hospital on the assumption that he had inhaled water into his lungs while splashing in the river.

During his hospitalization, he appeared depressed. Although generally oriented, he answered questions slowly and with poor detail. The medical evaluation identified a vitamin B_{12} deficiency. Treatment with B_{12} injections was immediately initiated. Within a few weeks improvement was noted. The man's mental alertness and spontaneity in conversation and activity returned, and he experienced no further episodes of bizarre confusion. Later, it was discovered that the man's brother also had suffered from pernicious anemia (vitamin B_{12} deficiency).[12]

The Amnestic Syndrome ("Amnesia")

The amnestic syndrome is an unusual, well-circumscribed form of brain syndrome that may be either rapid or slow in onset.

It is characterized by a profound alteration in orientation and recent memory.[13] While the person has no difficulty attending to the immediate situation and can readily solve simple problems, when she is tested for retention of new information, a striking defect is apparent. The ability to recall even one or two objects after 5 to 10 minutes is lost. The person is simply unable to hold onto recent experience; learning new information becomes impossible. There is also a severe disorientation to time and place, reflecting the close tie between orientation and the assimilation of new information. Consequently, persons suffering from the amnestic syndrome are prone to losing their way and, experientially, are continually meeting new people whom they have previously met and forgotten. Thus, this condition leaves the person quite capable of immediately recalling five digits and retrieving old memories out of the past, but between old and immediate experience a devastating memory void exists.

As a means of coping with this continual loss of new information, the person may begin to confabulate; that is, to make up responses in order to fill the memory gaps. This results in the creation of fanciful, if not outrageous, tales that can be mistaken for psychotic delusions by the unsuspecting clinician.

The amnestic syndrome can arise from head trauma, stroke, oxygen deprivation, or a deficiency of thiamin, vitamin B_1, usually associated with chronic alcoholism. The alcoholism-related amnesia is called Korsakoff's Syndrome, after the Russian physician who first described this condition in the late 1800s.

> A 50-year-old man with a long-standing drinking problem was hospitalized after several months of heavy alcohol consumption combined with increasing forgetfulness. The man had neglected his appearance and nutrition and had begun to talk to himself much of the time. When admitted to the hospital, he was noted to be "completely disoriented."
>
> After his admission, the patient persisted in explaining his hospitalization by stating that he had "been brought to the hospital after an injury to his leg at the shipyard," an event which had actually occurred, 10 years earlier. The day after he was transferred from one hospital building to another, he estimated that one week had passed since leaving the other building, and his memory for details of his former hospital setting already had begun to fade. In contrast, the man's memory for past years remained relatively

intact; he was even able to recall the exact address of the boarding house where he had lived sometime before his hospital admission.

The man would not admit that he had trouble remembering; instead, he made vague statements which he seemed to hope would appear consistent with the conversation. Sometimes, however, he made definite statements which were completely untrue. When tested by being shown three pictures, he could never recall the first two; only memory of the third picture remained. At times when confronted with obvious contradictions, he would change his explanation. The hospital diagnosis was Korsakoff's Syndrome.[14]

In this chapter we have considered brain syndrome as a clinical constellation involving one or more of five cognitive deficits in varying combinations: inattention, disorientation, recent memory impairment, diminished reasoning, and sensory indiscrimination. The recognition of these cognitive deficits is of con-

FIGURE 4-2 CLINICAL CHECKLIST

Brain Syndrome Cognitive Deficits

☐ INATTENTION

Failure at immediate recall of *five random digits* on *two* occasions.

☐ DISORIENTATION

Time: inability correctly to identify the *month, year, or general time of day* (day or nighttime).

Place: inability to identify one's *present location.*

Person: inability to recognize *persons* who should be *quite familiar.*

☐ RECENT MEMORY IMPAIRMENT

Failure to recall *four items* after *5 minutes* on *two* occasions.

☐ DIMINISHED REASONING

Inability to solve simple calculations:

- How many remain when you subtract 7 from 22?
- How many eggs would you have if you had one-third of a dozen?
- If you wish to divide 6 books so that twice the number are on the lower bookshelf as on the upper shelf, how many books should you place on each shelf?

☐ SENSORY INDISCRIMINATION

The presence of *illusions* or *hallucinations* (other than isolated auditory hallucinations).

siderable clinical import because they are highly correlated with a number of organic diseases, many of which are correctable.

We have discussed two prominent clinical versions of brain syndrome—ROBS and SOBS—as well as the amnestic syndrome, an unusual variation of brain syndrome marked by a striking disruption of recent memory and orientation. Although ROBS and SOBS have been portrayed as contrasting clinical presentations to facilitate our review of brain syndrome, this clear demarcation is not frequently found in the day-to-day world of clinical experience. Persons with SOBS are prone to the superimposition of ROBS resulting from various factors, including infections, medications, sensory deprivation, and nonspecific stress. In turn, ROBS may be the initial manifestation of a process that with time takes on the characteristics of SOBS. The clinician should be familiar with these two clinical versions of brain syndrome and recognize that they sometimes blend together.

Finally, we have reviewed various behavioral manifestations and personality changes that can mask the presence of brain syndrome.

In the next chapter, we will consider further clues to organic mental disorder which, along with recognition of brain syndrome, provide the clinician with a comprehensive basis for critical assessment.

> Once we got back to England, he was admitted to a mental hospital without delay. He had long since given up the struggle of trying to relate his ideas to reality, and had retired into a private world of unimpeded action. When last I saw him he had been put in charge of running the war after Dunkirk and was well pleased with the results.[4]

CHAPTER 5

FURTHER CLUES TO ORGANIC MENTAL DISORDERS

> *"Some circumstantial evidence is very strong, as when you find a trout in the milk."*
>
> *Henry David Thoreau*

In this chapter further clinical clues suggestive of organic mental disorders will be considered under two categories: alerting clues and presumptive evidence. Alerting clues are clinical findings that should prompt the clinician to a thorough search for an organic mental disorder. The greater the number of these clues in any given case, the more intense the suspicion that should be aroused in the mind of the clinician. Presumptive evidence is even more compelling in its implication. Until proven otherwise through medical evaluation, the presence of one or more of these factors must be interpreted as a sign of underlying organicity. The presence of brain syndrome is one important presumptive factor, but the clinician must not limit his clinical consideration to this factor alone. There are other observations which, when found in association with psychiatric symptoms, constitute presumptive evidence of an organic mental disorder, and they may appear in the absence of brain syndrome.

ALERTING CLUES

We will consider five factors which in association with psychiatric symptoms should suggest the possibility of organic disorder.

None of these clues, alone, indicates organicity, but their presence sensitizes the clinician to the possibility. Alerting clues serve as blinking red lights to the clinician, heightening the intensity of the search for presumptive evidence of organic mental disorder.

No History of Similar Symptoms

The initial occurrence of a psychiatric symptom should be carefully scrutinized. Generally, one of the best predictors of the future is the past; thus, if a person has never heretofore reacted to the stresses and strains of living with psychiatric symptoms, the emergence of such symptoms should suggest that something else is operating.

> A 54-year-old woman with no previous history of mental illness abruptly experienced a "delirious" episode lasting for almost 24 hours. Her confusion cleared, only to be replaced by striking changes in her mood and personality, manifest as depression and childlike dependency. After these changes had persisted and even worsened over a 10-month period, the woman was admitted to a hospital for evaluation.
>
> She was diagnosed as suffering from depression and treated with ECT. During the course of her treatment, however, she began to show obvious neurological deficits such as weakness in her left arm and leg as well as becoming markedly confused. At surgery a large, inoperable brain tumor was discovered infiltrating the right frontal, temporal, and parietal areas of the brain.[1]

The importance of prior history is heightened when the observed symptoms would have characteristically appeared prior to this time in the person's life. For example, "schizophrenia" is a diagnostic label sometimes indiscriminately applied to any person who exhibits delusions or hallucinations. The clinician would be well advised to question this characterization of psychotic symptoms when they occur initially in an individual over the age of 30. Schizophrenia, in the vast majority of cases, will express itself in the late teens and early twenties.

The emergence of new psychiatric symptoms also falls within the "no history" category. A history of one kind of psychiatric symptom should not be construed as representative of all psychiatric symptoms. For example, previous episodes of agitated, bizarre behavior should not obscure the initial emergence of an entirely different constellation of symptoms such as depression, confusion, and somnolence. The initial occurrence of any psychiatric symptom should be highly suspect despite a history of prior "mental illness."

No Readily Identifiable Cause

Psychiatric symptoms in the absence of problems in living should make the clinician uneasy. Even though the precise nature of the conflict may not be immediately apparent, with psychological reactions, there is usually evidence of stresses in the person's life. Particularly, psychological reactions that emerge without any "warning period" are almost always associated with a readily identifiable conflict or traumatic situation. In contrast, organic mental disorders often develop abruptly "out of the blue."

The concerned friends of a 31-year-old computer sciences student brought the young man into the hospital emergency room after they had observed noticeable changes in him over a 48-hour period. They related how he had abruptly started to hear strange voices mumbling to him and simultaneously had become quite withdrawn in his behavior. He seemed to avoid conversations; and when he did respond, he gave very short answers which did not appear related to the discussion.

Further questioning of the man's friends revealed that a week before, he had stopped his studies and quit his job as a taxi driver. He had also complained of a headache for which he sought help from several physicians without satisfaction.

The young man was described as a loner, but without a history of mental disorder. No precipitating stressful event that might account for these changes in him could be identified.

Although fully oriented to time and place when examined by a psychiatrist, he had considerable difficulty complying with simple requests. He did not seem to understand the questions being asked and was thought to have "loosening of associations." His memory proved "difficult to test."

He was admitted to a psychiatric unit with a tentative diagnosis of "acute schizophreniform psychosis."[2]

The abrupt onset of strange behavior in a person with no previous history of mental disorder combined with difficulties in cognitive functioning (as well as a change in headache pattern which we will discuss shortly) should have raised suspicion of an organic problem. Within 24 hours of admission he developed fever, and his neck became rigid. An emergency angiogram (a contrast study of the brain using dye which can be seen on x-ray) showed a large subdural hematoma. Reparative surgery was immediately performed with excellent results, leaving no residual symptoms. The hematoma had developed from a "leaking" artery, known as an "aneurysmal malformation," a somewhat rare congenital anatomical defect.

Although the absence of significant problems in living is suggestive of an organic mental disorder, *the reverse is not true.* The presence of problems in living that might be expected to elicit psychiatric symptoms cannot be taken as proof positive of a psychological reaction. As illustrated by numerous examples throughout this book, the most plausible psychodynamics are frequently identified in cases of organic mental disorder. The fact that a sound psychological explanation can be advanced should never blind the clinician to evidence for organicity.

Age 55 or Older

Although age 55 may be an arbitrary designation, it is true, nevertheless, that older persons are particularly susceptible to organic mental disorders. More than half the initial psychiatric admissions for persons age 55 or older are cases of organic mental disorder.

Several factors contribute to this increased risk among older persons. The wide margin of safety inherent within the support systems of the body is significantly reduced with age; consequently, maintenance of the optimal internal environment on which brain functioning depends is less efficient than in earlier years, and certain organ systems may actually fail. The nervous system itself becomes more sensitive to drugs and less adroit at adapting to troublesome side effects. The incidence of numerous diseases rises with age, as does the risk of accidental falls with head injury, which predisposes to organic mental disorders.

I do not mean to imply that psychological reactions are absent from older life; it is just that the percentage of psychiatric symptoms most appropriately explained from an organic perspective shows a dramatic increase with age.

Coexistence of Chronic Disease

Persons suffering from chronic diseases are frequently treated with medications that cause adverse side effects resembling psychiatric symptoms. Long-standing chronic disease also frequently predisposes a person to support system failure. Of course, the degree of risk for organic mental disorder depends on the specific type of disease. Some chronic diseases create minimal risk while others characteristically produce organic mental disorders. Consider the following case history.

> After the death of her husband, a 56-year-old woman became increasingly agitated over the next 48 hours. Her relatives brought her into a medical emergency room after she had insisted that her brother was her dead husband returned to life. The preceding day she had mistakenly defecated in a trash can, thinking she was in her bathroom.
>
> The woman was "cleared medically." She was given a diagnosis of "acute grief reaction," and admitted to the psychiatric service. There she was unable to recall one of three items after 5 minutes, and she was also found to have a peculiar yellow coloring of the sclerae of her eyes.[3]

This woman had a known history of chronic liver disease from a severe drinking problem. Her liver disease put her at risk for a variety of problems that can lead to organic psychiatric symptoms. Subsequent laboratory studies confirmed that she had contracted viral hepatitis, thus compromising her already debilitated liver to the extent that she went into hepatic (liver) failure. This was the cause of her psychiatric symptoms. The history of chronic liver disease should have served as an important alerting clue to the true nature of the woman's problem.

Excessive Use of Drugs

Psychoactive chemicals can create an elaborate array of mental and emotional effects ranging from the pleasurable to the frightening and extremely bizarre. Toxic reactions to drugs are probably the number one cause of organic mental disorders. Furthermore, with certain substances, addiction can ensue. If the person's drug supply is then interrupted, severe withdrawal states characterized by anxiety, confusion, or even psychosis may result. Although the wild, delirious state is easily recognized as a drug reaction, these conditions can be quite subtle in presentation.

In addition to the direct psychiatric effects, excessive use of drugs (including alcohol) predisposes a person to a myriad of medical problems as well as accidents, particularly related to driving.

The clinician should not overlook the fact that prescription and over-the-counter medications are *drugs.* Increasingly, these substances account for more and more organic mental disorders. This is particularly true in the psychiatric field, where the very medications we use for treatment purposes can cause additional psychiatric symptoms in the form of side effects.

Persons taking over-the-counter drugs sometimes do not consider these substances medications. They may unknowingly mislead the clinician by denying the use of medications even though they are taking self-prescribed, over-the-counter preparations, some of which have powerful "mind-bending" effects.

> For a period of 2 months he had slept infrequently. Sometimes he would work two consecutive shifts, one for pay, the other for free. He would throw himself feverishly into whatever he was doing. When he went bowling, he could bowl 50 games uninterrupted and would become impatient, resetting the pins if they were not all knocked down with the first ball.
>
> The parents of this 23-year-old man became concerned as they watched their son overspend his income and even begin to squander his savings. On the day prior to his admission, he disrobed in front of his mother at home and tried to climb into a small wash basin. After becoming quite agitated when his father restrained him, he was admitted to the hospital.
>
> The young man was described as fully oriented but with obvious paranoid delusions. There was no memory impairment or hallucinations. He denied using drugs.[4]

Eventually it was discovered that this man had recently experienced a peculiar acne-like rash in conjunction with his unusual behavior. This subtle clue led to a laboratory determination of "bromide toxicity." Within a week the man's normal behavior had returned. On further questioning, he revealed he had been daily ingesting a whole bottle of a bromide-containing, over-the-counter medication. It was unclear as to whether he initially hid this fact or did not think it of significance. The clinician should routinely inquire about the use of drugs and medications. This is an aspect of history-taking which, whenever possible, should involve a secondary source. Persons who abuse drugs are notoriously unreliable reporters.

The role of drugs and medications in producing organic mental disorders is so extensive that I have devoted a later chapter exclusively to this subject.

PRESUMPTIVE EVIDENCE

The clues discussed in this section are so strongly correlated with organic mental disorders that when detected in association with psychiatric symptoms, they should be accepted as indicative of organicity until proven otherwise. In this sense they have the same clinical significance as do the core elements of brain syndrome.

Head Injury

Following a head injury, the onset of psychiatric symptoms always raises the specter of medical emergency. Head trauma can cause increased pressure within the brain, most commonly due to an expanding extravasation of fluid such as seen in subdural hematoma. The most rapidly progressing cases produce symptoms readily recognized as neurological deficits and thus do not characteristically create a critical assessment problem. A major exception, however, is seen with alcoholics, where acute neurological symptoms may be mistaken for signs of drunkenness. For example, the inebriated person may pass out while standing upright or driving a car and sustain a traumatic injury to the head while unconscious. Upon arousing, the person may be unable adequately to communicate the injury or the resulting symptoms and may be written off as "just another drunk." The clinician should always look for signs of recent head trauma, such as facial lacerations, broken teeth, dried blood around the ear, or an unexplained lump on the head, particularly when intoxication is suspected.

In some cases of head injury, symptoms are slow to evolve and may be restricted to subtle changes in personality combined with vague complaints of headache. For this reason, clinicians should routinely inquire about head trauma. Automobile accidents frequently cause head injury, even though no external evidence may be seen and the person may not report a loss of consciousness. Sometimes direct questions—such as, Have you been in a recent automobile accident or otherwise injured?—will bring to light instances of injury that otherwise would have gone unacknowledged.

Change in Headache Pattern

A recent *change* in a person's characteristic pattern of headache should be throughly evaluated medically. Headache is a relatively common experience among adults. Typically there is a characteristic pattern of onset and distribution of pain that has existed for many years. The person comes to accept this symptom as a response to certain kinds of stress relieved by a reduction in tension or such simple symptomatic treatment as the taking of aspirin. When a person, particularly one seeking help from a human service professional, spontaneously complains of headache, the clinician should *listen.* Headache can be a symptom of serious brain diseases, particularly infections, brain tumors, and subdural hematomas. One researcher has estimated that approximately 60% of persons with brain tumors experience headache. Headache is the *initial* manifestation of brain tumor in one out of five cases! The percentage for subdural hematoma is even higher. As we shall discuss in Chapter 7, the type of headache most commonly associated with brain tumor has a characteristic pattern with which all clinicians should be familiar.

In addition to routinely inquiring about headache, the clinician should also be sensitive to nonverbal clues suggestive of this complaint. Once again, this is especially important when dealing with persons who are intoxicated, and with persons who are confused, drowsy, or psychotic. The person may intermittently pull at his ear or hold his head in his hands. In certain cases these gestures may be the only perceivable evidence of headache.

The following case history demonstrates how this complaint can be neglected when associated with dramatic, overshadowing psychiatric symptoms.

A young man in his early twenties, hyperactive and abusive, periodically threatening violence, was evaluated in an emergency room.

His wife said that on the previous day he had started complaining of a severe headache for which he was seen by his family physician and treated with a "pain shot." After returning home, he continued to suffer from the headache. A short time later the man abruptly began to scream, attacking both his wife and children. The Fire Department was summoned, and he was taken to the hospital.

On examination he appeared in good physical health but was incoherent in his responses to questions. Without provocation, he would become wild and scream out at other people in the emergency room. He was treated with an antipsychotic medication and admitted to the psychiatric service as a case of functional psychosis (schizophrenia).

Over the next 24 hours, the young man became progressively drowsy with fever and stiff neck. Special neurological studies showed an infection of the brain and its coverings known as meningoencephalitis. Fortunately, he was successfully treated with antibiotics and suffered no residual effects.[5]

Visual Disturbances

Any visual problem of recent onset should suggest the possibility of an organic disorder, but the clinician should be particularly watchful for complaints of double images or partial visual loss.

Eye movement is the product of complex muscle coordination requiring balanced input from several different nerves. The cranial nerves that control eye movement extend for varying lengths from their points of origin in the brain to their connections with the muscles of the eyes. As a result of encroachment by expanding brain masses or from certain degenerative diseases, these nerves become compromised. When this happens, the fine movement of the eyes is disrupted. To the observer, the eyes may appear out of line or crossed. The affected person may report "seeing double," since the muscle imbalance leads to image formation on slightly different areas of each retina.

The visual pathways carrying input from the retina of the eye to the occipital cortex and surrounding associative areas of the brain also can be interrupted by a variety of brain diseases.

In some instances, the visual loss may be so subtle that the person fails to notice the deficit. Nevertheless, the person will be left with a "hole" in their sight that may become apparent only after a series of unexplained accidents, such as bumping into objects or scraping the car, usually the same side on each occasion. This is because the person is now unable to detect objects in certain parts of the visual fields, right or left, depending on where the brain disorder is located.

In other cases the person will be well aware of a defect in vision. When this complaint is made, clinicians should be alert to the possible organic implications.

Speech Deficits

Speech deficits can be categorized roughly into two groups: problems in the mechanical production of speech sounds and problems with appropriate word usage.

Mechanical difficulty in articulating words is called *dysarthria.* The most common cause of dysarthria is drug or alcohol intoxication. The person's speech is slurred and "thick," sometimes to the extent of being impossible to decipher. This garbled speech can be mistaken for psychotic language, although the observant clinician should not make this error. The speech of persons in the throes of functional psychosis is strange in content and connections but mechanically intact. It is not dysarthric.

In contrast to dysarthria, aphasia is the loss of word comprehension and proper word usage. In one form of this disorder, known as *nonfluent aphasia,* the natural flow and rhythm of speech is lost in addition to the person's having difficulty finding the right word. Characteristically, a person with this problem mainly uses verbs and nouns, with a scarcity of modifers or connecting words. Nonfluent aphasia frequently results from a stroke that also leaves the person with a dramatic restriction in movement on one side of the body (usually the right side); for this reason, it seldom creates a significant critical assessment problem since it is readily identifiable as a neurological condition.

Not so, however, with *fluent aphasia,* which can easily be mistaken for a psychiatric problem. As a result, the person has little difficulty articulating words; the speech is smooth and naturally rhythmic. There is, nevertheless, a profound difficulty in finding the correct words and arranging them so as to communicate a desired meaning. When closely examined, the person's speech will have little substantive content; instead, it is filled with incorrect, inappropriate, or even made-up words.

The individual suffering from fluent aphasia adapts in several characteristic ways, yet surprisingly often seems unaware that anything is wrong. The person may talk around the word that cannot be mobilized. For example, in trying to say "key," the person might come up with "what you unlock the door with"; or, in referring to a spoon, "a handle with a little cup on it."

Word substitution may be used, so "hammer" is used for the related word "nail," or "fork" for "knife." Word substitutions are sometimes made purely on the basis of similar sounds. "Spoot" might be used for "spoon" or "heart" for "hard." Sometimes the substituted word will be quite obtuse, as in one writer's report of a patient who referred to his thumb as an "Argentinian rifle."[6] Prepositions and other connecting words are frequently misused, thereby creating peculiar grammatical transitions.

From a critical assessment perspective, one of the most confusing variations of fluent aphasia is the prominent use of artificial words known as "neologisms." These fabricated words can sound quite bizarre, and are easily mistaken for psychotic speech. The difference is that, while the psychotic person periodically uses strange words, there is generally no ongoing difficulty with basic descriptive language. For the aphasic, the simple use of language is problematic.

The most common form of fluent aphasia is limited to a problem with naming well-known objects, a condition called *anomia.* The person appears to have lost the meaning of what should be familiar objects. Anomia may occur alone or in combination with other forms of aphasia. It is an important condition for the clinician to recognize because it is a symptom found in a large number of neurological disorders.

The following is a hypothetical exchange that might be expected in a case of fluent aphasia with anomia.

Examiner: (holding up a pencil) What do I have in my hand?
Subject: It's a long think . . . you hold it with writing. (Frustrated) No, it's a uh, uh, nenpil, you write it.

When a person with aphasia is persistently unable to communicate what they want to say, frustration with a gradual raising of the voice typically occurs, and understandably so. Add to this clinical picture a tendency to use neologisms plus a variety of inappropriate expressions and you have a worthy challenge for critical assessment.

Differentiation of aphasia from psychiatric symptoms requires an active suspicion on the part of the clinician combined with careful listening. "The acute onset of abnormal speech in a middle-aged person is . . . almost invariably diagnostic of a fluent (receptive) aphasia."[6] Any detection by the clinician of a mechanical defect in speech, such as slurred or garbled speech or the inability to communicate simple facts or name common objects, must be considered a neurological problem until proven otherwise.

This next case history illustrates the last three presumptive factors we have considered: change in headache pattern, visual disturbances, and speech deficits.

> A middle-aged man required restraints made from heavy fish netting to control his violent, explosive behavior. As he was admitted to the hospital he was observed to snarl, show his teeth, and lash out at bystanders.
>
> Previously in the day, he had attacked his wife with a butcher knife for no apparent reason. When the police had arrived at his home in response to his wife's frantic call, the man was noted to have severely garbled speech.
>
> For the past several months he had undergone a striking personality change and had complained of blurred vision and severe headaches.
>
> This man was subsequently found to have a large right frontal lobe tumor extending into the temporal area as well. After the tumor was removed surgically, his symptoms disappeared, allowing him to resume his job as night watchman.[7]

Abnormal Body Movements

Many clinicians fail adequately to appreciate the association between various kinds of abnormal body movements and organic mental disorders.

Take simple, ordinary walking. This basic human capacity is disturbed in a number of conditions that characteristically produce psychiatric symptoms. Unsteadiness in walking is an important clue to drug and alcohol intoxication. When manifest by gross staggering, the clinical detection of this clue is easy; but when the person compensates by walking with his feet spread more widely apart than usual or by simply moving very slowly, clinical recognition may be more difficult.

Syphilis of the brain, pernicious anemia (vitamin B_{12} deficiency), alcoholism, and a number of other organic disorders manifest as psychiatric symptoms in combination with disturbances in walking. Normal pressure hydrocephalus is an unusual condition commencing in mid-life and characterized by declining mental ability, usually with depression, loss of bladder control, and a strange disturbance in walking. The person has considerable difficulty initiating each step. The feet seem almost stuck to the floor; hence the term *magnetic gait.*

Every clinician should develop a sense of what constitutes normal walking: how the arms swing, how far apart the feet are, what the relative length is of normal walking steps. On the basis of a brief observation, the clinician should be able to detect aberrations in walking (gait). In the interview situation, this is easily and unobtrusively accomplished by watching a person enter and leave the office.

But there are other kinds of abnormal movements of considerable consequence for critical assessment. Persons with Parkinson's disease may experience depression and emotional lability along with a characteristic tremor of the hands, sometimes described as a pill-rolling movement. The genetic disease known as Huntington's chorea leads to poor impulse control and eventually may manifest as violence and psychosis. A hallmark of this condition is spastic jerking and twitching of various muscles throughout the body, particularly the extremities and the trunk muscles.

This frequently found combination of psychiatric symptoms and unusual movements is not as surprising as it may at first seem. Brain areas specific for motor coordination and emotional elaboration both contain high concentrations of the same neurotransmitter, dopamine. It is presumed that disturbances in the level of this chemical in relation to other neurotransmitters simultaneously produce disturbed movements and psychiatric disorder. Tremors, tics, twitches, jerking movements, and problems in walking—these somatic symptoms should not be dismissed by the clinician concerned with critical assessment, for they often represent important clues to organic mental disorders.

Sustained Deviations in Vital Signs

Vital signs is a term referring collectively to heart rate, blood pressure, respiratory rate, and temperature. These four measures reflect the physiological integrity of the body. They remain within relatively narrow ranges, even under increasing stress. With extreme exertion or anxiety, significant increases in heart rate, blood pressure, and respirations occur temporarily, only to return to normal as the stressful situation passes. As a general rule, when one or more of these vital signs remains outside the normal range for a period of several hours or more, organic disease should be considered. This is a frequently overlooked clue to masquerading organic mental disorders.

In some instances, particularly those involving drugs, a change in vital signs may be the only indicator of the organic nature of psychiatric symptoms. Vital sign determinations are not highly technical measurements, and their use as screening measures with respect to critical assessment does not require special medical expertise.

I am not suggesting that nonmedical professionals assume primary responsibility for requesting and determining vital sign measurements. They should, however, make use of this valuable source of information when it is available and also recognize these indicators as potential aids in puzzling cases.

In Table 5-1 are listed ranges for the four vital signs that can be used by the clinician for detecting sustained deviations. These ranges should not be equated with normal values; readings within them can be abnormal. Nevertheless, determinations *outside* these ranges, if persistent, must always be considered pathological. They require further medical evaluation since they are likely indicators of organic disease.

Following 2 days of confusion, disorientation, and delusional thoughts that centered on the idea that he had a transistor radio

TABLE 5-1 VITAL SIGN VALUES
(for critical assessment screening)

Heart Rate:	50–100/minute
Blood Pressure:	90/50——160/95 (systolic)/(diastolic)
Respirations:	6–20/minute
Temperature: (Oral)	96°F (35.6°C)—100°F (37.8°C)

in his head, a young man was admitted to the emergency ward of a general hospital.

When examined, he appeared "delirious"; his memory for recent events was obviously impaired. Measurements of his vital signs were recorded: blood pressure—140/100, pulse—120, and rectal temperature—100.2°F. His pupils were widely dilated and did not contract to light.

Despite these abnormal findings, the initial clinical impression was that this man was in a state of psychotic excitement. Treatment with intramuscular haloperidol, however, was without effect.

Three hours later, his family brought in an empty pill bottle that had contained amytriptyline (Elavil). This discovery, combined with the man's clinical appearance and abnormal vital signs, led to a diagnosis of anticholinergic psychosis. Treatment with the chemical antidote, physostigmine, was given and within 45 minutes the delirium had cleared, only to return after two and a half hours, when the short-acting physostigmine had worn off. Repeated intervention, however, led to a complete resolution. He was discharged 36 hours later without symptoms.[8]

A clinician oblivious to the significance of this patient's abnormal vital signs might have persisted in the mistaken idea that this was another episode of psychotic behavior to be treated with antipsychotic medication. Fortunately, this clinical error was not perpetuated in this case.

A word of caution about vital signs. These measures are sometimes hastily made and may be recorded incorrectly. When a gross deviation is discovered, the first course of action should be to repeat the determination. This simple procedure can save considerable time and energy directed at false values.

Changes in Consciousness

Consciousness indicates a person's state of alertness or general awareness with respect to what is happening in the immediate present. Three important changes in consciousness should always suggest the presence of organic dysfunction. They are excessive somnolence, lapses in consciousness, and loss of consciousness.

Excessive somnolence occurs in conjunction with many brain disorders. The clinical history in such cases often includes falling asleep in the middle of the day, even during the course of conversation. Activities once performed with ease are increasingly difficult due to the person's diminished level of alertness. The person's sleepiness is typically exaggerated quite dramatically following the consumption of small amounts of alcohol or tranquilizing medication.

A lapse in consciousness is a momentary break in a person's awareness. There may be no memory of such lapses; thus, the person, particularly in cases where the lapses are quite brief, may be unaware of the problem. When observed by the clinician, lapses can be mistaken for blocking, a symptom seen in schizophrenia. The person will suddenly cease talking for no apparent reason, only to resume after a momentary pause as though nothing had transpired. More often than not, lapses in consciousness indicate seizure activity arising from deep in the brain.

> The family physician of a 26-year-old man referred him to an emergency room with the brief notation that he was "psychotic and needed hospitalization."
>
> While at work that day, the man thought he smelled acetylene gas. Concerned about a possible explosion, he crawled out on the roof of his shop to investigate the matter. While there, he visualized "tanks of gas" pouring over into the air conditioning system. He called the local police and fire departments, but when they arrived, they found nothing unusual. The man was referred to his physician and then to the emergency room.
>
> There was no history of mental illness or drug use. On mental status examination, the man appeared normal without disorientation, delusions, or hallucinations. Further questioning, however, revealed a history of short lapses in consciousness, one of which had resulted in an automobile accident.[9]

This man was suspected of having seizures, as was confirmed by an electroencephalogram showing "random sharp spikes" over the left temporal lobe area. The final diagnosis was temporal lobe epilepsy.

Fainting spells as well as loss of consciousness associated with certain kinds of seizures should, without exception, receive a thorough medical evaluation. These important danger signals are deserving of routine clinical questioning by the human service clinician. One would think that an unexplained loss of consciousness invariably would raise the suspicion of neurological disorder, but as the next case illustrates, this is not always true.

While on business in another country, an atomic physicist began to have paranoid thoughts about other people plotting to steal certain atomic secrets from him. After his problem had become obvious, he was quickly returned home, where he was diagnosed as schizophrenic and hospitalized for psychiatric treatment.

After his release several months later, he suffered a loss of consciousness with a grand mal seizure. His psychiatrist, however, was so convinced the man was experiencing a schizophrenic break, that he dismissed the possibility of an organic mental disorder. Only after the young man complained of a severe, unrelenting headache was he finally referred for more extensive neurological studies. He was found to have a highly malignant brain tumor invading the temporal lobe.[10]

SPECIAL CLINICAL TESTING

We have now considered five alerting clues and eight presumptive factors essential to the practice of critical assessment. These clinical clues, along with the core manifestations of brain syndrome, are the clinician's basic keys to unmasking organic masqueraders appearing as psychological reactions. There will be situations, however, where the evidence is equivocal or only suggestive, leaving the critical assessment in the balance. In such instances, three special tests can be valuable aids. These three tests are quite simple in design and can be administered in a brief period, ordinarily less than a total of 10 minutes. When any of these tests are positive the clinician should consider this to be presumptive evidence of an organic problem. When *negative,* however, these tests must not be construed as definitive evidence against organicity.

Write-a-Sentence Test

Despite an appearance of simplicity, the task of writing a sentence requires highly complex brain-eye-muscle interaction. Persons with a brain deficit often have difficulty executing this common task. The Write-a-Sentence Test is a particularly sensitive indicator of global brain dysfunction and typically shows improvement that parallels the person's recovery from the causative disease.[11]

The test is administered by giving the following instructions verbally: "Write the sentence which I give you as neatly and legibly as you can. The sentence is: "Men and women have equal rights but different needs." This sentence should be slowly stated *twice* to ensure that the person adequately registers it. The person should be provided with lined paper and a pencil. Of course, if there is a language preferred to English, the sentence must be given in that language.

When the person has completed the sentence or at the end of two minutes, whichever is first, the sentence should be reviewed for the following deficits:

Motor
: Clumsily formed letters; duplication of certain strokes, particularly in letters such as *m* or *w.*

Spatial
: Improper alignment of letters, with displacement either upward or downward from the line.

Linguistic
: Simple spelling errors; use of nonexistent words (neologisms); word deletions; word repetitions.

In evaluating the person's performance on this test, you should not engage in a microscopic analysis. Look for obvious errors as a basis for calling this test positive.

Draw-a-Clock Test

This test requires that a person handle spatial relationships, simple number sequences, the mechanical recording of numerals, and the representation of time. The task is not dependent on verbal skills and therefore is subject to relatively little cultural distortion. Although a simple task for most adults of normal intelligence, the Draw-a-Clock Test may prove highly problematic for persons with organic brain problems.

The test is administered by providing the person with a previously printed circle, approximately 3 inches in diameter. (It is a good idea to have a supply of these printed circles available in the clinic setting.) The person is given a pencil and instructed to enter the appropriate numbers as they ordinarily appear on the face of a clock and then draw the hands so that the time showing is 10 minutes past 10 o'clock. When the person has completed the task or at the end of 2 minutes, whichever comes first, the construction should be reviewed with the following facts in mind.

Persons with organic brain disease sometimes displace the numbers on the face of the clock so that the numbers fall outside the circle or gravitate toward the center. Crowding, repeating, or deleting numbers may also occur, as well as a rotation of the numbers around the face of the clock, so that 12 no longer appears at the top. Sometimes the person will draw the hands of the clock so that they are displaced from the center of the circle or represent an incorrect time.[12]

If a person is unable to complete this test without obvious errors, it should be considered positive, constituting presumptive evidence for an organic disorder.

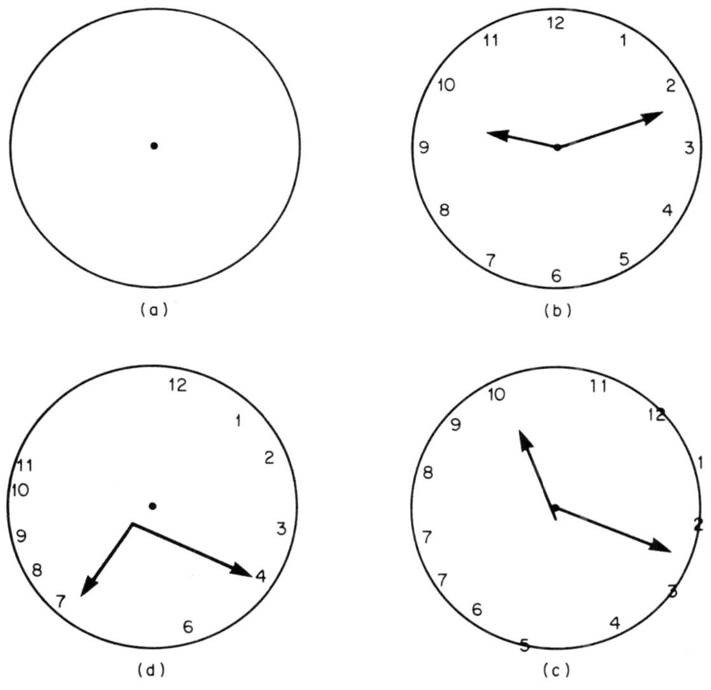

a. Printed circle with dot in center.
b. Adequate reproduction.
c. Displacement and rotation of numbers: repetition of a number (7).
d. Spatial crowding: displacement of hands; deletion of a number (5); incorrect time.

FIGURE 5-1

Copy-a-Three-Dimensional-Figure Test

This is a test of spatial appreciation. Adequate performance rests on the integrity of various associative areas of the brain. Since these areas are extensive in size and relatively silent with respect to obvious neurological functions, like motor movement and sensory perception, this simple constructional test can be an important screening device for organic dysfunction.

The test is administered by presenting the person with a previously printed, three-dimensional figure such as a cube. The person is instructed to reproduce the figure on a space provided just below the printed version. When the person has completed the task or at the end of 2 minutes, whichever comes first, the construction is reviewed.

Evaluation of this test is a global assessment as to whether the person has been able to reproduce the three-dimensional effect.

In these last two chapters we have discussed the crucial clinical evidence to be considered in the search for organic mental

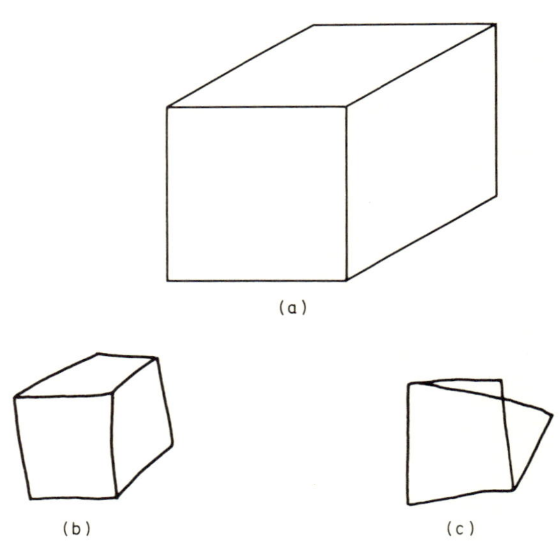

a. Printed cube which client copies
b. Adequate reproduction
c. Inadequate reproduction

FIGURE 5-2

disorders. Alerting clues sensitize the clinician to the probability of an organic masquerader. In turn, the identification of any one of several presumptive factors demands further medical evaluation. Although in certain instances, presumptive evidence will turn out to be misleading in that no organicity exists, in the majority of cases an underlying organic basis will be discovered. Persistent searching for these factors provides the human service clinician with a sound approach to critical assessment.

We have not reviewed the use of such highly specialized test procedures as the CAT scan, the EEG, and the lumbar puncture. While these are potent assessment tools, they are reserved for medical specialists in making specific diagnoses. In this book our focus is the clinical activity that leads to a more thorough medical diagnostic evaluation.

In the next chapter, we shall look at how the clinician can integrate the search for organic masqueraders, that is, critical assessment, into the basic interview format.

CHAPTER 6

PUTTING CRITICAL ASSESSMENT TO WORK

"Practice and thought might gradually forge many an art."
Virgil

HAVING WADED through the previous chapter, the reader may feel overwhelmed by the long list of factors to be considered in critical assessment. This would seem an appropriate point to pause, take a breath, and look at the nuts and bolts.

A complete check list is provided in Table 6-1. The clinician should resist the initial tendency to try to run through this list as a separate part of the interview. Although initially such an approach might prove easier, in the long run it is much more intrusive and is less efficient than an approach which weaves critical assessment observations and questions into the overall interview. With practice, your own natural style will prevail; critical assessment will become second nature and will require a surprisingly small amount of interview time.

In Figure 6-1, I have tried to specify where in the ordinary course of an interview various issues will typically be addressed. The person's age, and sometimes even vital signs, are frequently noted in the identifying information provided on the admission form or in the client's record. The first portion of an interview usually includes a discussion of the presenting symptom and possible causes in the person's life situation. It is also quite natural to inquire in these early stages of the interview about a history

TABLE 6-1 CRITICAL ASSESSMENT
(Check List)

WHEN ASSOCIATED WITH PSYCHIATRIC SYMPTOMS:

Alerting Clues to Organic Mental Disorder

1. No History of Similar Symptoms
2. No Readily Identifiable Cause
3. Age 55 or Older
4. Coexistence of Chronic Disease
5. Excessive Use of Drugs

Presumptive Evidence for Organic Mental Disorder

6. Brain Syndrome (One or More Core Deficits)
   - Inattention
   - Disorientation
   - Recent memory impairment
   - Diminished reasoning
   - Sensory indiscrimination
7. Head Injury
8. Change in Headache Pattern
9. Visual Disturbances
10. Speech Deficits
11. Abnormal Body Movements
12. Sustained Deviations in Vital Signs
13. Changes in Consciousness
14. Special Tests (One or More Positive)
    - Write-a-Sentence
    - Draw-a-Clock
    - Copy-a-Three-Dimensional-Figure

of similar symptoms if this should not be addressed as the person tells his own story.

Throughout the interview the clinician must continuously observe for changes in consciousness, abnormal body movements, speech deficits, and core manifestations of brain syndrome. Evidence of these factors may also emerge as part of the history; this is particularly true concerning changes in consciousness and brain syndrome. Other critical assessment factors tend to require specific questions which can be naturally woven through the interview. If indicated, special tests are administered toward the conclusion of the interview, because at this point the clinician can best determine their appropriateness.

HYPOTHETICAL CASES

Let us consider a hypothetical case as a way of reviewing the actual practice of critical assessment. You are about to interview

COURSE OF THE INTERVIEW

Early — Middle — Late

Early Issues

- History of Similar Symptoms ______
- Identifiable Cause ______
- Vital Signs (if taken) ______
- Age 55 or Older ______

Ongoing Observations

- Changes in Consciousness ______
- Abnormal Body Movements ______
- Speech Deficits ______
- Manifestations of Brain Syndrome ______

Specific Questions (if unanswered)

- ______ Head Injury
- ______ Change in Headache Pattern
- ______ Visual Disturbances
- ______ Co-Existence of Chronic Disease
- ______ Excessive Use of Drugs

Special Tests (if indicated)

- ______ Write-A-Sentence
- ______ Draw-A-Clock
- ______ Copy-A-Three-Dimensional-Figure

FIGURE 6-1

a new client. He arranged for an appointment the previous week and this is your first meeting. The receptionist calls your office, announcing that Mr. B has arrived. You go to meet him in the waiting area and, after introducing yourself, escort him to your office. You are both seated. His chart says he is a 45-year-old automobile salesman.

By this time—even though the formal interview has yet to begin—you should have made several pertinent observations. You have had an opportunity to observe the man's general appearance and dress as well as the way he walks. Are there any gross incongruities? Is his shirt wrong-side-out? Does he have difficulty walking? Positive answers to these questions suggest neurological deficits. The point is that even before you ask the first question of the interview, observations with respect to critical assessment should have been made.

You might start the interview with a question like, "What brings you here?" As the individual begins to tell his story, he may provide a prior history of similar symptoms or reveal the presence or absence of a stressful life situation. If these issues are not spontaneously touched on by the client, you will want to insert specific inquiries at appropriate junctures in the interview. For example, in our hypothetical case, the man might state that he has been feeling depressed. The interview would then proceed along the following lines.

INTERVIEWER: "In the past, have you ever been depressed the way you are now?"

CLIENT: "Well, I have felt blue at times, a little down . . . but never like this. I don't want to do anything. I avoid friends. Nothing seems to mean much anymore."

You have pretty well established that the man has no prior history of depression similar to that which he is now experiencing.

As the interview progresses, you continuously observe for unusual shifts in consciousness, abnormal body movements, and speech deficits. Each of these symptoms can manifest episodically and infrequently during the course of the interview and may be overlooked unless you are actively watching for them. This does not require an ongoing central focus, but rather a continuous suspicion, looking "out of the corner of one's eye," so to speak.

So, relatively early into the interview, you are collecting information with respect to several critical assessment items. As the client proceeds to tell his story, other information may be volunteered. As this occurs, you should note it, thereby avoiding later questions that, had you been listening and watching, would have already been answered.

Our hypothetical client elaborates on his depression by describing how nothing seems to go right for him any more: sales are down, his car has been in the shop twice in the last 3 weeks, one of his children has had a "brush with the law," and he has been having "a bitch of a headache" for the past 2 days. While describing situational events which might reasonably be expected to produce "downer" feelings, the client slips in an unexpected symptom: headache. It is now incumbent on you to explore this complaint.

INTERVIEWER: "About this headache you have been having, describe it for me."

CLIENT: "Oh, it's the kind I always get, right in the back of my neck. If I take three aspirin early enough, I can usually nip it in the bud, but otherwise, it goes on for most of the day. I've had these things off and on for 30 years. The doctors never have been able to find anything wrong; they say it's just stress."

INTERVIEWER: "Is there anything *different* about your headache this time?"

CLIENT: "No, it's the same every time. Just like clockwork, when I get loaded down with pressures."

Through this brief exchange, you have confirmed that the client is experiencing a headache quite familiar to him over the years. It does not represent a change, and unless it should persist beyond the usual duration which he has described, it would not constitute presumptive evidence for an organic mental disorder.

If by midway in the interview certain critical assessment issues have not been addressed, you want to begin to look for a natural transition during which you can inquire specifically about them.

INTERVIEWER: "Mr. B, I want to ask you a few questions about aspects of your health which might possibly have some bearing on the depression you are feeling. Have you had a recent head injury?"

CLIENT: "No."

INTERVIEWER: "Has your vision changed—has it decreased or have you been seeing double?"

CLIENT: "No, I haven't had anything like that."

INTERVIEWER: "Do you have any kind of chronic disease?"

CLIENT: "My doctor tells me I have chronic bronchitis and maybe even a touch of emphysema. It's because I smoke too much."

INTERVIEWER: "Do you take medications, either prescribed or those you get over the counter at the drug store?"

CLIENT: "No."

INTERVIEWER: "No medications for your lung problems or any other symptoms?"

CLIENT: "Well, I use aspirin and stuff for stomach acid, but I don't use either of them more than every few weeks."

INTERVIEWER: "How about alcohol or other drugs? How much do you use them?"

CLIENT: "I have a cocktail just about every evening and sometimes a beer or two on the weekends, but I don't take any kind of drugs."

INTERVIEWER: "Has a doctor ever told you something was wrong with your heart rate, blood pressure, or the way you breathe?"

CLIENT: "Never a time. Even with all my smoking, every time my doctor checks me, he says all my measures are pretty good."

This short series of questions would probably take less than two minutes to complete. From the answers supplied by our hypothetical client, the only item that would be considered positive with respect to critical assessment is the possibility of chronic disease (lung). Along with the fact that the man has apparently never before experienced a significant depression, it serves as an alerting clue to the possibility of organic mental disorder.

Let us assume, in this case, that no presumptive factors are identified. You have been particularly alert for evidence of brain syndrome. There is none. He is fully aware of the time and where he is. The manner in which he goes about telling his story demonstrates that he is completely alert. At one point in the interview you test his recent memory by giving him four objects to remember, and after 5 minutes he recalls them all on the first try. Throughout the interview you have observed for changes in his level of consciousness; nothing has been noted.

If his vital signs appear in the chart, you would want to check them to confirm that they are grossly normal. If during the interview you have heard anything that makes you suspicious of the man's statement about his drug and alcohol use, you might return to this with more insistent questioning or, better still, if his spouse is waiting outside, you might want to ask her this same question.

Assume that no further evidence is detected. You are left

with a middle-aged man whose life situation is compatible with depression, and who has never before had this problem. He may have some degree of chronic disease for which, however, he takes no medication. A decision as to whether to administer the special tests becomes a value judgment for you as a clinician. If you are still concerned about the possibility of an organic mental disorder, they should be given. Our hypothetical client completes all three tests quickly and without error.

At this juncture, you proceed with a consideration of this man's depression as a psychological reaction, realizing, nevertheless, that at some future date presumptive evidence for an organic mental disorder might yet appear. Critical assessment can never be considered complete. Clinicians must always be watching out of the corner of their eye for relevant clues.

In a case where presumptive evidence is uncovered, the clinician should guard against prematurely indicating his suspicion to the client. Instead, the person should be told of the need for further evaluation, and an appropriate referral should be arranged as soon as possible. It is important that the clinician take responsibility for following up on such a referral to ensure that the evaluation does take place. Of course, this will also provide the clinician with educative feedback concerning the critical assessment.

Consider a second hypothetical case. A woman, age 45, is brought in by her husband for psychological evaluation. On the intake form—which you are handed when the woman, escorted by her husband, enters your office—is listed the chief complaint: nervousness. The woman's husband immediately takes over the interview, quickly telling you that his wife has been hospitalized on two previous occasions for manic behavior. Each time she has gradually become more and more agitated, going without sleep, talking in nonstop fashion, sometimes with considerable irrationality. As the husband is talking, the woman appears anxious. You politely interrupt him by saying that you need to hear from his wife. When you ask her what seems to be the problem, she is hesitant to talk and, when she does so, is not able to tell a coherent story. As you attempt better to understand the problem by asking her clarifying questions, she becomes frustrated and begins to cry. Her husband breaks in, insisting that she be hospitalized immediately on the psychiatric ward since she is "obviously having another manic attack." When you ask him to tell you how this episode developed, however, he appears somewhat perplexed, stating that it was actually different from before. All of a sudden, the preceding day his wife began to talk "crazy" and became quite upset.

By this time in the interview, you have been able casually to observe for changes in consciousness and abnormal body movements. There are none. The woman appears oriented; there is no evidence that she is experiencing illusions or hallucinations. When you check her recent memory, she recalls four items, although she eventually points to a book (the fourth item), appearing to have difficulty getting the word out. You proceed to ask her specifically about recent head injury, changes in headache, visual problems, chronic disease and drug/alcohol use. She starts to answer, but her husband breaks in and answers for her. Other than the regular use of a laxative and infrequent excessive drinking on weekends, all questions are answered negatively.

You can't quite put your finger on it, but something doesn't add up. You decide to administer the three special tests. The woman has no trouble reproducing the stated time on a printed clock face or copying the three-dimensional figure. She does, however, have some difficulty writing the sentence you have given her. She has left out a word and she has given a strange spelling to a second word in the test sentence. As you are discussing this with her, you realize that she is having trouble understanding you as well as using the correct words to express herself. You check this out by asking her to name a few common objects in your office and find that she is unable correctly to identify several of them. The woman has a notable speech deficit, quite likely aphasic in nature. You now have presumptive evidence for organicity, evidence that requires further medical evaluation.

You inform the client and her husband that you suspect her problem may not be another manic attack and that she needs further evaluation that you will be glad to arrange for her that same afternoon.

SELF-TEST

Before proceeding to the next chapter, let us see how well you have mastered the various critical assessment factors. On the following pages, the reader will find three case histories. Try reading them and identifying any evidence which would indicate an organic mental disorder. Following each history you will find an explanation and a listing of the evidence that should have been noted.

CASE HISTORY #1

A 25-year-old college student was escorted by a friend to the emergency room of a hospital in a large metropolitan city. The friend related that the man's wife had come home from work only to find her husband acting strangely, stumbling about the apartment, alternately laughing and crying, almost incoherent at times.

When examined, the patient mumbled without making sense and frequently did not respond to direct questions. Periodically, he would drop to the floor as though trying to pick up nonexistent objects. Over the course of several hours his condition fluctuated from one of relative passivity to being combative and uncontrollable. His pupils were observed to be widely dilated.

Later, the man's wife arrived at the hospital and provided further information. She stated that her husband did not drink or take drugs and had never experienced similar symptoms. With further questioning, she related that she and her husband had been involved in a serious marital struggle over the preceding 2 weeks.[1]

DISCUSSION
CASE HISTORY #1

Initially, this patient received a diagnosis of acute schizophrenic reaction. There is little evidence in this case to support such a diagnosis, however. The sudden onset of *staggering incoherence* combined with clinical observations consistent with *visual hallucinations* and an *alternating level of consciousness* provide compelling evidence for an organic mental disorder. This is a classic picture of rapid onset brain syndrome. The dilated pupils suggest the possibility of drug intoxication. Unfortunately, the patient's vital signs were not reported; most likely, they would have shown striking deviations.

The man's wife finally reported that her husband had written an extended letter the day he was brought into the hospital addressed to his parents. The letter included the statement: "Whatever happens is not my wife's fault." She was instructed by the clinical staff at the hospital to return home and search for signs of drugs or medications that might have been taken. She did find a box with a few remaining Sominex tablets in a wastepaper basket. Based on this new information, the clinical diagnosis was changed to acute scopolamine poisoning. (Scopolamine is an anticholinergic agent found in many over-the-counter preparations, including Sominex.)

Within 24 hours the man had fully recovered. No signs of drug intoxication remained.

Condition: organic mental disorder secondary to drug ingestion ("anticholinergic psychosis").

CASE HISTORY #2

A 33-year-old woman, without any history of significant mental or physical ill health, was referred to a psychiatrist for symptoms of depression. She complained of losing interest in her work and friends. She also related how she had become obsessed with the suspicion that her husband was being unfaithful to her— apparently, a concern not without some basis. This issue had led to many arguments that had become more intense within the past several months.

She complained of feeling trapped in her role as housewife. The situation was leading her into an increased drinking pattern; she denied the use of other drugs, however. There was no evidence for disturbances in memory or orientation. She appeared above average in intelligence. She denied any change in headache pattern. There were no deficits in speech, vision, or walking and no history of head injury or unexplained shifts in consciousness.[2]

DISCUSSION
CASE HISTORY #2

The experiencing of significant psychiatric symptoms for the first time at age 33 is suggestive of an organic mental disorder, but this was not confirmed by other findings.

With the permission of the client, supplementary information from a close relative was obtained, which substantiated the woman's account of her problem. No evidence for heavy drug use was found. Her suspicion regarding her husband appeared based in fact. The relative denied any history on the part of the client of confused or psychotic behavior.

The woman entered psychotherapy and continued for 12 months. After reviewing her marital relationship—in the absence of her husband, who would not consider couple therapy—she decided to seek a divorce. She took training and was successful at securing a real estate license. Her symptoms of depression and obsessive thinking disappeared.

After 2 years of living independently, she married a man whom she had dated for a year. She retained her career with considerable success and without a return of her psychiatric symptoms.

Condition: Psychological reaction to marital problems.

CASE HISTORY #3

Obviously out of control, a 25-year-old man was admitted to a hospital psychiatric service one week after his return home from an Army summer camp. Within a few days of his return, he had begun to hear voices and to see things that were not visible to others. His wife described him as elated one moment and depressed the next. Finally, when he was unable to resume his normal work, he was taken by his family to the psychiatric emergency clinic.

Upon close observation, he smiled inappropriately and at times repeated his responses over and over. He was unable to provide the interviewer with coherent information and at one point required a seclusion room for unmanageable behavior. During this time he was observed removing his clothes and assuming strange, frozen postures, some of which were clearly sexual in nature. When treated with chlorpromazine, the patient became much calmer and seemed generally improved.

Further questioning of the family established that this behavior was quite uncharacteristic. Although the family stated that he was "fuzzy" on occasion, they portrayed him as generally reliable, stable, and without previous mental illness.

A thorough mental status examination demonstrated visual and auditory hallucinations with paranoid delusional thinking and an agitated, anxious demeanor. Periodically, the man appeared confused; he was highly unpredictable.[3]

DISCUSSION
CASE HISTORY #3

The admission diagnosis was recorded as acute schizophrenic reaction, but was changed to catatonic schizophrenia because of continuing episodes of posturing alternating with wild and violent behavior. But on the third hospital day, the patient developed a fever. He became increasingly violent, despite electroconvulsive therapy. After a steady deterioration in his condition, he died on the ninth hospital day, presumably of a severe, malignant, catatonic reaction.

At autopsy, evidence of a viral encephalitis was discovered. It was determined that an outbreak of encephalitis had occurred in the summer camp area while the patient had been stationed there. Furthermore, it was learned that just prior to leaving camp, the patient had experienced a sudden episode of abdominal pain with body stiffness and a brief loss of consciousness. Evaluation at a nearby community hospital revealed no basis for this attack. The suggestion by an Army physician that the patient have a follow-up assessment was apparently never pursued.

The *sudden onset* of uncharacteristic bizarre behavior with *no previous history,* in combination with clinical symptoms of *visual hallucinations* and *confusion,* strongly suggested organicity. *Fever* on the third hospital day (information the reader did not have) provided additional presumptive evidence in this case.

Condition: Organic mental disorder secondary to viral encephalitis.

CHAPTER 7

THREE MASQUERADERS

"And after all, what is a lie? 'Tis but the truth in masquerade."
Lord Byron

It is hoped, by this point, that the reader has accepted the proposition that organic diseases can capably masquerade as psychological reactions to problems in living. Fortunately, many of the conditions with the greatest propensity for masquerading are extremely uncommon. Not so, however, with the three masqueraders we consider in this chapter. Although they are by no means rare, when accurately identified they are often amenable to treatment. These three masqueraders represent three *kinds* of disease rather than three specific conditions. They are *brain tumors, epilepsy, and endocrine disorders.* In their most subtle guises, they can fool even the most astute observer. Usually, however, they exhibit certain telltale clues of organic disease. Developing a basic familiarity with these three masqueraders is probably the clinician's best guarantee against failing to recognize them when they manifest as psychiatric symptoms.

BRAIN TUMORS

Brain tumors are not inevitably malignant; nevertheless, due to their strategic location they often prove fatal when not detected early. Roughly one out of five brain tumors are benign meningiomas (tumors of the coverings of the brain, the meninges).[1] If discovered early, such tumors can be removed, resulting in a complete cure; but if the diagnosis is delayed, these tumors enlarge to where treatment becomes mechanically impossible without gross destruction of surrounding brain tissue. In these tragic cases, the question of whether the tumor is malignant becomes immaterial. Early detection of brain tumors is essential.

Brain tumors are either primary or secondary. Primary tumors arise from brain tissue, whereas secondary tumors spread through a process of seeding from other parts of the body to the brain, where they take up residence and grow. The emergence of unexplained mental symptoms in persons with past histories of cancer should suggest the possibility of secondary brain tumor. This is especially true of breast cancer in women and lung cancer in men—two cancers which account for a significant percentage of secondary brain tumors.

Symptoms arise primarily in one of two ways. First, depending on the exact location, local changes occur as a direct effect of the tumor. The expanding tumor may actually destroy brain tissue by invading, displacing, or compressing it within the closed space of the skull. In other instances nerve tracts in the oncoming path are falsely stimulated ("short-circuited"). For example, if the tumor is located in an area of the brain related to visual perception, partial loss of vision or, more rarely, visual hallucinations may arise from local stimulation.

The second way a brain tumor produces symptoms relates to changes in the fluid pressure system surrounding the brain. Tumor growth can cause significant increases in the intracranial pressure. Typically this leads to headache, vomiting, and—later—blurred vision. Although these symptoms are considered classic manifestations of brain tumor, they do not always develop; sometimes even if they do appear, it is extremely late. Of the three, headache occurs most consistently.

Approximately 60% of persons with tumors of the brain experience *headache.*[2] In 20% of cases it is the *initial* manifestation.[3] The headache associated with brain tumor is highly variable in severity, but, with increased intracranial pressure, a characteristic pattern frequently emerges. The headache is described as "pressure" or "throbbing." It is made worse by coughing, sneezing, straining, and exertion. Characteristically, the person finds that the pain is most severe upon awakening in the morning; it may even arouse the person from sleep. Usually, the headache will persist for several hours, gradually diminish, and disappear, only to recur the following day. Over time this symptom may last longer and longer until it becomes persistent. The clinician should be alert to this ominous headache, which can be identified with a few elaborating questions concerning its quality, when it occurs, and what makes it worse. Other headache patterns, of course, should not be ignored, particularly when they are of recent onset and are experienced by the person as unlike previous headaches.

Another symptom highly suggestive of brain tumor is *seizure* (in the absence of an established history of epilepsy). Although seizures are not associated with brain tumor as frequently as are headaches, they are highly indicative of brain pathology. Seizures may be focal (localized) or generalized. If focal, the clinical picture reflects the area of the brain being stimulated by tumor growth. Accordingly, the person might have abrupt episodes of involuntary movement in an extremity or peculiar shifts in consciousness or distortions in certain sensations. Generalized seizures, in contrast, produce a sudden loss of consciousness with total body collapse, followed by spastic jerking of the arms and legs. Either form of seizure when actually observed by a clinician or, as is more commonly the case, related in the history, should be considered indicative of organic disease and suggestive of brain tumor. The reader may be surprised to find, as shown in several cases included in this book, that seizures are sometimes construed as ancillary findings of minor consequence compared to the person's mental problems. This is a serious mistake in critical assessment.

Excessive drowsiness—especially after consuming an alcoholic drink, sedative, or tranquilizer—is yet another symptom seen with brain tumors. This symptom may lead to puzzling declines in a person's job performance or social life. Tolerance for alcohol and tranquilizing medication markedly diminishes so that even small amounts lead to considerable drowsiness.

Finally, *elements of brain syndrome* are present in a high proportion of persons with brain tumor. In one study of 326 cases, 77% of the patients had some detectable cognitive deficit; 59% appeared confused; 39% were disoriented.[4] Brain tumors with increased intracranial pressure are especially likely to produce brain syndrome.

Brain tumors located in areas primarily involved with motor movement or sensory perception stimulate changes easily recognized as neurological deficits; thus, with the possible exception of conversion reactions, these tumors are not often mistaken for psychological reactions. Tumors located in the frontal lobes are another matter.

Frontal Lobe Tumors

The reader will recall that the frontal lobes encompass an extensive anterior area of the brain that is relatively silent neurologically. This is not to say that nothing of neurological consequence is transacted in this area; it is, after all, that portion of the brain critically involved in abstract thinking, judgment, and social propriety, as well as the moderation of emotional expression. It is only silent in the sense that deficits are not manifest as such obvious neurological problems as paralysis or sensory anesthesia. Technically, this silent area is only the most forward portion of the frontal lobes, as opposed to a relatively smaller posterior area that does include the motor cortex. This is why, somewhat confusingly, the frontal area with which we are concerned is referred to as prefrontal (implying that it lies just anterior to the motor cortex).

During the clinical course of frontal lobe tumors, *70%* of patients experience psychiatric symptoms.[5] One researcher reporting on 56 cases of frontal tumors found that 46% of the patients received an *initial psychiatric diagnosis.* Mistaken diagnoses included depression (5), presenile dementia (6), schizophrenia (5), anxiety state (2), and inadequate personality (1).[6]

Two contrasting clinical pictures of psychiatric disturbance are described in cases of frontal tumors. The first, the more common of the two, is characterized by depression, apathy, indifference, emotional flatness, and reduced spontaneity and self-initiative. Along with these emotional and behavioral changes, a diminished intellectual capacity is sometimes seen. Understandably, such cases can be mistaken for psychological depression.

At retirement age, a government clerk was referred to a local emergency room by his family physician with a note stating that the man should be admitted to the psychiatric service for a severe depression that had lasted for 2 months.

More extensive history showed that for more than 3 years the man had shown a degree of drowsiness unusual for him prior to that time. He had also suffered from headaches for many years which, over the past 2 months, had become significantly more pronounced. Recently, he had undergone short attacks of memory loss and confusion. Apparently, these symptoms had played a part in the man's recent failure to be promoted at his job.

The man would not cooperate in the emergency room. He was described as depressed and easily irritated. A cursory neurological examination failed to show any abnormalities. Based on the man's history, a brain scan was requested, which revealed a "space-occupying lesion." At surgery a right frontal lobe tumor (astrocytoma) was found and removed. The man recovered without complications and was later described by his wife as his usual self.[7]

The findings of a recent change in headache pattern, combined with sudden shifts in consciousness, as well as an extended history of increased drowsiness provided the basis for a clinical suspicion of organicity.

The second clinical picture represents the opposite characteristics. The person becomes euphoric and light-hearted. Often this devil-may-care, don't-give-a-damn attitude leads to antisocial or outright criminal behavior. Social and sexual inhibitions disappear, and the person's personal hygiene deteriorates. This clinical pattern simulates that found in manic reactions. In some instances the euphoria evolves into a silly, childish manner with intellectual decline not unlike that found in hebephrenic schizophrenia.

The following case illustrates the manic features sometimes prominent in cases of frontal tumor.

A 29-year-old veteran was admitted to a V.A. hospital after a period of observation during which he was extremely agitated, talking rapidly in nonstop fashion and obsessively naming objects in the observation room. When asked what his problem was, he replied: "Nothing, sir, just ignorance; just gross ignorance around here." His response to a question about his occupation was: "I was a carpenter, like Jesus." He alternated between statements suggestive of a grandiose view of himself and those expressing ideas of

> persecution. He was fully oriented and appeared to have no difficulty with memory; his judgment, however, was extremely poor.
>
> The medical records showed a 6-year history of seizures thought to be related to drinking. These seizures usually began with a peculiar feeling of strangeness, quickly followed by loss of consciousness, collapse to the floor, and jerking of his arms and legs. Despite his seizures, he had been sent overseas during World War II and reportedly had suffered no further episodes during an 11-month period. Upon discharge he received a 50% service-connected disability for neurosis. The seizures subsequently resumed.
>
> Three months prior to his admission, the man was seen in a psychiatric outpatient clinic for anxiety, unresponsive to treatment. Gradually, his condition progressed to severe restlessness with increasing elation and flight of ideas. After taking a leave of absence from his job, he became openly hostile and belligerent at home. He went without sleep and became unmanageable, necessitating hospitalization.
>
> Neurological studies—including an EEG and pneumoencephalogram—led to a tentative diagnosis of frontal lobe tumor, confirmed at surgery when a "parasagittal meningioma" was removed from the right frontoparietal area. One month later, the man's mental condition appeared entirely normal.[8]

This was a difficult case. The clues to its organic origins were limited. The key is the history of seizures for which no explanation had been provided other than that they might be related to drinking. This man had a 6-year history of seizures, which in all likelihood were manifesting the slow development of a meningioma during that entire period. Slow-growing meningiomas are the most common form of frontal lobe tumor.

The relatively silent nature of the frontal area makes it imperative that the clinician be familiar with those few neurological deficits that can arise. Perhaps a brief recap of certain anatomical aspects of the frontal lobes is in order. Along the medial aspect of the frontal lobes, on either side, is situated a micturition center, that is, an area concerned with voluntary control of the bladder. This area is a favorite site for meningiomas; thus it is not unusual at some point for the person to lose bladder control. *Mental symptoms associated with incontinence must always be considered highly suggestive of organic disease.*

The major nerves and brain tracks involved in smell and

sight maintain a close anatomical juxtaposition to the underside of the frontal lobes. For this reason, frontal tumors may produce changes in vision and, more rarely, smell. Connections also exist between the frontal lobes and other parts of the brain instrumental in normal walking. When these connections are disrupted, changes occur similar to those seen in Parkinson's disease: shortening of steps and a progressive loss of balance.

Although the precise mechanism is unknown, frontal lobe tumors sometimes trigger catatonic-like episodes.

At age 22 the woman began to have peculiar attacks during which she would be unable to move or speak. Periodically, while eating, she would suddenly go into a daze, dropping the eating utensils from her hands. In addition she complained of vague sensations in her head as well as attacks of "a sleepy state." Since her condition was thought to be psychological, she was treated briefly by a hypnotist but without any change. Within a short period she began to hear strange voices muttering obscenities. She notified the police that she was being victimized.

Six months later, after becoming preoccupied with bodily sensations and constantly hallucinating, she was admitted to a psychiatric hospital. Her report read: "hallucinated in all senses, worried by visions of wild animals and indecent sexual activities."

On the unit she accused doctors and nurses of playing with her brain. She felt that her eyes were "being made to work in Morse code." At times she was frankly catatonic. Her diagnosis was recorded as schizophrenia.

Twelve years later, still in the hospital, she was claiming to be a lieutenant in the Army as well as a psychologist at Cambridge, Horatio Bottomley's sweetheart, and heiress to the British throne.

After 17 years she had become impulsively violent and her complaints now were all being interpreted by staff as psychotic productions.

So accustomed were her doctors to regarding all her utterances as manifestations of a sick mind that when she complained of failing sight they noted: "Still wildly deluded—she believes she cannot see her own image in the mirror."

After *26 years of institutionalization,* this woman received a neurological examination that showed the nerves conducting visual impulses from the eyes had completely deteriorated (optic atrophy). Even then, unbelievably, she was still presumed to be schizophrenic. Only after she began to have generalized seizures was she transferred to a research hospital, where studies showed a large intracranial mass identified at surgery as a frontal lobe meningioma. It proved to be inoperable. The woman never regained consciousness; she died 2 days later.[9]

This case extended over 43 years! For virtually this entire period—despite such clues as sudden shifts in consciousness with muscle weakness, visual failure, attacks of drowsiness, and eventually even generalized seizures—the diagnosis of schizophrenia was doggedly maintained. This case convincingly illustrates the extremely slow growth pattern of meningiomas, the most common tumor of the frontal area.

Limbic System Tumors

The limbic system, as you will recall, consists of a group of interrelated brain structures primarily concerned with individual and species survival. Areas of primitive human drives, with their attendant emotions, are located in this ancient brain system.[10] When tumors arise in the limbic brain, outward expressions are likely to be powerful, behavioral-emotional responses, such as fear, rage, or sexual aberrations.

Since the limbic system is highly compact anatomically, even extremely small tumors can create significant emotional and behavioral changes. Eventually, through encroachment, basic biological functions relating to eating, sleeping, drinking, and sexual behavior may also become compromised.

A study of 18 patients who had limbic tumors showed that in every instance an initial psychiatric diagnosis had mistakenly been given: schizophrenia (10), depression (4), severe neurosis (3), and mania (1).[11]

The following case is an example of a limbic tumor mimicking a functional sexual problem.

A 36-year-old married man was referred for psychiatric treatment because of sexual impotence. Married for 13 years, he had two children. His work history was exemplary, and he did not appear to be under excessive stress.

Sixteen months prior to his referral for treatment, the man noticed a gradual decline in sexual interest. Within 5 months, he was unable to obtain an erection at any time. He also began to have episodic attacks of anxiety, "feelings of dread" that persisted for 5 to 6 seconds and then disappeared. These attacks eventually increased in intensity and were characterized by a sense of panic. Sometimes these were preceded by a "compulsion to stare" and by the feeling that everyone around him was going through the same experience. The man's wife noticed that during these episodes her husband would undergo a sudden blanching of his face and cease talking.

After a complete medical evaluation, a diagnosis of brain tumor was made. This diagnosis was confirmed at surgery when a tumor of the limbic system was removed. The man's recovery was rapid. He had no further episodes of panic and his sexual interest and his potency returned.[12]

The temporal lobes have the highest incidence of tumors of any area within the limbic system. If the tumor happens to involve the posterior aspect of the left temporal lobe, fluent aphasia is likely to result. The reader will recall from our previous discussion that this condition can be extremely misleading with respect to critical assessment because it is easily misperceived as psychotic speech.

Most temporal lobe tumors stimulate seizure activity, thereby producing a clinical picture similar to temporal lobe epilepsy, a seizure disorder that we will take up in some detail in the following section.

A 53-year-old man with no previous psychiatric history began to experience "spells" during which he heard strange musical sounds. He would then become overwhelmingly depressed. The depression and the musical sounds would disappear after a short while, but these spells recurred with increasing frequency. Eventually, the man was committed to a state hospital with the diagnosis of involutional depression.

Over the next 3 months, he became lethargic and developed a pronounced weakness in his left arm and leg. Shortly thereafter, he deteriorated, slipped into a coma, and died. At autopsy, a large tumor of the right temporal lobe was discovered.[11]

This man had no previous psychiatric history. His "involutional depression" was highly atypical in that he experienced it in short-lived episodes, and the auditory hallucinations were inconsistent with a depressed mood. All of these factors argued against a psychological depressive reaction.

Before proceeding to a consideration of our next masquerader, perhaps a brief summary of what we have said about brain tumors would be worthwhile. Brain tumors are not rare conditions. Any brain tumor can give rise to psychiatric symptoms, although this is more typically the case in tumors of the frontal, temporal, and limbic areas. We have emphasized the importance of headache, seizures, increased drowsiness, and brain syndrome as clues to brain tumors. Slow-growing, benign meningiomas represent approximately 20% of all brain tumors, and their favorite place of occurrence is the frontal area, where they produce two distinctive patterns of mental and emotional changes: apathetic depression and antisocial mania. Nonsilent aspects of the frontal lobes provide clues suggestive of growing tumors, symptoms such as urinary incontinence, abnormal movement, deficits in vision and smell, disordered speech, and catatonic-like behavior.

TABLE 7-1 BRAIN TUMORS

Suggestive Findings
General
Headache
Seizures
Drowsiness
Brain syndrome
Frontal Lobes
Two characteristic clinical patterns:
Apathetic-depressive
Antisocial-manic
Loss of bladder control
Shortening of walking steps
Deficits in vision and smell
Catatonic reactions
Limbic System
Disturbances in instinctual behavior: eating, drinking, sex, aggression
"On-off" shifts in consciousness or perception
Aphasia (left temporal lobe)

EPILEPSY

A seizure is an electrical discharge within the brain giving rise to movement, feelings, or thoughts unrelated to the situation. In other words, seizures are a kind of short-circuiting. They result from a variety of causes, including infection, tumors, hypertension, hemorrhage, trauma, drug intoxication, and withdrawal. In the majority of cases, however, no precise explanation can be established. Such cases are referred to as idiopathic epilepsy.

The outward manifestations of seizures depend on the site of origin. The most common type of seizure disorder is known as grand mal epilepsy. Such seizures are global brain discharges involving virtually the entire cerebral cortex, including, most dramatically, the motor cortex. The person initially cries out, loses consciousness and, if standing, falls to the floor. The muscles of the body undergo a brief but sustained spasm followed by a wave of short jerking movements in the arms and legs that subsides after several minutes. The person is unconscious for this entire sequence and, therefore, retains no memory for what has transpired. In some cases, the person may experience one of a variety of strange sensations during a brief period, known as an aura, just prior to the onset of the seizure. Since the individual is fully aware during this brief prelude, this is often the last thing remembered.

In addition to the dramatic jerking movements, during a grand mal seizure the person may also drool from the mouth, make biting movements, and lose bladder or bowel control. As the seizure subsides, the person appears flushed; slowly, usually over a period of several minutes, consciousness is regained, but usually with a degree of confusion. This twilight period can lead to strange behavior stemming from the person's confusion. Sometimes this period following a seizure is extended, resulting in a sustained period of erratic, strange behavior and incoherent statements suggestive of schizophrenia. Suspiciousness and unprovoked aggression may emerge, reflecting in part the person's uncertainty about the situation.

Although cases of grand mal epilepsy can be mistaken for psychological reactions, particularly when the person is observed during the period immediately following the seizure, this potential is considerably greater in complex partial seizures.

Complex partial seizure is an official neurological designation for what is more popularly known as temporal lobe epilepsy or psychomotor seizure. This somewhat convoluted term has been selected to emphasize the intertwined cognitive and behavioral (complex) aspect of this condition, while at the same time indicating the circumscribed nature of the seizure (partial) as contrasted to grand mal epilepsy. Anatomically, these seizures arise out of the limbic brain.

The specific area with the greatest propensity for complex partial seizures is the temporal lobes, a sizable component of the limbic system. The temporal lobes play a pivotal role in perceptual integration; it is here that various kinds of sensory information are synthesized and interpreted. Unusual and distorted perceptions arise in temporal lobe epilepsy during the first phase, known as the aura. There is a suddenness to the aura: abruptly, without explanation, the person experiences peculiar sensations. Although a tremendously wide range of perceptual changes can occur in any given individual, the same subjective sensation is usually repeated each time. The person may feel as though he is in a dream. A sense of familiarity may engulf the person so that what is being experienced for the first time seems as though it is the identical recurrence of a past situation (dejà vu); or, precisely the opposite sensation may emerge, so that the person suddenly has a sense of strangeness despite being in familiar surroundings. Powerful emotions may erupt, such feelings as fear, loneliness, or anger. Sometimes visual changes dominate the aura: objects may seem far away and small, or the opposite, close at hand and gigantic. Conversation may become extremely muted or very loud. Strange sounds, voices, and even music are sometimes heard. The person's body may feel distorted, or a sense of abdominal distress may grip the person. Foul smells are particularly common during the aura and are often described as the smell of "rotting eggs" or "burning rubber." The aura or first phase of a temporal lobe seizure typically lasts only a matter of seconds and is immediately followed by a second phase.

The second phase also persists for only a matter of seconds, beginning with the person's loss of awareness. Usually, this is manifest by a blank stare. If the person has been talking, this is abruptly interrupted, although in some cases of temporal lobe seizures the person will continue to verbalize somewhat incoherent, repetitive sounds.

The third stage is the longest. It may persist for several minutes and, in exceptional cases, for hours. This stage is characterized by mechanical, automaton-like behavior. Particularly common are movements of the neck and face: lip-smacking, teeth-grinding, chewing, tongue-sucking, and jerky, turning motions of the neck from side to side. These movements are probably the most characteristic, observable aspect of temporal lobe epilepsy, but the clinician should be aware that they can be quite subtle. In rare cases highly complicated sequences of behavior lasting for hours have been described, activities such as driving an automobile or carrying out difficult tasks.

The fourth and final stage occurs as a gradual transition over several minutes. The automatic activity recedes, and consciousness returns. The person feels groggy and has little memory for what has transpired other than the initial aura.

Clinicians, more often than not, are presented with a history of strange "spells" that they are not able to observe first hand. It is this history of on-off behavior, uncharacteristic of the person and inappropriate to the situation, that must capture the clinician's attention if he or she is to suspect a seizure disorder.

A single man in his early twenties was admitted for the thirtieth time to a psychiatric service. These admissions had occurred over a 5-year period and always involved the same bizarre behavior with hyperactive, frenzied movements. The man was well known to the local police as well as the psychiatric staff.

The patient was started on what had become a routine treatment plan for his schizophrenia, beginning with 100 mg of chlorpromazine (IM) and seclusion in a side room until the medication could take effect. Due to a shortage of beds on this particular admission, the patient was sent to a different ward, where he was evaluated by a physician who had not treated him previously.

The patient was observed "muttering, grunting, groaning, or humming" as he rolled and crawled about the floor. At times he seemed to make masturbatory gestures and pelvic thrusting movements of a sexual nature. He was also noted to have strange expressions on his face, sucking, blowing, and grinning in a peculiar fashion. He scratched and scraped the walls, muttering over and over again: "Hare Krishna, Hare Krishna, Hare Krishna. . . ." But within 3 hours all of this strange behavior had disappeared. Almost as though awakening from a turbulent sleep, the patient rubbed his eyes and calmly asked for a cigarette. The observing psychiatrist judged him at this time to have no disturbance in thought, mood, or speech. There was only the faintest recollection of what had transpired over the past several hours.

The patient was removed from seclusion and spent five days on the psychiatric service without showing any further symptoms.

A review of his hospital records revealed that he had 29 previous admissions, as recorded in 12 volumes. He had received a variety of diagnoses, including: acute schizophrenia, chronic undifferentiated schizophrenia, psychotic reaction, obsessive-compulsive personality and, on his most recent previous admission, "hypomania in the context of chronic schizo-affective illness." The pattern of events leading up to hospitalization was identical on each admission. He would suddenly begin to have auditory hallucinations, after which he ran wildly down the street in the nude.

Again, the patient was discharged without detection of his actual problem. Ten days later, however, he was readmitted for similar symptoms and, based on the observations recorded during the previous admission, he was moved to a long-term unit for careful observation. In a relatively short period five additional episodes had taken place. They were judged to be identical reruns of each other. All attacks were ushered in by a period of withdrawn behavior, during which the patient communicated ideas of hopelessness and gradually became less coherent. Invariably, the full-blown picture of bizarre behavior and strange movements appeared within a matter of minutes or hours.

Despite several attempts, no seizure pattern was found on the patient's EEG; nevertheless, a diagnosis of complex partial seizure was made based on the clinical observations. Three subsequent seizures were quickly terminated with a rapidly acting antiepileptic agent (diazepam), and during a 6-month follow-up period, the patient was successfully controlled on an epilepsy treatment regimen (acetazolamide).[13]

This case well illustrates the history and observations characteristically found in temporal lobe epilepsy. The dramatic contrast in the patient during the episode and afterwards—the on-off effect—is an extremely important observation and should always alert the clinician to the possibility of a seizure disorder. Severe, acute psychiatric disruptions are seldom so characterized, nor are the episodes as stereotyped as is typically found in epilepsy. In addition, they rarely ever run their course in a few hours. In the foregoing case, the man went from a widly psychotic, raving condition to completely normal within a 3-hour period. Even drug-related psychiatric disturbances characteristically require a longer period for the drug to clear the system.

The reader should not be misled into concluding that all cases of temporal lobe epilepsy result in seizures with four clearly definable stages. Wide-ranging variations in clinical presentation occur. Virtually any of the symptoms seen in temporal lobe epilepsy can become the most prominent aspect of an individual's seizures. Given the myriad of connections between the temporal lobes and other parts of the limbic system, unusual clinical symptoms are to be expected. Take the following case:

> A woman called the police after her neighbor's husband had removed his clothes in his backyard and exposed his genitalia to her for the second time in a single week. The man was taken into custody. A police report had been made 4 months earlier, after the man was found standing by the side of the road naked from the waist down. He had remained in this position for several minutes. Under questioning, his wife related that approximately one year earlier he had bizarrely, without explanation, removed all his clothes in front of his children and appeared confused at the time.
>
> A psychiatrist evaluated the man and diagnosed him as a case of exhibitionism. Further neurological evaluation was performed, however, when it was found that at 17 years of age he had been knocked unconscious for several minutes by a falling tree. An EEG showed a wave and spike pattern over the left temporal area. A revised diagnosis of temporal lobe epilepsy was made, and he was started on Dilantin. After almost 2 years the man had experienced no more episodes of exhibitionism.[14]

The most important clinical clue to the epileptic nature of these peculiar behavioral episodes was the confused, trance-like state that came over the patient. An additional important piece of information related to the previous history of having lost consciousness for several minutes following a severe blow to the head. Head trauma sometimes leads to scarring of brain tissue and years later can manifest as seizures.

Another form of seizure, presumably originating in the limbic system, presents as rage attacks. These episodes of violence last from a few seconds to hours. Often, the attack appears completely unprovoked; in other cases, a minor provocation inappropriately precipitates a vicious assault. Alcohol and minor tranquilizers increase the frequency of these violent seizures. Sometimes, the individual will show an extremely low tolerance for such drugs, so that even minimal usage brings on an attack.

This condition has been termed *episodic dyscontrol.*[15] Persons suffering from it frequently have a history of childhood hyperactivity, arrest records for violence-related crimes, extensive traffic violations, and automobile accidents. The primary evidence for the epileptic nature of episodic dyscontrol is derived from clinical findings, including treatment responses to antiepileptic medication. The attacks are commonly preceded by a trance-like state or aura, which may consist of visual hallucinations, body numbness, or a heightened awareness of sounds. Once the episode is terminated, the person often complains of drowsiness and a headache.

In one study of 22 persons with episodic dyscontrol, after a 2-month trial period of treatment with an antiepileptic medication (Dilantin), 19 of the patients had shown at least a 75% reduction in the frequency and severity of their attacks.[16] This is a particularly impressive finding given all these persons had previously received other forms of therapy without beneficial results.

Repeated instances of irrational violence, especially when associated with shifts in consciousness and intensified by alcohol or tranquilizers, argue for the presence of episodic dyscontrol.

> A 23-year-old, unemployed mechanic beat his wife severely with a metal candlestick, leading to multiple lacerations and unconsciousness. The man's wife was later able to recall how he initially "went into a blank stare" prior to attacking her.
>
> A few weeks later, the same man shot and fatally wounded his friend. Abruptly, for no reason, he assaulted the victim, grabbed his hunting rifle, and shot him. This occurred after the two men had finished drinking a couple of cans of beer. He was jailed but soon released on bond. Shortly afterwards, he hurled his small daughter out of the window of a moving automobile. His explanation was that she had "talked back."
>
> This man had an extensive history of childhood truancy and had suffered from hyperactivity. He quit school in his early teens and had been jailed on numerous occasions for assault and for drunken driving. He was evaluated by a psychiatrist and diagnosed as a case of episodic dyscontrol.[16]

Despite such cases as this, the reader should realize that the relationship between violence and epilepsy is not well established. This is a highly controversial topic among neurobehavioral specialists. Violence and epilepsy should be kept in perspective. The vast majority of persons who are violent are not violent because of seizures, and most individuals who suffer from epilepsy are not violent either between or during seizures.

ENDOCRINE DISORDERS

Hormones exert powerful emotional and behavioral effects. The slightest imbalances can result in dramatic psychological changes as well as alterations in physical appearance.[17] Such changes are seen with numerous endocrine disorders; in this section, we will focus on three conditions that occur with some frequency and that have a predilection for producing alterations in mood, behavior, and thought. We shall review *hypoglycemia, hyperthyroidism, and hypothyroidism.* These conditions provide the reader with illustrative examples of the tremendous masquerading potential of endocrine disorders.

Hypoglycemia (Low Blood Sugar)

Glucose, a simple sugar, is an essential nutrient for the nervous system. Whereas other parts of the body readily utilize other sources of energy, the nervous system relies almost exclusively on glucose, requiring a constant supply for normal functioning. This statement about the essential reliance of the nervous system on sugar may strike the reader as difficult to reconcile with all the nutritional warnings about the dangers of excessive sugar

TABLE 7-2 COMPLEX PARTIAL SEIZURES

Suggestive Findings
Temporal Lobe Epilepsy
Unprovoked, episodic behavioral changes
Trance-like appearance
On-off shifts in consciousness or perception
Stereotypical movements of the face and neck
Episodic Dyscontrol
Unprovoked spells of violence associated with an altered state of consciousness
Precipitation by alcohol or minor tranquilizers

consumption. It is true that the body can be overwhelmed by large loads of glucose, thus setting into play a series of disrupting hormonal changes. Also, pure sugar provides calories without essential nutritional value, so called naked calories, so that over-reliance on sugar as a source of calories can lead to nutritional deficiencies. In order for the nervous system to be assured of an optimal supply of energy, a variety of food substances must be consumed in the diet and later converted into glucose as the demand arises. Nevertheless, glucose, itself, is essential; the brain must have a stable supply. Situations leading to wide fluctuations in the glucose level of the blood create neurological havoc.

Hypoglycemia is not a specific disease; rather, it is a physiological state that can result from a variety of causes. If the organs responsible for the absorption of glucose from ingested food fail to perform their job, hypoglycemia results. Similarly, if the pancreas—the endocrine gland that manufactures and releases insulin, the major regulator of glucose—becomes overproductive, as occurs with certain tumors, low blood sugar ensues. If the liver, a storage reservoir for glucose in the form of glycogen, fails to function properly, hypoglycemia is again the end result. Hypoglycemia can also be a *man-made* problem, as when excessive amounts of insulin are received by persons with diabetes mellitus. This results from errors in dosage or from a change in factors affecting the amount of insulin required and is probably the most common cause of hypoglycemia. Diabetics are at high risk for hypoglycemia.

Regardless of the specific cause, hypoglycemia evokes a powerful emergency response from the sympathetic nervous system. This automatic discharge sets into motion changes aimed at counteracting hypoglycemia and is outwardly expressed as perspiration, tremulousness, increased heart rate and blood pressure, dilation of the pupils, and a subjective sense of feeling ill, usually with nausea and anxiety. If due to its severity the hypoglycemic state persists, after a time the initial sympathetic reaction subsides, giving way to more flagrant mental symptoms due to the brain's dwindling energy supply. At this juncture the clinician may encounter an extremely diverse group of symptoms, including confusion, bizarre behavior, irrational fear, delusions and hallucinations, and, in the most serious cases, coma. These manifestations of hypoglycemia have misled even the finest of clinicians. If detected, the emergency treatment is simple; but first, the clinician must consider the possibility.

Some of the most dramatic recovery stories from hospital emergency rooms are cases of hypoglycemia. The person may be brought in by the police or even passersby previously unfamiliar with the person. In the absence of any history, the clinician is confronted with a highly unpredictable, incoherent individual who appears quite crazy. Preparation is made to admit the person to a psychiatric unit, blood is drawn for a series of routine laboratory tests; then, if the individual is lucky, the physician in charge injects a small test dose of glucose. This is a procedure adopted by many physicians who recognize the tremendous masquerading potential of hypoglycemia. Within seconds this psychotic person is transformed. Calmly and coherently, the person inquires as to what is going on, since his memory for what has transpired is usually defective. No trace of bizarre, delusional behavior remains. The person may relate, as is so often the case, how he is a diabetic and recently has been having trouble regulating his daily dose of insulin. Obviously, given what subsequently transpired, he took too much.

Hypoglycemia also results from a type of tumor that secretes an insulin-like substance. Consequently, the person develops an excess of insulin-hormone activity and low blood sugar. A review of 91 cases of insulin-producing tumors, revealed that 36 cases initially had been misdiagnosed, half of them being mistaken for functional psychiatric problems.[18]

> A young man in his early twenties with a history of excellent health began to undergo a personality change, as noted by his wife. He, himself, began to complain of weakness, especially in the morning upon awakening. On one occasion he unexplainably fainted while shaving.
>
> Over a 3-month period, he underwent periods of confusion and became withdrawn and negativistic in his relationships with his family. Although after these bouts of confusion, he appeared more like his old self, he could not recall what happened and overall seemed to deteriorate.
>
> Finally, he was taken to a hospital, where he was diagnosed as suffering from a schizophrenic reaction. Despite treatment he gradually became more unresponsive and withdrawn, until one morning he was found in a coma. Upon receiving a 50% glucose

solution, intravenously, he fully recovered within a matter of minutes. His blood sugar level was determined to have been one-third of normal.

A complete workup demonstrated a large mass in his lower posterior abdomen, which at surgery was diagnosed as a retroperitoneal fibroma. The tumor had been secreting an insulin-like substance, accounting for the man's episodes of hypoglycemia.

Eighteen months later, he reported no further problems and had returned to full-time employment.[19]

I do not wish to leave the reader with the idea that hypoglycemia always creates dramatic or psychotic behavioral changes; to the contrary, this condition is quite capable of producing much more subtle alterations that are more complicated with respect to critical assessment.

For reactive hypoglycemia no precise cause can be identified. It is presumed that persons with this problem have a physiological imbalance predisposing them to periods of low blood sugar. It is as though the body overreacts to sugar with an excessive production of insulin and a precipitous drop in the blood sugar, particularly after the ingestion of food with a high sugar content. Symptoms seen with reactive hypoglycemia typically include anxiety, irritability, and a sense of not feeling well. In more severe cases cognitive deficits occur. The person may find it difficult to concentrate and think through simple problems; he may become suspicious and develop mental confusion and memory gaps.

The next case is an unusual history. I have included it not as a representative example of reactive hypoglycemia but rather as an illustration of the far-ranging variations seen in this often clinically baffling disorder.

As she was nearing her home on a return trip from a nearby neighboring town, a woman was stopped in her automobile by the local police. They were investigating a hit-and-run accident that had resulted in the death of a cyclist earlier in the evening. On being questioned the woman did recall passing the scene of the accident on her return; but seeing help had arrived, she decided not to stop and continued on her way home.

She was a social worker by training and the wife of a practicing family physician, well respected in her community, a "citizen of excellent character." She fully cooperated with the police, even submitting to two breath analyzer tests for alcohol (negative results). The police then escorted her home, where they continued to question her about the accident. After more than an hour of extensive interrogation, the questioners were unable to detect any knowledge on her part of the actual occurrence of the lethal accident, although the woman readily admitted that she had likely been in the area at the time the fatality was believed to have happened. Within a few days, however, evidence strongly suggestive of the woman's involvement surfaced when damage to her car was found to be compatible with findings at the scene of the crime.

This woman had no history of psychiatric disease, but her close friends and family described what they considered "uncharacteristic behavior" over the preceding three years. During these periods, she had difficulty following her line of thinking and was easily irritated. She would become irrationally suspicious, angry, and even threatening but then, usually within a short period, would seem her normal self. She apparently had no recall for these stormy altercations, for she never mentioned them. On occasion, she complained of nausea and appeared tremulous, suggesting to those who knew her well a bit of a hangover. Even her complaints of exhaustion and depression, with attacks of breaking out into a cold sweat, were considered the product of drinking too much. Although the woman, herself, admitted to the regular use of alcohol "as a sedative" before retiring, she firmly denied excessive use.

During the days immediately preceding the accident, she had been under considerable stress, appearing preoccupied to the extent of failing to eat properly. In fact, on the day of the accident, she had not eaten anything. When she left for the neighboring town, her family noticed that she was not quite herself, but no one felt that she was incapable of driving.

Due to the inconsistencies in this case, an extensive medical examination was requested by the authorities. A 5-hour glucose tolerance test revealed a profound rebound hypoglycemia (30 mg%) 4 hours after the ingestion of a standard glucose meal. This finding led to a diagnosis of reactive hypoglycemia. The court accepted a plea of guilty, imposed a nominal fine, and disqualified the woman from driving because of her hypoglycemic disorder.[20]

Two aspects of this case should be emphasized because they are frequently complicating factors in cases of reactive hypoglycemia. The regular use of alcohol exacerbates reactive hypoglycemia, as do extended periods without eating. Symptoms shortly after awakening are common because food has not been ingested during the sleeping hours. In the foregoing case, the woman had gone most of the day without eating, which predisposed her to an attack of hypoglycemia. Somewhat paradoxically, symptoms also tend to occur several hours after a heavy intake of sugar, as illustrated in the special glucose tolerance test performed on this woman. This is the result of the excessive release of insulin.

Hypothyroidism

The hormone regulating the speed of physiological processes —the metabolic rate—is produced by the thyroid gland. Too much of this hormone produces a revving up of the body; with too little, body functions are slowed, even retarded in severe cases.

The thyroid gland is situated in the midline of the neck at the level of the Adam's apple. It is comprised of two lobes, one on either side of the windpipe, connected by a narrow bridge of tissue. Unless abnormally enlarged, the gland cannot be seen; in certain disorders, it may be observed as a prominent bulge in the neck.

In medical terminology the terms *hypo* and *hyper* indicate too little and too much, respectively. Hypothyroidism is a state of thyroid deficiency. It can result from different diseases but, ironically, most commonly develops as the aftermath of treatment for hyperthyroidism. Since this treatment is difficult to administer precisely, and too much of the thyroid gland may be destroyed, it may lead several years later to the emergence of hypothyroidism.

Regardless of the specific cause, hypothyroidism characteristically has a gradual onset. Symptoms may appear one after the other, making it difficult correctly to surmise that they are all part of the same problem. Generally, there is an overall slowing of physiological functioning. It is as though the body's pacemaker has been turned down, so that the processes of life go on at a much slower speed. The heart rate is lessened; the blood pressure depressed. The gut slows down, causing constipation. Since less energy is being expended in living, weight gain results, despite the maintenance of the person's usual food intake. The body temperature is reduced, leading to complaints of feeling cold when others appear comfortable or even warm. The person may have a sense of being slowed down, fatigued.

Women develop hypothyroidism five times as often as men. Frequently, they complain of changes in their menstrual pattern, particularly excessive flow.

Despite the numerous somatic changes seen with hypothyroidism, psychological symptoms can be the most prominent findings. Typically, the person feels blue; the ability to concentrate and solve even simple problems may be compromised. At this stage, hypothyroidism can be mistaken for a depressive reaction.

> A 48-year-old housewife noticed that her energy was gone. She found herself easily fatigued, listless, and irritable. In looking for a likely explanation, she blamed her symptoms on menopause, even though her menstrual periods were uninterrupted. Finally, she went to her physician, who told her she was depressed and started her on a tricyclic antidepressant medication. Her symptoms remained.
>
> Eventually, she sought out a second physician, who upon observing certain physical changes in her apperance—notably paleness in her skin color and a puffiness about her face—decided to evaluate her thyroid gland. The laboratory results showed that the woman was hypothyroid. She was started on thyroid hormone treatment, and within a short period, her symptoms began to disappear.[21]

As hypothyroidism deepens, a person's physical appearance undergoes dramatic changes. The skin becomes dry and thickened; it takes on a creamy hue, especially noticeable in the face. The hair becomes brittle and dry and begins to shed. Puffiness develops in the face, especially prominent in the eyelids. The eyebrows begin to thin and the outermost portion may even fall out. The person's voice deepens, becoming husky and raspy in character, making speech at times difficult to understand.

Psychological changes show a similar intensification and can reach psychotic proportions ("myxedema madness"). Paranoid delusions are often prominent; they may lead to threatening, violent behavior. The psychotic symptoms sometimes mask a characteristic decline in functioning intelligence, which if treated early enough is usually reversible.

> Following a rageful attack during which furniture was destroyed and family members were threatened, a middle-aged man was forcefully admitted to a mental hospital.
>
> Eight years earlier, this previously healthy and highly productive gentleman, an academic administrator, complained of fatigue and a peculiar tingling sensation in his arms. A medical examination failed to identify any organic problem.
>
> Over the next several years, the patient underwent a number of significant changes. He became sluggish of movement and his intellectual ability declined. He grew suspicious of people and eventually exhibited angry tantrums, during which he smashed things about the house and, on occasion, beat his wife. His outward appearance slowly altered. His skin grew pale, dry, and excessively wrinkled; he gained weight, and his hair started to fall out.
>
> When admitted to the mental hospital, the man was observed to have blatant paranoid delusions and to speak in a deep, rasping voice.[22]

Found to have severe hypothyroidism, he was started on treatment with replacement thyroid hormone. Ten weeks later he was discharged and described at that time as mentally normal. Within 6 months his weight and appearance had also returned to normal; and, soon after, he resumed his work in the academic field. This case had an unusually satisfying outcome given the long delay in diagnosis and treatment.

Hyperthyroidism (Thyrotoxicosis)

Hyperthyroidism is roughly the flip-side of hypothyroidism. The body's overall metabolic rate is increased; the pacemaker seems to be stuck in an "on" position, so that excessive caloric energy is continuously consumed. It is as though the person is being readied for a stress or struggle that never materializes.

As with hypothyroidism, hyperthyroidism develops in women much more often than in men. It occurs most commonly at puberty and in middle life and, of special interest to the clinician, it frequently is preceded by a severe emotional stress.

The physical symptoms can be quite prominent, but, as with other masqueraders considered in this chapter, such symptoms are sometimes neglected due to the dramatic, overshadowing psychological changes. The individual experiences excessive sweating and sensitivity to heat. The heart rate, blood pressure, and temperature are often elevated. A fine tremor in the hands is typical and the person's eyes sometimes become prominent, even bulging. The skin is flushed and *warm,* in contrast to the cold and clammy skin condition associated with acute anxiety, a condition otherwise easily confused with hyperthyroidism. Often, there is a history of weight loss despite a ravenous appetite; insomnia may be a problem, and heart palpitations or shortness of breath can occur. Women undergo changes in their menstrual pattern, sometimes even actual cessation of monthly periods.

The most characteristic mental and emotional expressions of hyperthyroidism are anxiety, irritability, tension, and a certain emotional fragility, characterized by episodes of prominent emotional expressions such as crying or laughing without provocation. Despite the overall appearance of tension and nervousness, the person may describe a strange feeling of *energized fatigue.* The simultaneous occurrence of restless impatience and a sense of exhaustion suggests the possibility of hyperthyroidism.

In cases that persist for an extended period without diagnosis and treatment, the clinical picture of anxiety may gradually give way to one of depression and apathy. It is as though the continuing hypermetabolic state eventually exhausts the body's reserves. This somewhat paradoxical presentation of hyperthyroidism is frequently seen in the elderly.

Sometimes hyperthyroidism is mistaken for a manic reaction; the person will be expansive and grandiose in his thinking, but almost always *without* the element of euphoria typical of mania.

The cognitive changes in hyperthyroidism vary from mild distractability to paranoid delusions and symptoms of brain syndrome.

For no apparent reason, the wife of a resident physician began to feel extremely anxious. She had difficulty sleeping and at times was tremulous and given to heavy perspiration.

She eventually brought herself to discuss these symptoms with her husband, who interpreted these changes as manifestations of the stress of being the wife of a resident. He started her on a minor tranquilizer for her anxiety.

But the symptoms did not improve; in fact, the woman became more agitated, anxious, and eventually obsessed with the thought that she was probably mentally ill.

Finally, almost as a self-fulfilling prophecy, she was admitted to a psychiatric hospital. No significant "emotional conflicts" were identified, but she was found to have an unexplained elevation in her heart rate and significant weight loss. Laboratory studies confirmed a diagnosis of hyperthyroidism. She was treated with radioactive iodine, after which her "anxiety" subsided.[21]

TABLE 7-3 ENDOCRINE DISORDERS

Suggestive Findings:
Hypoglycemia
Episodes of sweating, nervousness, and nausea
Unusual behavior after long periods without food and relieved by eating
Unusual behavior several hours after heavy intake of sugar
Unusual behavior in a person with diabetes mellitus
Hypothyroidism
Depression with weight gain, sensitivity to cold, and characteristic physical changes
Previous history of treatment for hyperthyroidism
Intellectual decline with characteristic physical changes
Hyperthyroidism
Unexplained anxiety or manic behavior with warm, flushed skin, weight loss, and increased heart rate
Complaint of energized fatigue
In older population, unexplained apathetic depression with intellectual decline

The capacity for masquerading is by no means limited to the conditions we have considered in this chapter; but we hope this discussion of brain tumors, epilepsy, and certain endocrine disorders—in addition to providing the reader with specific information about these three masqueraders—should serve to broaden the reader's overall clinical perspective on how the body sometimes distorts the mind.

CHAPTER 8

DRUG-INDUCED ORGANIC MENTAL DISORDERS

"There are some remedies worse than the disease."

Publilius Syrus

DRUGS AND MEDICATIONS can cause organic mental disorders; in fact, they frequently do so without being recognized—thus the need for a special chapter devoted to this subject.

Under the designation *drugs* we shall consider a variety of chemical substances, medicinal and nonmedicinal, in four categories: psychiatric prescription medications, general prescription medications, over-the-counter preparations, and street drugs. Our discussion will not be comprehensive, but rather a selective consideration of those drugs having a special propensity for mental side effects.

Coffee, nicotine, tea, vitamins, alcohol, headache remedies, cold preparations—all these are drugs, as are the medications purchased at the pharmacy with a doctor's prescription. In reality, street drugs are a relatively small part of the overall drug scene. In 1976, 7 billion capsules of tranquilizers alone were manufactured in the United States.[1] Drugs have become such a pervasive part of our society that clinicians have difficulty keeping up with them. We are particularly prone to overlook the everyday substances people take into their bodies, and we often restrict our clinical questions about drug use to a passing, half-hearted inquiry. As a background to assessing mental problems, the clinician should be aware of the pervasive utilization of drugs and should recognize that virtually any drug, when taken in sufficient quantity or in combination with other substances, can produce psychiatric symptoms. With respect to critical assessment, *drugs are always suspect.*

Even in settings of confidential communication people underreport their use of drugs. A study of 225 persons entering a community mental health program revealed that 13% were covertly using hard drugs (opiates, cocaine, and amphetamines); that is, the therapists from whom they were seeking help had not been told of this practice.[2]

But failure to disclose drug use is not restricted to illicit drugs and is not always the result of deception. Sometimes the person taking a substance simply does not think of it as a drug. This is particularly common with over-the-counter medications, which, unfortunately, can produce serious side effects. Certain medications may not be mentioned because the individual separates physical health concerns from mental problems. Medicine taken regularly for high blood pressure, for example, may go unnamed because the person can see no relevance to the emotional problem for which he or she is seeking help.

In certain instances the person may actually be unaware that a chemical or drug is being taken into the body. Parents may have no idea that their child is being intoxicated with lead as a result of eating lead-based paint from the apartment walls. Similarly, an employee may unknowingly absorb an industrial or agricultural toxin as he goes about his work. A person may report the use of one drug, such as marijuana, unaware that it has been laced with another substance.

In addition to the pervasive and often hidden nature of drugs, the clinician should be sensitive to the untoward effects drugs sometimes exert on one another.[3] One drug may increase or decrease the effect of another drug, or when given simultaneously, the two may produce an entirely different reaction. As more and more potent drugs are produced, the risk of hazardous drug-drug interactions increases. Particularly in the area of mental health care, this has emerged as a significant complication due to a tendency toward multiple-drug treatment, a practice often leading to bothersome or sometimes serious drug reactions. As we review various drugs, undesirable drug-drug interactions likely to create a problem in critical assessment will be noted.

PSYCHIATRIC PRESCRIPTION MEDICATIONS

Despite their beneficial qualities, psychiatric medications have significant side effects, certain of which can be easily mistaken for psychological reactions. The resolution of an initial target symptom should not divert the clinician from observing newly emerging symptoms related to drug treatment. Untoward effects of medication often occur simultaneously with the desired action.

Neuroleptics

Neuroleptics, also called antipsychotics or major tranquilizers, are routinely prescribed for the management of psychotic behavior. A number of side effects are encountered, often dose related, but these are highly unpredictable. Certain individuals simply have an extreme sensitivity to these drugs and react adversely to even low doses.

Extrapyramidal reactions occur with considerable regularity, particularly in young persons treated with high-potency neuroleptics. EPR's, as they are often called, emerge abruptly, usually within a few days of the initiation of treatment. When full-blown, they can be extremely frightening to the patient. The neck may haltingly twist to one side as though being pulled by an invisible force, and the body torso may turn and tilt to the side with one shoulder considerably lower than the other. Speech may become extremely garbled due to an involuntary protrusion of the tongue. Since this strange complex of symptoms develops as the patient is being treated for psychotic behavior, the clinician runs the risk of misinterpreting this reaction as more bizarre behavior or posturing, a symptom seen in catatonic schizophre-

TABLE 8-1 NEUROLEPTICS
(Selected List)

High Potency	*Low Potency*
Haldol (haloperidol)	Mellaril (thioridazine)
Prolixin (fluphenazine)	Serentil (mesoridazine)
Navane (thiothixene)	Thorazine (chlorpromazine)

nia. In some instances, because of the anxious, dramatic overlay, EPR's are perceived as hysterical behavior.

EPR's are not inevitably full-blown; they may be limited to a single symptom, such as a protruding tongue, body stiffness, grimacing, or labored speech.

One dose of medication is sometimes sufficient to produce EPR's. This is an important point to keep in mind, because neuroleptics are frequently given as single injections in emergency rooms because of their effectiveness against nausea and vomiting. An EPR which follows shortly thereafter may be inappropriately labeled as "psychiatric."

Brain syndrome can result from neuroleptics, particularly in older persons. Risk of this complication is greatly increased when these medications are given in combination with one another or with an antidepressant or antiparkinsonian agent, because all tend to have anticholinergic action, which is additive.

> A 23-year-old man had been followed for several years by a local mental health agency for impulsive and psychotic behavior.
>
> One evening he was brought involuntarily to a hospital emergency room, violently agitated and disoriented, with evidence of visual hallucinations. His pupils were widely dilated, his pulse 120 per minute, and his temperature elevated.
>
> Recently, the young man had been maintained on multiple medications, including Haldol (haloperidol), Mellaril (thioridazine), and an antiparkinsonian agent.
>
> Emergency treatment (physostigmine) and discontinuance of the patient's maintenance medications eliminated the mental symptoms and restored normal vital signs.[4]

This patient's problem could have been mistaken for the reemergence of functional psychosis; fortunately, it was correctly diagnosed as an anticholinergic psychosis, stemming from the combination of the three maintenance medications. Later in this chapter, under over-the-counter preparations, we will further discuss the problem of anticholinergic drugs.

High potency neuroleptics, particularly in large doses, can produce a bizarre, catatonic-like state, easily confused with catatonic schizophrenia and mistakenly treated with even higher doses of the symptom-producing medication. The person assumes unchanging, peculiar postures for extended periods, usually without speaking or acknowledging the presence of others. Even if the person is able to speak, the description of this strange reaction is likely to be misinterpreted as a further elaboration of psychotic thinking.

> Five years earlier, a 44-year-old woman was hospitalized for severe obsessive-compulsive symptoms. She received more than 60 electroconvulsive treatments with "moderate improvement"!
>
> Gradually, over the next several years, her obsessive-compulsive behavior returned, until finally she was rehospitalized and treated with Haldol (haloperidol), 20 mg. daily. After being discharged, she continued the medication, but her obsessive-compulsive problem returned and along with it, a robot-like appearance. She assumed strange postures and began to drool from her mouth. Eventually she lost control of her bowel and bladder functioning and was once again hospitalized.
>
> When evaluated she appeared rigid and motionless, staring with her mouth open. She had considerable difficulty speaking and initiating any movement on her own. From time to time, she assumed strange postures.[5]

The medication was discontinued and an antidote, Symmetrel (amantadine), an antiparkinsonian agent, given. Within three days the woman spoke in her normal voice, and after one week, she no longer showed signs of rigidity, posturing, or difficulty initiating movement. Although she continued to have mild obsessive-compulsive symptoms, she required no maintenance medications.

Akasthisia—a pervasive, relentless, internal restlessness—is a frequent and bothersome side effect of neuroleptics, leading many individuals to stop their medication. This restlessness produces prolonged periods of anxious pacing, one of the few activities that give some relief from this drug-related tension. This symptom can be mistaken for a sign of increasing psychological anxiety indicative of a need for additional medication, thus setting into place a vicious cycle. Unrecognized akasthisia is probably the underlying basis for many episodes of "loss of control" in persons treated with neuroleptics. Regrettably, restraints and the use of locked side-rooms in psychiatric hospitals are sometimes inappropriately used simply because this pattern is not recognized clinically. One can only imagine the frustration and rage generated within the person who is the target of such a treatment mistake.

The lower potency neuroleptics have various sex-related side effects, which, when reported to a therapist unfamiliar with these unusual drug-related symptoms, may be dismissed as hypochondriacal or even delusional. Breast enlargement (gynecomastia)—sometimes with lactation—is not infrequent. When this occurs along with the failure to menstruate, another side effect seen with these medications, the uninformed patient may assume that she is pregnant. Men also have their share of bothersome effects, such as difficulty achieving an erection and ejaculating. This problem has been extensively reported in association with the drug Mellaril (thioridazine).

When taken for extended periods, all neuroleptics carry the risk of causing tardive dyskinesia, especially in older persons. This is a syndrome of purposeless movements usually most severe in the region of the face but sometimes extending to virtually all parts of the body. The person so affected typically evidences smacking of the lips, blowing of the cheeks, tongue protrusion and grinding movements of the chin and jaws. Writhing movements in the arms and legs or around the torso of the body also occur, though less frequently. In the majority of cases tardive dyskinesia constitutes a problem of embarrassing disfigurement, but with increasing severity it becomes disabling and even life threatening.

With the continued usage of neuroptics, eventually tardive dyskinesia becomes irreversible. For this reason it is essential that the clinician recognize its cardinal signs so that, if at all possible, this form of treatment can be discontinued. It is important to remember that the symptoms of tardive dyskinesia, oddly enough, are improved with higher doses of neuroleptic; thus, the causative agent temporarily at least may make the symptoms disappear. If tardive dyskinesia is present, most likely it will best be observed when a patient has stopped his medication or has recently reduced the dosage.

The side effects of neuroleptics have become so universally observed by clinicians that there is a growing tendency to view these drug-induced symptoms as an aspect of the mental condition being treated. This clinical misperception unnecessarily condemns patients to the agony of bothersome side effects and, in the case of tardive dyskinesia, to an irreversible neurological disability.

Antidepressants and Lithium

Whereas, only a few years ago, psychotherapy was the standard treatment for depression, large numbers of people are now managed with antidepressant medications.

Antidepressants generally fall into one of two main chemical types: the tricyclics and the MAO-inhibitors. The tricyclics, by far the most widely prescribed in this country, possess potent anticholinergic properties which, as previously mentioned, can in relatively small doses precipitate symptoms of brain syndrome, especially in elderly persons. Both types of antidepressants can cause a sensation of anxious agitation. In persons prone to cyclical mood swings, antidepressant medication may precipitate a full-blown, manic attack. Since many persons treated with these medications suffer from manic-depressive disorder, it is important that the clinician be sensitive to this potential adverse drug reaction, if it is not to be mistaken for just another manic episode.

Lithium has become a pharmacological mainstay in the management of manic-depressive disorder. Although not particularly impressive as an antidepressant, this salt-like element has proven efficacy in the treatment of acute manic attacks and is a preventive deterrent against future attacks. Unlike other psychiatric medications, lithium requires a close monitoring of the exact blood level. As long as the lithium level remains within a narrow therapeutic range, few adverse effects are associated with this drug; when this range is exceeded, a host of uncomfortable and sometimes serious symptoms emerge. Generally, the first manifestations of lithium toxicity relate to the stomach and intestinal tract—nausea, vomiting, and diarrhea. The person appears physically sick, often with an ashen gray countenance. Unfortunately,

TABLE 8-2 ANTIDEPRESSANTS

(Selected List)

Tricyclics	*MAO-Inhibitors*
Tofranil (imipramine)	Marplan (isocarboxazide)
Elavil (amitriptyline)	Nardil (phenelzine)
Sinequan (doxepin)	Parnate (tranylcypromine)

these early warning symptoms do not always appear. Instead, the clinician may confront an unexplained deterioration in the patient's ability to think clearly and an outward appearance of apathy and depression with tremulousness. In these instances, it is essential that the underlying culprit be quickly recognized, because the margin of safety between therapeutic and toxic levels of lithium is relatively small.

An important drug interaction effect to remember concerning lithium is the toxicity-enhancing influence of various diuretics (drugs which increase urine output) used for treating hypertension. Lithium becomes toxic in the relative absence of sodium and potassium, minerals which are depleted by diuretic treatment. Combined treatment with lithium and a diuretic requires close medical monitoring.

Minor Tranquilizers

The most widely prescribed medication in the United States is Valium (diazepam), one of a number of antianxiety preparations in the benzodiazepine chemical family. Probably the greatest danger associated with this class of drugs is the temptation on the part of patients and physicians to use them inappropriately. They do have certain side effects that represent potential problems in critical assessment. Many benzodiazepines are long-acting; that is, they or their active metabolites remain in the body for extended periods. Thus, if the same dose is taken day after day, a gradual accumulation of the drug occurs and the individual may feel drowsy, slowed down, depressed or, in extreme cases, confused. This problem is intensified when alcohol is consumed in addition to the medication. Rarely, individuals treated with the benzodiazepines will experience a paradoxical reaction, characterized by restlessness, agitation, and even rage.

Overall, the most serious problem associated with antianxiety agents is the addiction that can develop with long and heavy usage. In these cases sudden cessation of the drug produces a

TABLE 8-3 BENZODIAZEPINES

(Selected List)
Valium (diazepam)
Librium (chlordiazepoxide)
Tranxene (chlorazepate)

dramatic withdrawal reaction easily taken for functional psychosis. Later in this chapter, we shall consider in some detail the clinical features of drug withdrawal from physically addicting substances.

GENERAL PRESCRIPTION MEDICATIONS

Antihypertensives

Medications used in the treatment of high blood pressure have considerable potential for producing mental side effects. The chemical depletion or inactivation of stimulating substances in the body, while effective in lowering blood pressure, may simultaneously lead to depression. In fact, the first modern tranquilizer—rauwolfia—was accidentally identified after it was discovered that persons treated for hypertension with this substance experienced an additional calming influence, an effect that with time often evolved into depression. A derivative of rauwolfia (reserpine) is still widely used in the treatment of hypertension.

Aldomet (methyldopa) is a popular antihypertensive that has caused depression, sometimes with symptoms of brain syndrome. The risk of this adverse reaction appears to be considerably increased when methyldopa is used in combination with Haldol (haloperidol). A similar drug-drug interaction could be expected with other neuroleptics.

The diuretic drugs constitute the first line of treatment of hypertension, and although they act through a different mechanism, their extended use can promote a clinical picture of apathy, fatigue, depression, and confusion if proper attention is not paid to adequate potassium replacement.

Anti-inflammatory Drugs

Steroids have magical effects on certain diseases, especially those characterized by chronic inflammation—such as rheumatoid arthritis and ulcerative colitis. Unfortunately, this powerful therapeutic action causes severe physical and mental side effects when these medications are used extensively. Manic behavior—psychotic in intensity—can be induced by steroids, usually evolving out of a general euphoria experienced to some degree by most individuals placed on large doses of these drugs.

Cases of profound depression and hallucinations have been described in association with Indocin (indomethacin), a nonsteroidal, anti-inflammatory drug widely used in the treatment of rheumatoid arthritis.

Miscellaneous Medications

Stimulant medications play an important part in the management of asthma and other chronic respiratory diseases, such as bronchitis and emphysema. High dosages over extended periods can produce paranoid symptomatology. Stimulants also continue to be prescribed as diet pills despite their questionable effectiveness in achieving sustained weight loss. These drugs cause restlessness, irritability, sleep deprivation and, with prolonged use, the insidious onset of suspiciousness and paranoid psychosis. In recent years, similar stimulant preparations have appeared as over-the-counter "appetite suppressants." Their potential for adverse reactions is the same as for prescription diet pills. We shall discuss stimulants at greater length in the later section on street drugs.

Dilantin (phenytoin) is an effective anticonvulsant taken by many patients with seizure disorders. Its efficacy depends on the maintenance of blood levels, which—if exceeded by only a small degree—lead to disruptive side effects, including gross incoordination, mental dullness, and hallucinations. In addition, by interfering with the intestinal absorption of the vitamin folic acid, Dilantin can cause brain syndrome along with the loss of sensation and muscle strength in the extremities.

A sizable percentage of cases of Parkinson's disease—a degenerative condition of increasing muscular rigidity, tremor, and body imbalance—responds well to levodopa (L-dopa). In approximately 20% of cases, however, psychiatric disturbances are reported.[6] The most frequent problem is brain syndrome. Second in rate of occurrence is depression. This is an interesting finding from a theoretical perspective since, theoretically, levodopa would be expected to elevate mood. At present there is no satisfactory explanation for this apparent discrepancy.

Tagamet (cimetidine), a histamine (H_2-receptor) antagonist capable of drastically reducing gastric acidity, has recently revolutionized the medical approach to gastrointestinal ulcer disease. This accounts for the meteoric rise in the use of this medication, which is not without complications. Particularly in older people, cimetidine can produce confusion, with visual hallucinations and disturbed speech. There are also reports of loss of sexual interest and the emergence of impotence, which may result from the blocking of masculinizing androgenic hormones.

The clinician should also be alerted to the adverse mental effects seen with two popular analgesics (pain medications), Darvon (propoxyphene) and Talwin (pentazocine). Darvon is widely prescribed for headache and minor pain; chemically, it is related to the narcotic methadone, and has proven itself capable of producing addiction and severe withdrawal reactions after prolonged, heavy use. Certain people react to even small doses of this drug with psychosis; similarly, this reaction has been described with Talwin.

OVER-THE-COUNTER PREPARATIONS

Thousands of different products are available as over-the-counter medications. The consumer has ready access to this vast array of drugs, most of which can produce adverse effects. The clinician should be attuned to the widespread use of over-the-counter preparations and aware that people taking these self-prescribed drugs may fail to consider them medications, presumably because they have not been prescribed by a physician. A negative reply to the question, "Are you taking any medication?" is frequently misleading. This crucial clinical question requires further elaboration to ensure that the client's definition of "medication" does not exclude certain drugs.

Certain widely used over-the-counter medications have a predilection for producing reactions that mimic psychiatric problems. In this respect, perhaps the most important class of over-the-counter drugs are the so-called anticholinergics. Hundreds of these preparations are sold under various trade names, most commonly as sleeping pills, "cold" medication, and muscle relaxants for stomach, intestinal, and menstrual cramps.

Reports of the intoxicating properties of anticholinergics date back to ancient times. Found in certain plants scattered throughout the world, these substances, with their delirium-inducing powers, are mentioned in Chinese and Sanskrit writings, and Homer portrays their potent effects in the *Iliad* and the

Odyssey. As a quick survey of the shelves at any local drug store will indicate, the two most prevalent anticholinergics are methapyrilene and scopolamine, but there are many other drugs with similiar anticholinergic properties.

Anticholinergic side effects are captured in the following rhyme:

"Mad as a hatter,
Blind as a stone;
Red as a lobster,
Dry as a bone."

Back in the 19th century, the art of hat-making required exposure to highly neurotoxic mercurial compounds; consequently, going "mad" became a recognized occupational hazard associated with hat-making. In their most dramatic expression, mental changes associated with anticholinergics take the form of a delirious psychosis, typically including frightening visual hallucinations. In less florid cases, mild disorientation with apathy and drowsiness results. The pupils become widely dilated and are generally unaffected by bright lights, which normally cause the pupil to constrict. Having lost the ability to adjust through changes in pupillary size, the person's visual field is flooded with excessive light, and vision is diminished. In addition, the small muscle controlling the thickness of the lens becomes paralyzed, preventing appropriate accommodation and leading to a blurring of visual images.

Frequently, the person's skin will become flushed especially about the face, probably as a result of the dilation of small blood vessels in the skin and increased blood flow. This flushing re-

TABLE 8-4 ANTICHOLINERGIC OVER-THE-COUNTER PREPARATIONS

(Selected List)

Sleep-Eze
Compoz
Sominex
Alka-Plus
Excedrin-PM
Nytol
Ex Tension
Alva Tranquil

sponse may also partly stem from the elevated temperature seen in anticholinergic intoxication.

Increased perspiration is expected in association with an elevated temperature; not so with anticholinergics. Perspiration may be markedly decreased or even absent despite agitation and fever. Unexplained mental changes with widely dilated pupils, elevated temperature, and decreased sweating usually indicate drug intoxication secondary to anticholinergics.

> A 17-year-old man was forcibly brought to a hospital emergency room. Disoriented to time and place, he also exhibited delusional thinking, agitation, and hallucinations, both visual and auditory. At times the patient's agitation erupted into frank assaultive behavior. His pulse was 120, and he was noted to have widely dilated pupils. His skin was flushed and warm; but despite a rectal temperature of 105°F, he showed no sign of perspiration.
>
> The following morning the man was completely lucid and willingly reported that he had purchased Asthmador pipe tobacco from a local shop, returned home and, rather than smoking it, had used the tobacco to brew a tea-like drink. He freaked out after drinking one cup of this unusual brew. The man vividly recalled hallucinating strange things crawling about on his body.[7]

Asthmador is a special pipe tobacco containing anticholinergic medication, designed for asthmatics, to reduce the irritating effects of pipe smoking. This man's unorthodox and ill-advised use of Asthmador resulted in a classic case of anticholinergic psychosis.

Elderly persons exhibit a heightened sensitivity to anticholinergics as illustrated in one medical report of toxicity from the use of atropine eyedrops.[8]

STREET DRUGS

The street scene is a constantly evolving drama; today's favorite drugs give way to tomorrow's fads. Many street drugs are readily synthesized in backyard laboratories and thus become widely available. Since there are no required quality controls in the illegal production of homemade psychoactive substances, the most recent batch may not be precisely the same as the one before it;

what is in the "bag" may not even be the same substance. There is widespread adulteration of drugs after they are synthesized. One drug is mixed with another drug or substance, usually cheaper than the original, to create an added "kick" or simply to increase the overall profit margin for the seller.[9]

Given these confounding aspects of the world of street drugs, the clinician is well advised to supplement client histories with careful clinical observation, because the client may not know what he has taken or, if he does, may not be willing to divulge this information. Physical manifestations of street drugs are often quite prominent and can provide the clinician with evidence for a drug-induced mental problem. Changes in pupil size and vital signs, as well as other autonomic nervous system manifestations, are frequently encountered in these cases.

Street drugs can be categorized into stimulants ("uppers"), depressants ("downers"), and hallucinogens. Substances in each of these categories produce significant mental and emotional changes.

"Uppers"

Uppers are perhaps best typified by the amphetamines. These drugs produce an energized euphoria with heightened activity, rapid speech, grandiosity, and sometimes belligerence. Since the amphetamines stimulate the sympathetic nervous system, the person's eyes are usually widely dilated and the pulse and blood pressure elevated. From a clinical perspective, an "upper trip" appears like a manic episode, but the physiological

TABLE 8-5 STREET DRUGS
(Selected List)

"Uppers"
"Speed" (methamphetamine)
"Bennies" (amphetamine)
"Coke" (cocaine)
Hallucinogens
LSD (lysergic acid diethylamide)
PCP (phencyclidine)
"Buttons" (psilocybin)
"Downers"
"Barbs" or "Reds" (barbiturates)
Quaalude or Sopor (methaqualone)
"Booze" (alcohol)

changes are usually much more striking than in mania. If the drugs have been injected, track marks on the arms and legs aid the clinician in confirming the drug-induced nature of the problem.

Chronic use of stimulants, particularly high doses, leads to increasing suspiciousness and paranoid psychosis virtually indistinguishable from paranoid schizophrenia. This clinical presentation does not entail the physiological changes seen in conjunction with an upper trip, since these acute effects disappear as the body gradually adapts. The cognitive deficits of brain syndrome are *not* usually a part of amphetamine psychosis; in fact, an unusual degree of mental clarity may be preserved along with an obsessive interest in minute details.

Due to the appetite-suppressing quality of stimulants, extended use may also lead to considerable weight loss so that the person's clothes no longer fit properly.

After 2 months of unusual behavior, a 20-year-old woman was referred for psychiatric evaluation. She explained that she had felt increasingly "uptight." Upon meeting people for the first time, she strongly sensed she had met them previously.

She related other strange events. She was certain that because they did not like her the students at her college were playing tricks on her such as turning the clocks back. Her mother, she had come to believe, was planning to poison her.

Intuitively, the woman explained these strange happenings as manifestations of a great struggle going on within herself involving the Holy Spirit, the Devil, and her own will. Each of these competing forces was expressed through a different language.

During the psychiatric interview, she appeared anxious, perplexed, and scared. Although frankly delusional, she was fully oriented and coherent in her thinking. She had no previous history of psychiatric problems and stated that she had been in excellent physical health. On direct questioning, she denied using street drugs or prescribed medications. After a diagnosis of acute paranoid schizophrenia was made, the woman was started on Stelazine (trifluoperazine). Three weeks later, when the mental aberrations had subsided, she revealed to her therapist that she had been taking "diet pills," Ionamin (phentamine), for three months. She had not thought of the diet pills as medication.

The revised diagnosis was "diet pill (stimulant) psychosis."[10]

All stimulants—over-the-counter, prescription, or street drugs—can cause this type of paranoid psychosis with extended use.

One other word about stimulants. There are cases that come to the clinician's attention after stimulant use has been discontinued, not as a typical withdrawal reaction—this does not occur with stimulants—but as a problem of severe depression. Unless the clinician is alert to the possibility of a *poststimulant depression,* he may become engaged in a fruitless search for nondrug-related events in the person's life to explain this mood change.

Hallucinogens

An extensive number of street drugs are capable of creating an unusual array of perceptual distortions. Despite the name "hallucinogen," not all of these effects are actually hallucinations. Illusionary phenomena, for example, constitute a considerable portion of the hallucinogenic experience. Hallucinations are only one of several kinds of perceptual distortions involving vision, taste, touch, smell, and self-awareness. Synesthesias, in which one sensory form is perceived as another, are frequently experienced with hallucinogens. Music may sound like the taste of honey or the smell of lemon, or a strawberry may taste like the smell of vanilla or the sound of rain. Obviously, such experiences when communicated to someone else, particularly a person who is not having the same experience and may not be aware that the person has taken a drug, can appear more psychotic than aesthetic.

A person under the influence of a hallucinogen is strongly influenced by factors other than the drug itself. Setting, prevailing mood, and the nature of the relationship with other participants all contribute to the overall effect. Given the wrong mix, drug encounters become extremely frightening episodes and can quickly evolve into agitated psychosis. In other instances the individual may respond by becoming immobilized and mute, leading the unsuspecting clinician to a hasty impression of catatonic schizophrenia. This is especially likely when the person experiencing the "bad trip" has a previous history of mental disorder.

Many of the commonly used hallucinogens cause observable physiological changes, such as widely dilated pupils and deviations in vital signs. This is not, however, a consistent finding.

Flashback plagues a small percentage of persons who take hallucinogens. The specific cause is not known. Days, weeks, sometimes even months or years after taking one of these drugs, a sudden fragmentary episode reminiscent of the actual drug experience erupts. Usually the flashback lasts no more than a few seconds and disappears. The frequency of these attacks is quite variable, but generally they seem to decrease and eventually disappear with time. Unaware of their origin, an individual may become quite troubled and begin to suspect he is losing his mind, and the clinician, hearing a flashback described, may mistakenly suspect an impending functional psychosis.

Phencyclidine—PCP—is presently one of the most widely available hallucinogens, due mainly to the ease and cheapness with which it can be synthesized. This drug is both a potent analgesic and anesthetic agent that creates a kind of chemical sensory deprivation when taken in large doses. Bizarre, "spaced-out" behavior with a predilection for unprovoked violence characterizes bad trips from this drug. There may be long periods of blank, dazed expression and fixed posture; then, when the person does move, he is usually unsteady on his feet. There is a general tendency not to speak; and, overall, responses to any kind of stimulation are reduced. The symptoms of ROBS are characteristically present, with dramatic alterations in level of consciousness.

Unlike many other hallucinogens, PCP does not produce dilated pupils; there is, however, a characteristic up-and-down and side-to-side jerkiness of the eyes, known as nystagmus. Nystagmus is not specific to PCP intoxication; it is seen with other drugs and in a variety of other neurological conditions.

"Downers"

These drugs create a "loose" feeling with a sense of euphoria. After large doses the pleasant sensation quickly gives way to decreasing awareness, drowsiness, loss of consciousness, and sometimes coma and death. Numerous depressant substances are available, often diverted into the black market from production by pharmaceutical manufacturers.

Usage is often denied; thus recognition of a downer drunk requires an index of suspicion and careful observation. The person is usually unsteady and shows slurred speech. It is important for the clinician to remember that downers are not used exclusively by the so-called drug culture, an impression conveyed by the popular press. Extensive use of these substances occurs throughout the adult population, often in conjunction with alcohol.

Alcohol is such a pervasive part of the social scene that it is often not even perceived as a drug; in fact, it is the most extensively used drug in this country as well as the rest of the world.

The emotional and behavioral concomitants of chronic alcohol abuse—depression, anxiety, and suspiciousness—are frequently mistaken for functional problems. Persons who have come to abuse this drug are notorious in their need to deny their involvement with alcohol, making clinical recognition a complicated task. Tell-tale signs, such as increasing absenteeism, automobile accidents, and declining performance on the job or at school, are important indirect indicators of alcoholism. Family problems and other interpersonal difficulties sometimes clinically obscure the underlying difficulty with alcohol. These must be recognized as important but secondary problems.

Persons suffering from alcoholism are not immune to other diseases; in fact, they experience a much higher incidence of serious organic conditions. These include subdural hematomas and hypoglycemia as well as liver disease. Failure to suspect a serious medical problem hidden by a drunken condition is an all too common critical assessment mistake.

Alcohol potentiates the effects of most psychoactive drugs, including antidepressants, neuroleptics, minor tranquilizers, and particularly, other downers. In combination with these drugs, alcohol produces an overdose condition, manifesting as confusion and drowsiness and, in more tragic instances, becoming an unintentional cause of death.

DRUG WITHDRAWAL

Certain drugs require increasing amounts to achieve the same physiological and psychological effect. This is called "tolerance" and is a defining aspect of physically addicting substances, most of which are associated with a euphoric or pain-relieving effect. Included among these drugs are various pain medications, barbiturates, street narcotics, minor tranquilizers, and alcohol. The amount of time required to develop tolerance varies tremendously from substance to substance; whereas, with heroin or morphine, tolerance rapidly ensues within days or weeks, alcohol tolerance occurs over a period of years. The end result, however, is the same.

The body adapts physiologically to the suppression by addicting substances. It is this adaptation that leaves the person susceptible to withdrawal reactions. When the substance is suddenly stopped after extended usage, the brain is no longer under this suppressing influence; now, the increased neuronal activity that had arisen as an adaptation to the addicting substance is excessive; "overshoot" occurs. In this sense drug withdrawal can be viewed as an uncontrolled burst of neuronal activity productive of a variety of mental and physical aberrations.

Drug withdrawals have four characteristic components; but, in any given case, one or more may fail to appear.

Agitation

In the early stage of withdrawal, the person is tremulous and anxious, often easily startled by noises or unexpected events. He looks ill and is in obvious discomfort.

Physiological Changes

Often there is quickening of the pulse, a rise in blood pressure and temperature, and excessive sweating. These changes may also indicate a supervening infectious disease such as pneumonia. Withdrawal alone, however, can produce them.

Cognitive and Perceptual Disruption

Perceptual deficits, although usually emerging after the onset of agitation and physiological symptoms, can be the initial sign of withdrawal. Drug withdrawal, particularly delirium tremens, typically leads to ROBS with its characteristic cognitive deficits. Psychotic behavior with paranoid delusions is also a common finding. Cognitive distortions begin with misperceptions of things in the immediate environment and then progress to hallucinations. Voices may be hallucinated, often accusatory in tone. Gradually, the voices become more threatening and abusive. Visual hallucinations are commonplace in drug withdrawals. The perennial objects of alcohol jokes—pink elephants and little green men—are, in fact, a part of the world of withdrawal. Generally, the more severe the withdrawal reaction, the more frightening the hallucinations. Snakes and spiders crawling on the walls, the ceiling, or the floor may be witnessed; or, even more disturbing, the individual may sense an infestation by bugs which no one else will confirm.

Heroin withdrawal is a notable exception with respect to cognitive disruption and psychosis. These symptoms are seldom seen in individuals going off heroin; physical symptoms are characteristically much more prominent.

Seizures

Seizures develop in a relatively small percentage of appropriately treated cases of drug withdrawals; but in untreated cases—particularly involving alcohol or barbiturates—this complication is much more frequent and can become life-threatening.

> A disheveled man in his fifties was discovered lying in an alley way, grasping at his chest and complaining of pain. An ambulance was called, and the man taken to the emergency room of a county hospital. He was found to have suffered a severe heart attack for which he was admitted to the hospital.
>
> Over the next 2 days, the patient's chest pain subsided. He was cooperative, fully oriented, and able to carry on a normal conversation. He denied any previous history of serious illness, trauma, or alcohol consumption; but since he had smelled of alcohol on admission, his story was considered suspect.
>
> By the end of the second hospital day, a change in behavior was observed. The patient became increasingly anxious and at times verbally abusive with hospital staff, quite different from his previous calm and cooperative demeanor. That evening he was found standing in his bed, undaunted by the leads from the heart monitor and the I.V. going into his arm. He was sweating profusely and shouting out commands indicating that he considered himself the captain of a ship and the immediate hospital surroundings an ocean-going vessel. Staff and other patients were addressed as ship personnel. The man's eyes shifted about as though he were responding to visual hallucinations, and he carried on conversations with imaginary persons and threatening voices. The patient used graphic expletives and dramatic gestures. His pulse rate, blood pressure, and temperature were elevated.

For his own safety, the man was subdued and restrained in bed. Over the next 24 hours, despite aggressive treatment for delirium tremens, his condition remained relatively unchanged. His situation then became complicated by the development of pneumonia. He quickly deteriorated and expired on the fifth hospital day.

It was assumed that the man had been an alcoholic who had suffered a severe heart attack. After the abrupt cessation of his alcohol consumption due to hospitalization, he had developed a severe withdrawal reaction that in combination with a complicating infectious process led to his death.[11]

The clinical presentations of drug withdrawal are highly variable. The typical situation, much like the preceding case, involves a person brought in for treatment—sometimes confinement in jail—because of severe inebriation. Over the next 12 to 36 hours, as the symptoms of intoxication disappear, the stage is set for withdrawal.

Clinicians sometimes dismiss the possibility of drug withdrawal if all the characteristic symptoms are not present or if it is clear that the person has not completely stopped his drug or alcohol intake. These are misguided clinical practices, for drug withdrawal can manifest as a single symptom and can develop after only a *reduction* in the amount of drug consumed. Abstinence is not a requirement.

The severity of withdrawal reactions depends on the particular substance and the amount and duration of use. A commonly held misconception is that withdrawal from opiate drugs such as heroin is the most serious form of drug withdrawal; not so. The death rate from cold turkey heroin withdrawals is extremely low; in contrast, withdrawal from barbiturates carries a significant mortality rate, even higher than that seen in delirium tremens. Since the barbiturate addict frequently does not fit the stereotypical image of the "drugger," this potentially lethal withdrawal is often overlooked.

Finally, the clinician should be aware of what can be a particularly baffling form of drug withdrawal. Usually, the case involves a person who has ingested pills as a suicide attempt or is acutely intoxicated on alcohol or some other drug. The person is discovered and admitted to a treatment facility, confused, drowsy, and intoxicated. Unknown to the clinician, as well as to the family and friends of the patient, there is an extensive history of substance abuse, frequently including mixed use of barbiturates, pain medications, and alcohol. As the immediate effects of the overdose wear off, the clinical condition begins to shift radically. Since the patient no longer has access to his supply of drugs, withdrawal symptoms begin to displace the initial clinical picture of intoxication. This shifting clinical presentation is not uncommon and can leave the unsuspecting clinician quite bewildered.

Drug use is pervasive; it is epidemic. The clinician must maintain a high index of suspicion for drug-induced organic mental disorders. They are easily overlooked.

CHAPTER 9

THE OTHER SIDE OF THINGS

"Judge not according to appearance."

St. John

For most of this book we have been discussing ways in which organic problems masquerade as psychological reactions. In this chapter we are considering the reverse side of the coin: the translation of psychological conflicts into physical or somatic symptoms in the absence of an underlying organic disease. This is called *somatization.* These conditions are listed in DSM-III as "Somatoform Disorders."[1]

At this point the reader might realistically inquire as to how a consideration of somatization fits into the scope of this book. Since somatization results in the development of "physical" symptoms, there would seem to be little danger with respect to critical assessment. The problem is that, with the popularization of such terms as "psychosomatic" and "hysterical," the criteria for their use have become less precise. Anyone who complains of vague somatic symptoms increasingly runs the risk of being considered a case of somatization.

This chapter acquaints the reader with the major clinical types of somatization so that *atypical findings,* which should lead to a serious reconsideration of the somatization hypothesis, can be readily identified. When the human service clinician is confronted with "psychosomatic" cases he should verify certain characteristic clinical findings and confirm that an adequate medical evaluation has failed to reveal an organic basis for the problem. Clinicians should never fall into the trap of automatically viewing vague physical symptoms as reflections of problems in living. You will recall in a study mentioned earlier in this book that of 85 persons thoroughly evaluated medically and initially diagnosed as having hysteria, over one-third were eventually found to suffer from an organic disease.

As we review the clinical patterns of somatization, the essential findings that are present in most cases will be noted, for when these are absent, the diagnosis of somatization must be considered highly tentative. It is much more important for a nonmedical professional confidently to conclude "this is probably *not* a case of somatization" than to speculate that "this might be a case of somatization." The latter should be left to those who are responsible for medical evaluation.

SIMPLE SOMATIZATION

From time to time most of us experience somatic symptoms related to psychological stress. Perhaps under increasing pressure we simply become more cognizant of minor aches and pains we might otherwise ignore; or, perhaps the added conflict in our lives produces greater muscle tension that results in various somatic symptoms. Whatever the exact mechanism, many people who seek medical help apparently suffer from this problem.

Simple somatization is not a psychiatric disease; rather, it is a common experience in living. Although it may be accompanied by depression, this is certainly not an invariable association. The clinician should look for certain characteristic features of simple somatization, the most important one being that the complaints arise out of a stressful situation, perhaps a job change, marital problems, a significant personal loss, or a major life transition. Often when the stressful situation is openly identified and discussed, the symptoms dissipate.

Another characteristic feature of simple somatization relates to the temporary nature of the symptoms. The long-standing doctor joke—"take two aspirin and call me in the morning" —is based on an important principle that physicians have taken advantage of for centuries: the body tends to heal itself, psychologically as well as physically. This is certainly the case with simple somatization. Even if a stressful situation persists, the person gradually adapts and the severity of the somatic complaints diminishes. Generally, the clinical picture of simple somatization is not characterized by persistence or increasing severity in symptoms; this is much more characteristic of organic disease.

The complaints are usually vague. Even if the person is encouraged to be more specific, they are likely to be unable to do so. When a person relates a major somatic symptom with *specificity,* simple somatization is not the most likely explanation.

For the nonmedical clinician the message is this: *if somatic symptoms occur without an identifiable stress, if they persist or intensify, or if they are specifically described, consider the possibility of organic disease rather than simple somatization.* Also, of course, if the person has a history of organic disease that produced similar symptoms, a recurrence of the disease must be ruled out.

One word of warning: what on the surface appears as a vague complaint with slight elaboration by the clinician often proves to be a specific physical symptom. Take fatigue. Such a complaint can become a projective test for clinicians, plunging them into premature conclusions: "Fatigued? Yes, well how long have you been depressed?"

Fatigue does not necessarily imply depression and certainly should not be equated with it. When a client complains of fatigue, the clinician should encourage the person to elaborate.

CLINICIAN: "What do you mean when you say you feel fatigued?"

CLIENT: "Well, I don't have any energy."

CLINICIAN: "What makes you say you don't have any energy?"

CLIENT: "At the job, I can't carry the heavy containers that I use to . . . mainly seems to be my left arm. Guess I'm just getting old."

In the course of this short hypothetical exchange, the initial, vague-sounding complaint of "feeling fatigued" has been circumscribed as weakness in the left arm, a very specific physical complaint that cannot be assumed a manifestation of simple somatization.

Consider a second vague symptom.

CLIENT: "I'm not my old self; I'm just not well."

CLINICIAN: "Not well?"

CLIENT: "Yeh, I hardly even get out of the house."

CLINICIAN: "You mean because you are not well?"

CLIENT: "I can't walk more than a few steps without getting completely out of breath. Can't even make it up the stairs at home without being winded."

What was presented as, "I'm just not my old self; I'm just not well," with brief clarification is found to mean, "I get completely out of breath." Breathlessness is a specific physical complaint commonly seen in various heart and lung conditions; it deserves a complete medical evaluation.

Organic diseases causing persons to feel apathetic, fatigued, breathless, or weak can easily be misinterpreted as psychosomatic conditions. Anemia is a good example. This is a common medical problem, especially among women, characterized by a reduced red blood count. The most frequent cause of anemia is iron deficiency, which often develops as a result of the chronic depletion of blood some women have from heavy menstrual periods. Other conditions, such as ulcers, hemorrhoids, and certain internal cancers, also produce chronic blood loss and resulting anemia. Regardless of the precise etiology, anemia usually leads to certain core symptoms: pallor (loss of the natural pinkish hue of the skin, nail beds, and mucous membranes), fatigue, lassitude, and breathlessness upon mild exertion. Problems in critical assessment arise when the fatigue, lassitude, and reduced activity are construed as reflections of "depression with somatic overlay." Vague somatic symptoms should always be pursued with clarifying questions. If a person is encouraged to elaborate and specify somatic symptoms, more often than not this will be forthcoming in cases of organic disease.

Hyperparathyroidism, although not nearly as common a

TABLE 9-1 ESSENTIAL CHARACTERISTICS OF SIMPLE SOMATIZATION

Has no identifiable organic basis
Occurs in association with increased life stress
Fails to persist beyond the stress period
Manifests as nonspecific, vague complaints

condition as anemia, can also present as depression and somatization. The parathyroid glands (small, pea-shaped nodules located in the neck adjacent to the thyroid gland) play a central role in the body's regulation of calcium and phosphorus. In hyperparathyroidism an excessive amount of parathyroid hormone (parathormone) is released, causing abnormally high concentrations of calcium in the blood and urine. The calcium tends to precipiate within the kidneys, causing stones that produce abdominal and back pain as they are passed from the body. Complaints of scattered discomfort and tenderness result from the mobilizing of calcium from the bones. Approximately 25% of patients with hyperparathyroidism develop peptic ulcer, providing yet another source of somatic symptoms. When such complaints are joined by muscle weakness and characteristic mental changes of lethargy and depression, critical assessment becomes difficult.

> Apathetic, depressed and feeling herself losing strength, a 68-year-old widow explained her deteriorating condition as the product of her loneliness.
>
> For 4 years she had also suffered from an intermittent upper abdominal discomfort. While being evaluated by her internist, the woman was seen by a consulting psychiatrist who diagnosed her as moderately depressed. But during the course of her medical evaluation, a duodenal ulcer was identified on a radiographic study of her gastrointestinal tract.
>
> Further investigation established an abnormally high serum calcium level (12 mg/100 ml) and led to a diagnosis of hyperparathyroidism. At surgery a parathyroid adenoma (a benign tumor) was removed. The woman recovered without complication and showed prompt healing of her ulcer. Her symptoms of lethargy, weakness, and depression lifted completely without further therapy.[2]

Here we have illustrated the importance of distinguishing muscle weakness from complaints of lethargy, apathy, or fatigue. Until proven otherwise, muscle weakness must be considered a neurological deficit. There is a tendency on the part of nonmedical human service professionals to view somatic complaints as peripheral concerns, but somatic symptoms are often indicators of masquerading organic problems. If ignored, the recognition of the underlying organic disturbance may be overlooked. The syndrome of hyperventilation serves as a good example in illustrating the pitfalls of ignoring somatic symptoms. Hyperventilation syndrome is an episodic organic condition, typically evolving out of a state of psychological anxiety. As the anxiety builds, the person starts to overbreathe; the breathing progressively becomes deeper and more rapid. Symptoms result from the blowing off of excessive amounts of carbon dioxide. When the proper balance between oxygen and carbon dioxide is disrupted, the body's delicate acid-base relationship becomes too alkaline. Among other changes, this chemical shift creates a sense of apprehension, thus setting into motion a vicious cycle leading to higher and higher levels of anxiety. Characteristic organic symptoms emerge, but they may be overshadowed by the person's state of anxiety. A sensation of lightheadedness and peculiar feelings of numbness around the mouth and in the fingers and toes are the most frequent findings. These may be accompanied by blurred vision, breathlessness, chest pain, and headache. In severe cases, the person experiences muscle spasms that turn the wrists and ankles inward. Consciousness may be lost momentarily, and in rare instances the person hallucinates.

When the entire spectrum of symptoms are present, the organic nature of hyperventilation is usually suspected. In more typical cases however, the clinician encounters an extremely anxious person who usually can describe some reasonable problem-in-living basis for the reaction. The somatic symptoms may be minimized by the patient, or if commented on, neglected by the interviewer. A point to remember is that once a person has overbreathed to the extent of precipitating symptoms, continuous rapid breathing is no longer required to sustain the symptom-producing chemical imbalance. A few deep sighing breaths taken periodically will do the trick.

> Accompanied by her boyfriend, a 22-year-old woman sought medical care at a local hospital emergency room for what she felt was a heart attack.
>
> Obviously frightened and anxious, she complained of shortness of breath and chest pain. She also described a tingling sensation around her mouth and lightheadedness. The woman related that her symptoms had developed soon after discovering that her boyfriend had been with another woman.[3]

If a person is hyperventilating, a reduction in the rate and depth of breathing will quickly ameliorate the symptoms. The patient should be encouraged to relax and breathe more slowly. In certain cases the person will be too anxious to follow this direction. If so, the person can be instructed to breathe into and out of a brown paper bag for a few minutes. This time-honored technique ensures the rebreathing of carbon dioxide. The result: a dramatic disappearance of symptoms.

As a way of convincing the patient of the role of over breathing, once the symptoms have disappeared, they can be rapidly re-introduced by having the person purposely take several rapid, deep breaths.

The hyperventilation syndrome is a common clinical problem and should be considered in all cases of acute anxiety, particularly when associated with vague somatic complaints. This clinical picture can also result from specific organic diseases. In one study of 30 patients with hyperventilation, 7 were found to have underlying organic disorders.[4] Although it is possible that in some of these cases the symptoms arose out of anxiety concerning the physical disease, it must be assumed that in most instances the disease itself caused the problem. This possibility should be considered especially if symptoms of hyperventilation do not come under control easily or if they tend to recur after only brief periods of relief.

Although physical expressions of problems in living are a common occurrence, the clinician should guard against interpreting all cases of vague somatic complaints as simple somatization, particularly in the absence of the essential characteristics listed in Table 9-1.

BRIQUET'S SYNDROME (HYSTERIA)

The term *hysteria* has been variously applied by mental health professionals, often having little scientific value and at worse serving as a pejorative adjective. For example, "hysterical personality," although giving the impression of a well-delineated personality type, is a global concept indicating widely varying degrees of histrionics, seductiveness, superficiality, and ego-centeredness. Since no precise criteria for this so-called personality disorder have been established, the use of the term is largely a matter of subjective value judgment. At best, "hysterical personality" represents a gross stereotype that can be quite misleading.

Due to the vagueness of "hysteria", its usefulness seems limited. For this reason, the suggestion has been recently made to replace this term with that of "Briquet's syndrome," after the French physician who described a striking form of somatization in 1859.[5] This syndrome typically begins during the teen years and is characterized by the emergence of various physical complaints that are inevitably found to have no organic basis; nonetheless, various diagnoses, hospitalizations, and treatments (including surgery) accumulate, usually along with an ever-growing list of physicians. The person with Briquet's syndrome becomes compulsively preoccupied with ill health; complaining about physical symptoms becomes a way of life.

Dramatizing and overexaggerating symptoms is an essential aspect of Briquet's syndrome, as is a history of significant interpersonal conflict, particularly in the area of sex. One researcher has even suggested that this diagnosis be seriously questioned when a satisfactory sexual life is related by the individual.

Although extensive somatization is the dominant characteristic, the clinician must not make the mistake of equating multiple somatic symptoms with Briquet's syndrome, which is more than complaints. It is the total absorption by the person—continuing over years—in this aspect of his or her life. People with this form of somatization invariably have thick medical and therapy records.

An unemployed, 31-year-old divorced man experienced multiple psychiatric and somatic complaints over several years. During a divorce, he had become depressed and on several occasions disappeared for extended periods. Each time, upon his return, his memory was quite fuzzy for what had transpired.

The man had been admitted to a psychiatric hospital nine times, during which his inpatient treatment was inevitably disrupted by the evaluation procedures required to investigate numerous somatic complaints. No organic basis had ever been documented.

There was an extensive medical history dating back to the age of 12, when he had been hospitalized for abdominal pain suspected of being appendicitis. Afterwards, he was discharged without treatment. Five years later he was again hospitalized, this time for long-lasting headaches. Once again no organic basis could be determined. At age 30 a recurrent bout of abdominal pain led to another round of exhaustive but unproductive medical workups. More recently, he was operated on for gallstones, but at the time of surgery, the gallbladder was found to be normal. Over the years, this man had been extensively evaluated for endocrine, cardiac, and respiratory problems and a variety of gastrointestinal complaints. In all instances no organic pathology was found. On one occasion, however, at age 24, this man did have severe pain found to result from renal stones.

Upon being interviewed, he alleged the current existence of more than 30 different physical symptoms, many of which were described in exaggerated terms. For example, when asked if he had experienced fatigue, he responded: "Yes. Sometimes I have more energy than Carter has pills, but sometimes I don't have enough energy to pick up a pin."

He related a past personal history of considerable uncomfortableness and embarrassment about sex. After being exclusively homosexual between the ages of 16 and 21, he acceded to pressure from his mother and started seeing women. Soon thereafter he married. The relationship was marked by marital discord. He found himself indifferent to sex and even impotent much of the time.

From a mental perspective he was described as being fully oriented without delusions or hallucinations. He appeared "flamboyant," "enthusiastic," and "friendly." At times he was overly emotional, easily moved to tears or laughter without provocation. Surprisingly, he expressed a belief that most of his problems—mental and physical—had psychological causes.[6]

Although this case history of Briquet's syndrome contains the essential features—early onset, extensive number of somatic complaints, numerous negative medical evaluations, dramatic presentation, and a history of chronic sexual dissatisfaction—it also includes certain notable deviations. First, the patient is a man. By far, most cases of Briquet's syndrome are described in women; obviously, there are exceptions. Second, this patient seemed to have an awareness of the psychological nature of his problem. Perhaps more extensive interviewing would have revealed this to be deceptive, but to the degree that it was present, it is an unexpected finding. A characteristic aspect of this condition is an unwillingness, often with an element of active hostility, to entertain the possibility of psychological explanation.

Finally, an important aspect of this case is the occurrence at age 24 of a bona fide organic disease, renal stones. *Even people who somatize excessively sometimes become physically ill.*

Certain diseases attack multiple organ systems and precipitate numerous complaints that could be confused with Briquet's syndrome if the essential characteristics listed in Table 9-2 are not adequately considered. Take the following case:

> Shortly after the aircraft manufacturing firm for which he worked began to lay off employees, a 32-year-old aeronautical engineer, father of three, visited his family physician complaining of transient episodes of double vision, dizziness, leg weakness, and "tingling" sensations in his legs over a 3-month period.
>
> During this same time the man had been engaged in two minor automobile accidents while driving alone in his car. On both occasions he had sustained minor lacerations.
>
> His marriage of 11 years had been satisfactory; other than periodic arguments with his wife about limited finances, they seemed to get along well.
>
> The patient had been in good health. He denied ever having experienced transient episodes of blindness, deafness, fainting spells, convulsions, paralysis, or speechlessness. Two years prior, his father, with whom he had been quite close, had died from a stroke.
>
> The man was alert and fully oriented; his memory was excellent. Early in the interview he expressed the idea that his symptoms might be caused by stress over the threat of losing his job. The physical examination, including a careful neurological assessment, revealed no abnormal findings.[7]

In his early thirties, this patient had no previous history compatible with a diagnosis of Briquet's syndrome; furthermore, rather than rushing to the doctor with a dramatic elaboration of symptoms, he had delayed for 3 months and sought out his family physician with some reluctance. His 11-year marriage suggested a degree of interpersonal stability, and his willingness to consider the possibility of a psychological explanation for his symptoms suggested considerable psychological awareness.

Based on these findings, a mental health consultant who had been asked to evaluate this case concluded that there was strong evidence *against* this being a hysterical reaction.

Subsequently, the patient was discharged without a definitive diagnosis, but several months later, he experienced a full-blown neurological disease with partial paralysis and selective sensory loss. He was diagnosed as having multiple sclerosis.

Multiple sclerosis (MS) is a degenerative neurological disease of undetermined cause. It destroys the nerve coverings, thereby producing a kind of short circuiting in patches throughout the nervous system. The resulting symptoms are diverse in character. Multiple sclerosis begins in young adulthood and tends to manifest episodically in the early course of the disease. Symptoms abruptly arise and then often disappear after a short while, only to recur again months or even years later. Initially, temporary deficits in vision and other sensory modalities may be the only symptoms; with time, however, additional neurological deficits arise and gradually become more severe, eventually leading to death. To date, no effective treatment for multiple sclerosis has been discovered.

Given the diverse and shifting symptomatology of this disease and its propensity for defying diagnosis in the early stages, it can be mistaken for an elaborate form of somatization like Briquet's syndrome or, as we shall soon discuss, conversion reaction.

A group of diseases collectively known as "autoimmune diseases" attack different parts of the body, creating an array of symptoms that, as with multiple sclerosis, often mystifies medical evaluators. It is thought that autoimmune diseases result from a failure in the body's own immune system. Early in embryonic development, the immune system establishes the difference between the body's own cells and foreign invaders from outside, such as bacteria and viruses. This essential distinction allows the immune system discriminately to seek out and destroy agents of disease.

For reasons not fully understood, when there is a breakdown in the immune system's ability to distinguish between "self" and "not self," this essential surveillance system becomes disoriented and attacks the person's own body as though it were a foreign invader. The result: a spectrum of degenerative diseases whose symptoms vary according to which of the body's organ systems are most assaulted. Either as a result of direct damage to the brain itself or as the secondary manifestation of support system failure, mental symptoms are not unusual in autoimmune diseases, along with various somatic symptoms.

In a study of patients with the autoimmune disease known as systemic lupus erythematosis (SLE), medical researchers discovered that roughly one-fifth had experienced psychiatric symptoms at some time during the course of the disease. With reference to our present discussion on somatization, a variety of intermittent somatic symptoms easily mistaken for somatization occurred. Joint pains (arthralgias) were found in 92% of cases; pleuritic pain in 54%, and symptoms of anemia in 32%.[8]

Abdominal pain is one of the most common complaints made by persons with Briquet's syndrome but, of course, all instances of abdominal pain are not manifestations of this condition. Many serious medical and surgical diseases produce a similar distribution of discomfort. Cancer of the pancreas, for example, typically causes vague abdominal discomfort early in the course of the disease and is frequently misinterpreted as a psychiatric problem due to the depression that often accompanies it. The person may also report an uncanny, frightening sense of doom. This emotional response can appear hysterical in quality to the clinical observer. As the disease progresses with such other symptoms as nausea, back pain, and weight loss, a diagnosis of Briquet's syndrome may be considered, particularly since pancreatic cancer is three times more frequent among women than men. Cancer of the pancreas, however, is quite rare before the age of 45, a point that should serve clinically to distinguish it from Briquet's syndrome.

A 59-year-old woman with no previous history of mental illness began to have insomnia, nervousness, and depression. She also complained of weakness, vague abdominal symptoms, and a striking loss of appetite, resulting in a 10-pound weight loss over a 4-month period.

Finally, she was admitted to a hospital for a medical workup. There she was noted to be fully oriented with intact memory, but she did give a history of crying spells associated with her depression and informed her doctor that she thought something terrible was about to happen to her.

A complete physical examination, including a series of gastrointestinal studies failed to reveal any organic disease. She was discharged with a diagnosis of neurasthenia and anxiety neurosis. But 2 months later, after increasing abdominal discomfort and continued weight loss, the woman was reexamined; a hard mass was found in the upper left side of her abdomen. At surgery carcinoma of the body of the pancreas was found which, due to its advanced stage of growth, was inoperable. She died at home a few weeks later.[9]

The clinical presentation of abdominal discomfort, lassitude, depression, and weight loss in a middle-aged or older person—especially without a previous history of similar problems—should make the clinician suspect pancreatic cancer.

The clinician must resist labeling symptoms as hysterical or accepting the diagnosis of Briquet's syndrome in the absence of the essential characteristics summarized in Table 9-2.

TABLE 9-2 ESSENTIAL CHARACTERISTICS OF BRIQUET'S SYNDROME

Has no identifiable organic basic
Presents as extensive number of somatic complaints (minimum 10)
Dates back to teens or early twenties
Includes extensive dramatic elaboration of symptoms
Has history of chaotic interpersonal relationships, particularly with respect to sexuality

CONVERSION REACTION

Conversion reaction—sometimes called hysterical conversion neurosis—refers to the sudden, usually dramatic appearance of a "neurological problem" that when evaluated is found to have no underlying organic basis. Since the time of Freud, the most widely accepted explanation has held that this condition represents repressed psychological conflict translated into somatic language. The idea is that somehow the conflict is more acceptable to the person expressed as a somatic symptom rather than as a psychological problem or by the carrying out of an unacceptable, fantasied action.

Unlike Briquet's syndrome, conversion reaction usually produces a single prominent symptom or symptom complex rather than multiple widespread complaints and has an abrupt, explosive quality rather than a chronic presentation. Conversion reactions, however, can be superimposed on a clinical background of Briquet's syndrome. This condition, like Briquet's syndrome, is much more common in women than men.

Conversion reactions can be categorized roughly into three clinical types.

In the *loss of function* conversion reaction, the resulting deficit involves movement or sensation; thus, the person may have an inability to walk, complete loss of movement in an arm or leg, blindness or deafness, or the absence or severe distortion of sensation over a certain area of the body. This type of conversion reaction appears primarily in individuals with limited psychological sophistication and limited educational background. Interestingly, these demographics represent a striking change from the turn of the century, when Freud and other investigators described conversion hysteria occurring among sophisticated, well-educated clientele.

When evaluated neurologically, the conversion deficit is found to be only a rough approximation of what would be expected based on neuroanatomical relationships. The person may appear unable to move a leg, yet when the examiner draws attention to some other area, the leg inadvertently moves. A disturbance in sensation may not conscribe to the anatomical distribution of nerves, so that, for example, the person fails to register the sensation of a pinprick over a square or circular patch on the body even though the nerves are not distributed in that fashion. In the absence of documented neurological inconsistencies, conversion reaction of this type should be seriously questioned as a diagnosis.

A young man—previously an acrobat and dancer in the circus —enlisted in the Army during peace time. He quickly found his new lifestyle monotonous compared to his traveling life with the circus; and the discipline of military life was a rude awakening. He considered desertion but could not muster the courage to act.

Without warning, he abruptly became unable to walk and

TABLE 9-3 TYPES OF CONVERSION REACTIONS

1. Loss of function
2. Pseudoseizure
3. Pain reaction

could not feel anything in his legs. There was no previous history of explosive symptomatology. Struck with this catastrophic event, he appeared surprisingly unconcerned. He was hospitalized and shortly thereafter discharged on a surgeon's certificate of disability.

The man's symptoms were never reconciled with any organic deficit. Gradually he regained function in his legs along with a return of normal sensation. Within a few months he left the hospital fully recovered. His diagnosis was conversion reaction.[10]

Pseudoseizure (hystero-epilepsy) is a second type of conversion reaction, occurring in a similiar population as the first type, but characterized by a simulated seizure. The person collapses on the floor or begins to experience thrashing or jerking movements. Inevitably the episode is quite dramatic and hardly ever transpires in the absence of other people.

In many of these cases even a passing familiarity with organic seizures will lead the observer to suspect a nonorganic origin. For example, the person, while outwardly appearing to have a grand mal seizure, may show such obvious signs of consciousness as speaking in a faint voice or responding to verbal command. The clinician should not forget, however, that other seizure patterns (like temporal lobe epilepsy) can manifest as unusual forms of behavior. All instances of sudden shifts in consciousness or behavior that recur in episodic fashion must be evaluated neurologically. The clinician should be especially sensitive to cases labeled conversion reaction but which include a history of loss of bladder control, self-injury, or occurrence in the absence of other people. While frequently found in organic epilepsy cases, these findings are highly uncharacteristic of conversion reaction. The reader will recall that in the previous case of multiple sclerosis thought to be hysterical, the man had injured himself in two minor automobile accidents while driving alone. This would have been strong evidence against a diagnosis of conversion reaction.

Conversion reactions involving a *specific complaint* of pain—the third type—are particularly difficult medical diagnostic problems. As a general rule, the nonmedical professional should insist that pain symptoms be evaluated by a physician. Medical specialists have at their disposal sophisticated testing procedures for differentiating organic from psychogenic pain; this is not a legitimate area of assessment for the nonspecialist. Any persistent, unexplained pain must be evaluated medically. Even when an organic basis is not initially determined, if the pain persists or recurs, it should be reevaluated periodically by medical personnel. Pain is an elusive phenomenon, one whose organic basis sometimes remains unidentified for long periods despite intensive investigation.

Invariably, conversion reactions, regardless of type, are associated with significant interpersonal conflict; often, the resulting symptom provides at least a partial resolution to the conflict. The resolution may be symbolic: a long-suffering woman confronted again and again with her husband's unfaithfulness suddenly becomes paralyzed in her right hand, rendering her unable to pull the trigger of the gun she had fantasied as the lethal weapon. Or, the conversion resolution to the conflict may be more literal in nature: a man confronted by the desire to tell off his tyrannical boss, but realistically unable to do so, becomes mute, thereby actually as well as symbolically resolving his conflict.

In addition to resolving conflict, conversion symptoms often lead to secondary gain; that is, the person derives a new advantage or personal attention from having become "ill." The role of medical patient affords a person certain privileges not otherwise available.

Finally, it is unusual for a person to have a single episode of conversion reaction; thus, unless it is the initial occurrence, a previous history of unexplained somatic symptoms is characteristically found. Without a previous history, the initial episode of conversion reaction must always be met with considerable suspicion even when a neurological evaluation reveals no organic basis.

The human service professional must seriously question a diagnosis of conversion reaction that does not include the essential characteristics outlined in Table 9-4.

TABLE 9-4 ESSENTIAL CHARACTERISTICS OF CONVERSION REACTIONS

Has no identifiable organic basis
Occurs with sudden, dramatic onset in the midst of interpersonal conflict or other high-stress situation
Manifests as a single, prominent symptom, usually neurological in nature

Shortly after returning home from church, a 16-year-old girl complained of a severe headache accompanied by nausea. She went to the bathroom to take medication (Fiorinal) and was discovered by her parents soon after, unconscious, lying on the bathroom floor. She was rushed to a nearby hospital, where she regained consciousness in a couple of hours. A neurologist examined her and recorded a presumptive diagnosis of conversion reaction. He had the patient transferred to a psychiatric hospital.

Let me interrupt just to state what is probably obvious to the reader. At this juncture in the case history, even when recorded by a neurologist, the diagnosis of conversion reaction is inappropriate. The fact that the patient lost consciousness in the absence of anyone else, combined with a failure by the neurologist to record any context of interpersonal stress or previous history of similar episodes, should have raised serious questions about this diagnosis. This is precisely what occurred when the patient was subsequently seen at a psychiatric hospital.

The patient gave a 2-year history of headaches. No neurological basis had been discovered. She had been followed by a physician and treated with Fiorinal, from which she obtained partial relief. She described her headaches as present on only one side, often associated with nausea, blurred vision, and unsteadiness in walking. Her friends had stated that during these headaches she sometimes walked as though she were intoxicated.

The hospital staff characterized the patient as attractive and intelligent, depressed at times, but genuinely concerned about her condition. She talked openly with her psychologist about competing with her sister and described the special attention that she received from her mother when her headaches first started. She was given an MMPI psychological test, which showed a "conversion V" (allegedly seen in persons prone to conversion reactions). Members of the nursing staff consistently described her, however, as a "healthy, normal teenager," based on her behavior on the unit.

Further neurological evaluation of this young woman led to a diagnosis of "migraine headaches, basilar type."[11]

Basilar migraine—a somewhat unusual variant of migraine—is characterized by a "sick" headache, usually only on one side with unsteadiness and visual disturbances. It is primarily seen in adolescents, particularly girls.

This case illustrates the importance of resisting the diagnosis of conversion reaction unless the positive evidence is compelling and includes as a minimum the essential characteristics we have noted. Although no organic basis had been found on previous examinations and the patient did openly express ongoing conflict with her sister, other findings strongly argued against conversion reaction. She had a multiple-symptom clinical picture: headache, nausea, blurred vision, and unsteadiness. Furthermore, no increase in the conflict with her sister or other stressful situation was identified to account for the present reaction. Other considerations arguing against the diagnosis were the woman's psychological awareness and concern over her problem.

This case points out once again the diagnostic difficulties encountered in dealing with the symptom of pain. In a study of 250 patients with protracted head pain, after repeated negative medical consultations, 25% were eventually discovered to have an organic brain disorder accounting for their symptom.[12] The clinician should always be uneasy with pain as a conversion reaction.

> An 18-year-old Jewish college student was considered to have a conversion reaction based on a 6-year history of peculiar internal rotation of her right hand, which initially manifest only when she was writing. This deficit did not develop when she engaged in other activities, such as eating, typing, or playing a musical instrument. After a neurological examination was reported as normal, she was referred for psychotherapy, which she continued for 1 year without any change in her condition. Four years later the strange posture had extended to guitar-playing and had even come to affect her other hand.
>
> When interviewed the woman appeared intelligent and sophisticated. She was noted to have additional movement abnormalities, including a slow, forward-thrusting motion of her right shoulder and out-turning movements of her right wrist.
>
> She was diagnosed as having idiopathic torsion dystonia, a rare neurological disease of unknown etiology, with an increased incidence among Ashkenazic Jews.[13]

Although the woman's symptom was unusual, there was no identifiable, dramatic onset; the symptom was gradually progressive. She was described as intelligent and sophisticated, adjectives not characteristically applied to persons with conversion reaction. No particular interpersonal stress was identified. In short, there was never sufficient evidence for considering this woman's problem a conversion reaction.

In this chapter we have considered three forms of somatization, with the main objective of familiarizing the reader with their clinical patterns, especially their essential characteristics. The human service professional should be less concerned with making these diagnoses and focus more on recognizing glaring inconsistencies that argue against them. This is best accomplished through a positive approach of identifying characteristic findings. As demonstrated by the case histories, failure to detect organic disease alone is a fragile basis on which to conclude the presence of somatization. The casual use of the concept of somatization or the term *hysterical* is to be avoided; such practice opens the door to tragic mistakes in critical assessment.

CHAPTER 10

THE OLD AND THE YOUNG

"They say an old man is twice a child."

William Shakespeare

THE PRINCIPLES we have considered in this book for identifying organic mental disorders are generally applicable regardless of a client's age. This chapter should be considered an addendum that highlights clinical issues having special relevance for the critical assessment of older people and children.

AGING AND ORGANIC MENTAL DISORDERS

With respect to aging, the single most important principle for critical assessment is this: *aging is not synonymous with mental deterioration.* One author has recommended "prophylactic injections against the notion that old age involves imbecility." The clinician must never accept the normal process of aging as an adequate explanation for psychiatric symptoms. Old age is not the cause of senility!

Approximately 10% of persons 65 or older have senile dementia.[1] Several diseases can produce this clinical picture which is similar to that described for SOBS in Chapter 4. Unfortunately, some forms of senile dementia are not correctable, although with the tremendous strides in basic research today, this may change in the near future.

Irreversible Dementias

The two major forms of irreversible dementia among the aged are Alzheimer's disease and multiple infarct dementia. It is estimated that more than one million Americans 65 or older suffer from Alzheimer's disease. Furthermore, research evidence suggests that this condition, involving widespread progressive destruction of brain cells, is identical to that which strikes certain persons in mid-life and is called *presenile dementia.* Alzheimer's disease—the etiology of which is unknown—accounts for approximately 50% of all cases of dementia.[2]

This degenerative condition virtually always manifests initially as failing memory and a deterioration in the sense of orientation; but, these deficits are usually so subtle when they first appear that it is only in retrospect they are recognized as significant changes in the person. Eventually, the deficits become more obvious. Appointments may be forgotten, stories repeated or the person may lose his way when out of familiar surroundings. Having finished shopping, for example, the person may have no memory for where the car is parked.

Transient periods of depression or anxiety appear. The person becomes less spontaneous; the facial expression may take on a vacant appearance. Activities and people that in the past were important become of little interest; apathy settles in, only to be interrupted periodically by unexplained moments of panic or hyperexcitability.

With the relentless progression of Alzheimer's disease, there is difficulty understanding what is read; and aphasic problems appear. Eventually, judgment and simple problem-solving skills show significant decline. Movement becomes impaired, characterized by unsteadiness and a shortened and rigid gait. In certain cases, seizures develop. Later, bowel and bladder control are lost.

Early in the evolution of Alzheimer's disease, it can be mistaken for reactive depression. As it progresses, however, the evidence for organicity builds; in later stages it is usually readily identifiable as a neurological condition.

Multiple infarct dementia is associated with arteriosclerotic changes in blood vessels. Such changes increase the risk of blockage and the resulting death of small areas of the brain supplied by the affected vessel. (The term *infarct* refers to dead tissue produced by arterial insufficiency.) Usually, persons with multiple infarct dementia suffer from high blood pressure.

This form of irreversible dementia accounts for roughly 15% of all cases of dementia and in another 20% of cases occurs in conjunction with Alzheimer's disease.[2] The clinical symptoms in these two tragic conditions are virtually indistinguishable but have somewhat different courses. Whereas Alzheimer's disease proceeds as a gradual deterioration, multiple infarct dementia progresses in stepwise fashion, usually punctuated by dramatic episodes of mental decline. Clinical detection hinges on the identification of core features of brain syndrome, which may be somewhat overshadowed by psychological symptoms arising in response to declining cognitive ability.

Treatment for both of these forms of dementia is limited, but practical counseling can be extremely helpful; thus, early recognition is important. If these irreversible dementias are correctly identified rather than being mistaken for crazy behavior or getting old, clients as well as family members can be educated as to how best to cope with anticipated problems.

Reversible Dementias

Approximately one out of every ten cases of persons with symptoms suggestive of senile dementia have a potentially correctable organic disorder.[3] Probably the most common reversible cause is medication. Although persons age 65 or older make up only 11% of the American population, they consume 25% of all prescription drugs sold and probably an even higher percentage of over-the-counter medications.[4] Dosages of medication well tolerated by youthful persons often stimulate toxic reactions in the aged, because drugs—especially psychoactive drugs—remain in the body longer, exerting stronger and more prolonged effects. Several factors contribute to this delayed metabolism of drugs in the elderly.

As they circulate through the body, chemical substances are metabolized or excreted. Due to the decline in heart proficiency, circulation time lengthens in older people, so that it takes longer for a drug to pass through the body's "breakdown stations," mainly the kidneys and liver. Also, these organs themselves undergo aging changes, rendering them less efficient. The kidneys gradually become inefficient filters, and the liver produces less of the enzymes essential to drug metabolism.

With aging comes a relative increase in body fat, a change which also contributes to an exaggerated response to drugs, especially psychoactive drugs, because these substances are stored in fat. Thus, in older persons these medications tend to be sequestered and only slowly released, creating a sustained effect.

> A twice-widowed man in his mid-eighties, known to his friends and family for his aggressive pursuit of living, became apathetic and withdrawn. He would sit in a chair most of the day, showing little concern for food, friends, or any other of his previous interests. Earlier, on several occasions, he had parked his car and then forgotten where it was. The third time he reported it stolen to the police, they threatened to revoke his license.
>
> His local doctor diagnosed the problem as old age, but, subsequently, the man was referred for more extensive assessment. He was coherent but did show some degree of confusion. No evidence for infections or other common physical diseases encountered among elderly persons was discovered. The man denied the use of medication, but further inquiry showed that after the death of his first wife, many years before, he had started taking a single butabarbital tablet nightly because of his inability to sleep. When, after the death of his second wife, the problem returned, he added another sedative tablet (Quaalude).
>
> Based on the additional history, this trifling amount of medication was discontinued despite strong protests from the old man. Within 10 days his zest for activity had reappeared, his appetite had returned to normal, and his confusion had cleared. He started actively socializing again and had no further incidents of misplacing his car.[5]

Older people are particularly sensitive to drugs; for them there are no "minor" tranquilizers. The medications they take often create new problems manifest as mental dysfunction. It is not within the scope of this chapter to discuss all the potentially treatable conditions that pose as senility, many of which are listed in Table 10–1. We will, however, consider two examples: chronic subdural hematoma and normal pressure hydrocephalus.

The reader will recall that a subdural hematoma is a collection of blood in the space just under the outermost covering of the brain, the dura. Subdural hematomas usually result from traumatic injury to the head that tears the small veins traversing the subdural space. Symptoms, which can be primarily mental or behavioral in nature, arise from increasing intracranial pressure and encroachment on surrounding brain tissue.

The increased number of accidental falls among older people places them at risk for subdurals. This risk is even greater if the person also has a problem with alcohol. Given a history of mental deterioration or significant behavioral change in an older person, the clinician should always inquire about accidents or falls. But the clinician should not make the mistake of dismissing the possibility of subdural hematoma simply because there is no recall of a fall or a blow to the head. In one study of 75 cases in patients 65 years or older, one out of every three cases of subdural hematoma was without such a history.[6] Sometimes bruising about the head or eyes will suggest head trauma even when the person cannot remember the event. The clinician should be on the alert for such tell-tale signs.

In contrast to acute subdural hematomas, the chronic variety evolves much more slowly and is often more subtle in its clinical presentation. Chronic subdural hematomas typically become symptomatic over a period of days to weeks. Symptoms are varied, but may include confusion, social withdrawal, disinterest, depression, and intellectual decline. Psychotic manifestations can appear. Headache is a frequent accompaniment, and it may be intermittent. Such neurological findings as weakness in the arms, legs, or muscles of the face sometimes readily indicate the organic nature of this condition. Such signs, however, are not invariably in evidence.

> An elderly man, age 77, active and in good health, had occupied himself with garden work and odd-jobbing for his neighbors. Immediately prior to Christmas, while digging under an apple tree, he struck his head sharply on a low-hanging branch. Momentarily, he felt dazed but quickly recovered without losing consciousness. The following day while walking home from a neighbor's house he inexplicably fell over in the road. When he got up and continued on, an observer noticed that he seemed to be walking funny.
>
> Over the next few days, the man became confused, excessively sleepy, and "completely unlike his former self." He also lost control of his bladder.
>
> Three weeks later he was admitted to a hospital, where he was found to have weakness of muscles on the right side of his face. Arteriography showed a large subdural hematoma on the right side of the brain. It was evacuated surgically. The man had an excellent recovery and experienced no residual deficit.[7]

The treatment results for chronic subdural hematomas are gratifying. One study of 52 elderly patients treated surgically showed that 75% were restored to their prior level of functioning.[8]

Normal pressure hydrocephalus results from an internal blockage of the flow of cerebral spinal fluid. It usually affects persons in their sixties and seventies. Although several different diseases can produce this problem, the precise cause is usually unknown; nevertheless, the condition can often be corrected surgically.

Psychiatric symptoms, particularly depression, are often the first sign of normal pressure hydrocephalus. As the condition progresses, forgetfulness and cognitive decline emerge along with a peculiar deficit in walking. This so-called *magnetic gait* makes it difficult to initiate each step; it is as though the person's feet are stuck to the floor. Later, the loss of bladder and bowel control appears.

Although depression is probably the most common psychiatric symptom associated with normal pressure hydrocephalus, other manifestations include anxiety, paranoid delusions, visual hallucinations, and unprovoked violent outbursts.

If detected early, normal pressure hydrocephalus can be successfully treated with a neurosurgical procedure known as "shunting," which restores the normal flow of cerebral spinal fluid.

A 58-year-old man became delusional maintaining, incorrectly, that he had given his wife a strange illness. He also expressed the thought that people in his home town were talking about him and meant to do him harm. When he was finally admitted to a hospital, it was established that he had been suffering from depression for the past 8 months. He was noted to have difficulty remembering things and was unable to concentrate for even the shortest time. His walking was unsteady.

A series of neurological studies were performed, including an EEG, brain scan, and skull x-rays. All were judged to be normal. Together, the neurologist and psychiatrist concluded that there was no organic brain disease and diagnosed the problem as psychotic depression.

Over the next 6 months, the man was treated with haloperidol (antipsychotic) and imipramine (antidepressant) and showed some improvement in his symptoms. A year later, however, he was readmitted with a return of his psychiatric symptoms and a deterioration in his ability to walk. During this hospitalization, he was treated with ECT and discharged again after reportedly being improved.

Within 2 months he returned to the hospital, acutely agitated and paranoid, having impulsively attempted suicide with pills. He evidenced a striking memory deficit as well as significant impairment in his ability to think abstractly. Specialized studies produced findings consistent with a diagnosis of normal pressure hydrocephalus. A year later, after a shunting procedure, he was reported 80–90% his normal self.[9]

Losing One's Senses

Older persons are prone to diminishing sensory acuity. As hearing and vision decline, the person may become depressed in response to this impairment of self or, sometimes, may entertain paranoid thoughts in an attempt to cope with the confusing absence of sensory information. Here, paranoia is a way of making sense, albeit irrational sense, out of a chaotic world stemming from sensory gaps. *Paraphrenia* is a term applied to old-age paranoia that develops in the absence of a history of schizophrenia. Several studies have shown that partial deafness probably plays an important causative role in this condition.[10]

Failing sight can also precipitate psychiatric symptoms. Dramatic evidence for this comes from studies of elderly persons who undergo surgery for cataracts. Following surgery, it is imperative that the eyes be covered with black patches. In this state of iatrogenic blindness, rapid-onset brain syndrome is likely to emerge.

Another clinically misleading aspect of aging is the decline in the body's ability to signal the presence of disease through symptoms. For example, the characteristic manifestations of pneumonia—fever, chills, increased respiratory rate, and pain on breathing—may be quite muted or even absent. Instead, the elderly person may become lethargic and incoherent.

This softening of symptoms can mask such serious physical disorders as heart attack, heart failure, and pulmonary (lung) insufficiency. Whereas with a younger person these conditions are readily identifiable as organic problems, among the elderly

TABLE 10-1 CAUSES OF REVERSIBLE DEMENTIA[3]

Intracranial Conditions
- Meningiomas
- Subdural hematomas
- Hydrocephalus
  - Communicating
  - Noncommunicating
- Epilepsy
- Multiple sclerosis
- Wilson's disease

Systemic Illnesses
- Pulmonary insufficiency
- Cardiac arrhythmia
- Severe anemia
- Polycythemia vera
- Uremia
- Hyponatremia
- Portosystemic encephalopathy
- Porphyria
- Hyperlipidemia

Deficiency States
- B_{12} deficiency
- Pellegra
- Folate deficiency

Endocrinopathies
- Addison's disease
- Panhypopituitarism
- Myxedema
- Hypoparathyroidism
- Hyperparathyroidism
- Recurrent hypoglycemia
- Cushing's disease and steroid therapy
- Hyperthyroidism

Drugs
- Methyldopa and haloperidol
- Clonidine and fluphenazine
- Disulfiram
- Lithium carbonate
- Phenothiazines
- Haloperidol and lithium carbonate
- Bromides
- Phenytoin
- Mephenytoin
- Barbiturates
- Clonidine
- Methyldopa
- Propranolol hydrochloride
- Atropine and related compounds

Heavy Metals
- Mercury
- Arsenic
- Lead
- Thallium

Exogenous Toxins and Industrial Agents
- Trichloroethylene
- Toluene
- Carbon disulfide
- Organophosphates
- Carbon monoxide
- Alcohol

Infections
- General paresis
- Chronic meningitis
- Cerebral abscess
- Cysticercosis
- Whipple's disease
- Progressive multifocal leukoencephalopathy

Collagen-Vascular and Vascular Disorders
- Systemic lupus erythematosus
- Temporal arteritis
- Sarcoidosis
- Cogan's syndrome
- Behçet's syndrome
- Carotid artery stenosis (?)

"Potentially Recoverable Dementia"
- Cerebral anoxia
- Trauma
- Excessive electroconvulsive therapy
- Encephalitis

only the psychological and behavioral changes due to secondary brain failure may be prominent. This is why the clinician should pursue even the most innocuous appearing physical complaints in an older person.

> A 75-year-old widow had been living alone. Although she was said to hold somewhat eccentric religious beliefs, she had never exhibited psychotic behavior. Never, that is, until she abruptly expressed religious delusions and became suspicious and agitated. After being found trying to set her house on fire because of alleged "instructions from Jesus Christ," she was admitted to a psychiatric unit.
>
> Her heart rate was quite rapid (160 beats per minute), and an EKG showed that she had supraventricular tachycardia, which was causing heart failure. After 3 days of treatment with Digoxin (a drug used for certain irregularities in heart rhythm as well as heart failure) her rate had slowed to 86 beats per minute, and her symptoms of failure were disappearing. Simultaneously, she had become much more lucid. By the following week her acute psychotic manifestations had disappeared, leaving an aging woman with a slightly eccentric personality.[11]

CHILDREN AND ORGANIC MENTAL DISORDERS

As a general rule, psychiatric symptoms in a child, when occurring for the first time or when associated with general signs of illness, should be thoroughly evaluated medically. Furthermore, in the absence of notable stress or a well-defined precipitating event, behavioral or psychological aberrations in children are more likely organic than psychological.

Declining School Performance

School performance is a sensitive indicator of the well-being of a child. With the exception of reactive depression, which is usually readily apparent, a *substantial decline in a child's school performance is virtually always a reflection of organic dysfunction.*[12] In one report of children with neurological disease, all of whom had initially received psychiatric diagnoses, declining school performance had appeared early in the course of the disorder in every case. Explaining declining school performance in terms of family dynamics is risky business in the absence of a neurological evaluation.

> A 12-year-old Yugoslavian-born child was brought up in Iceland by his aunt until his parents, who had emigrated to the United States several years earlier, called for him. Although the boy had some initial difficulty overcoming the language barrier, he progressed in school until 6 months after starting, when his performance rapidly deteriorated.
>
> At first this was attributed to psychological difficulties associated with cultural shock. Counseling was started along with psychotropic medications; nevertheless, the boy's intellectual capacity continued to decline.
>
> Another 6 months passed before a neurology consultation was sought. Based on specific EEG and spinal fluid findings, along with the clinical observation of spastic movements, a diagnosis of subacute sclerosing panencephalitis was made, for which, unfortunately, there is no known cure.
>
> Over the next 3 years, the child became severely demented and suffered frequent seizures.[13]

The outcome of this mysterious, slow virus infection is always fatal. In this case its initial clinical manifestation was a significant decline in school performance.

Psychosis in Children

Before the age of 12, psychotic symptoms are relatively rare. When a child has hallucinations or delusions or relates to the surrounding world in a grossly inappropriate manner, organic disorder is the most likely explanation.

Autism is one form of organic psychosis occurring in early childhood.[14] Although the precise neurological deficit has yet to be firmly established, the fact that autism seems to be present from birth, is characterized by highly stereotypical patterns of behavior, and exhibits significant genetic loading argues strongly for an organic explanation.

Autistic children exhibit expressive and behavioral abnormalities that can be grouped primarily in four ways: speech disturbance, distorted responsiveness to stimulation, disturbed relatedness, and peculiarities of motion.

Autistic children usually fail to develop meaningful speech, remaining either mute or producing verbal expression punctuated with weird, high-pitched sounds having no recognizable meaning. In those few instances where speech does appear, usually it is late in onset and has notable peculiarities. The child repeats phrases over and over again in echo-like fashion ("echolalia"), and there is an absence of normal rhythm and tone, giving a highly mechanical quality to what limited speech exists.

A failure to appropriately respond to the immediate environment is illustrated by the autistic child's periodic obliviousness to obvious sounds or normally compelling sights. Periods of intense staring from which nothing can distract the child are typical. It is almost as though an invisible barrier rises up between the outside world and the child. In order to overcome this insulation from stimulation, the child resorts to strange, self-stimulating activities, such as endless whirling, rocking, or head-rolling, as a means of feeling something.

Typically, physical contact with other persons is shunned by the autistic child. There seems to be a preference for constancy that is upset by the inclusion of other people. Not surprisingly, normal social skills fail to emerge, including even the fundamental greeting smile.

The autistic child often walks on the toes of his feet for extended periods. Body-rocking, characterized by a swaying to-and-fro, is also common, as is a peculiar kind of movement where the child "flaps" his hands in front of his face. At times these excesses of motion may be replaced by extended periods of motionless posturing.

Autism is usually fully manifest by the age of 3. Treatment is limited, but proper identification avoids considerable frustration and unnecessary expense on the part of the family. Furthermore, once it is recognized that the child is not a psychological problem, a realistic management program can be instituted.

A host of other organic conditions, including brain tumors, central nervous system infections, and drug intoxications produce psychotic symptoms in children. The important point to remember is that psychosis in children should never be interpreted in psychological terms without evaluating for an organic mental disorder.

Childhood Seizures

As with seizures in adults, if gross motor movements occur during the attack, usually the professional as well as the family have no difficulty recognizing the problem as neurological. There are seizure disorders occurring in childhood, however, which manifest predominantly as psychological or behavioral changes. The symptoms seen in temporal lobe epilepsy are similar to those described for adults in Chapter 7. This disorder occurs in children and should always be suspected in cases of unexplained shifts in consciousness, especially when combined with semipurposeful movements and an aura that precedes the attacks.

Petit mal epilepsy is a seizure disorder that occurs *predominantly* in children. The seizures are marked by sudden, brief lapses in consciousness, during which the child momentarily will stop what he is doing. If an episode comes on while the child is talking, he may stop in mid-sentence. If the period of "absence" is quite brief, the child may resume talking where he has left off; when the attacks are longer, some degree of confusion or bewilderment usually persists when consciousness returns.

If attacks of petit mal epilepsy follow one another in rapid-fire fashion, so that the child never quite recovers from one before being overcome by the next, it is called "status," an allusion to the sustained nature of the condition. It is not difficult to envision how a child experiencing status petit mal could become disoriented and act in a peculiar fashion.

Although most attacks of petit mal arise spontaneously, they can have unusual precipitants. Music, light, even reading and emotional stress have reportedly stimulated seizures in predisposed children. Some cases of petit mal include sudden collapse, where the child for no apparent reason falls to the ground or floor. Due to their dramatic nature, these seizures are sometimes misconstrued as hysterical or even faking.

> For several years, a 9-year-old girl had frequently passed out just as she was leaving home in the morning for school. Although concerned at first, her parents eventually decided she was faking. Her family physician concluded that she was probably suffering from a school phobia.
>
> After several years, the child was referred for a complete neurological evaluation. A detailed history disclosed that these episodes happened only on bright, sunny days. With the aid of a series of EEG studies, it was established that exposure to bright light did indeed precipitate these seizures. Each morning when the child had stepped out her front door into a bright morning sun, she lost consciousness and fell to the ground.[15]

Psychiatric Symptoms and Disorders of Movement

The unexpected but readily explainable association between psychiatric symptoms and abnormal movements, previously discussed with reference to adult disorders, is also found in certain childhood conditions.

Wilson's Disease This disease results from a genetic abnormality affecting the transport of copper within the body that causes a destructive "plating-out" of copper onto body tissues, mainly within the liver and brain.

Approximately 20% of these cases initially manifest *solely* as such psychiatric symptoms as anxiety, depression, mania, or paranoid thinking.[16] In other cases psychiatric symptoms are found in conjunction with strange movements—tremor, jerkiness, or subtle twisting of the extremities. Sometimes, symptoms of hepatitis, stemming from liver damage, will also be a part of the clinical presentation.

As Wilson's disease progresses, the child's facial expression becomes vacant and the control of emotional expression is increasingly tenuous, with inappropriate crying and laughing. Full-blown psychotic symptoms are not uncommon in the course of this disease.

> For 2 years the child had appeared "emotionally disturbed" to school officials. In addition she was noticeably uncoordinated when participating in physical education activities.
>
> When her emotional problems persisted and even seemed to worsen, she was sent to a children's psychiatric unit, where she was treated for childhood schizophrenia. The increasing severity of unexplained jerky movements, however, finally led to a suspicion of neurological disease. An eye examination showed the characteristic "golden ring" in the cornea of her eyes. Laboratory tests confirmed the diagnosis of Wilson's disease.
>
> Unfortunately, by this time the condition was far advanced; despite the introduction of a chelating agent (for the elimination of excessive body copper), the child continued to deteriorate, expiring a month later.[17]

Early detection of Wilson's disease is crucial; otherwise the patient is condemned to a premature death.

Tourette Syndrome This is a highly unusual disorder consisting of nervous-like tics (sudden, small muscle movements), especially about the face, and involuntary utterances ranging from inarticulate sounds to explicitly dirty words, expressed in a compulsive and often explosive manner. Characteristically, the child first experiences excessive eye-blinking, facial tics, or grimacing, followed by the addition of a compulsive desire to touch or smell things or to repeatedly squat, hop, or bend the body.

Usually within a period of months, uncontrolled utterances develop that at first may be mistaken for coughing, throat clearing, or sniffing. Roughly half of children with Tourette syndrome eventually will experience an unrelenting need to verbalize dirty words ("coprolalia"). Usually, the child struggles not to make these expressions, covering his mouth or running away from the social situation. If unsuccessful in fending off the compulsion, a flood of graphic words fills the air.

Inappropriate referrals for psychotherapy are frequently made for this condition. In one study of Tourette syndrome, the researcher found that initial symptoms were often mistakenly considered expressions of tension or nervousness.[18]

Although the precise mechanism is not understood, a high percentage of children with Tourette syndrome respond quite favorably to the drug haloperidol as well as to several other pharmacological agents.

Attention and Sensory Deficits

Hyperactive child syndrome and *minimal brain dysfunction* are terms applied to children with extremely short attention spans, making extended periods of concentration impossible. Although these children can be impulsive in their behavior, rapidly moving from one activity or object to another, *hyperactivity is not an invariable aspect of this condition.*[19] When it does exist, however, the child may be mistakenly labeled as anxious, tense, or incorrigible. Frequently, children with a primary deficit in attention span also have difficulty with motor coordination; typically, they are considered clumsy.

Attention disorder in children is not well understood or even well defined. The clinician should understand that it is probably inappropriately diagnosed as often as it is overlooked. Nevertheless, certain children will profit considerably from remedial interventions, which may include the use of stimulant medications. Direct clinical observation is essential for establishing an appropriate suspicion of this disorder. At a minimum, the clinician must confirm that the child, even when engaged in an activity that he finds highly rewarding, cannot sustain attention for any significant period of time.

Some children become behavioral problems in response to sensory defects, such as defective hearing or vision. An inability to see or hear adequately can create considerable frustration in a child; but, since there is no basis for comparison, the child may never complain directly about these primary deficits. Hearing and vision should be routinely tested in children presenting with psychiatric symptoms. The clinician can grossly screen for problems by having the child visualize an object or printed words on a wall across the room. Similarly, a soft whisper when the child is not looking, if not responded to, can provide evidence of a hearing deficit. These simple screening tests, however, should not supplant the use of standardized testing for vision and hearing when there is any evidence that the child suffers from a sensory deficit.

To summarize, critical assessment with respect to children begins with the assumption that significant behavioral or psychological symptoms in a child not under significant stress is quite likely an organic problem. With the exception of reactive depression, which is usually relatively obvious in a child, a striking decline in school performance is virtually always an indicator of organicity. Psychotic symptoms—anytime they appear in children—demand a complete medical workup. The clinician should be sensitive to the association of abnormal movements and psychiatric symptoms in children and should be on the lookout continuously for lapses or "spells" indicative of a seizure disorder, particularly petit mal and temporal lobe epilepsy. The basic inability to properly attend and concentrate results in secondary psychiatric symptoms; similarly, children who have problems with seeing or hearing may develop behavioral problems out of frustration. The integrity of these basic sensory modalities should always be confirmed in child psychiatric cases.

CHAPTER 11

A SUMMING UP

"Look to the essence of a thing, whether it be a point of doctrine, of practice, or of interpretation."

Marcus Aurelius

PSYCHIATRIC SYMPTOMS are not always best explained psychologically. Certain organic disorders produce symptoms similar to those typically associated with psychological reactions. Anxiety, depression, paranoia—these as well as other psychiatric expressions can arise either as psychological responses to various problems in living or reflections of mechanical errors in the brain itself.

The existence of masquerading organic mental disorders creates a problem of critical assessment for all human service professionals, a problem by no means rare in occurrence. As we have seen, studies show that in psychiatric clinic settings one out of every ten clients, if thoroughly examined, are found to have causative organic conditions. In other settings the percentage is even higher. This is to say nothing of those persons with organic disorders which, although not causative of psychological problems, significantly aggravate them.

The human service professional must above all retain a porous mental set, allowing for the possibility of organic mental disorders. An active degree of clinical suspicion is an essential starting point for the development of a sound approach to critical assessment. To this suspicion must be added a clinical familiarity with brain syndrome, a variable constellation of symptoms highly correlated with global brain dysfunction. The five core deficits, one or more of which appear as manifestations of brain syndrome, are:

Inattention
Disorientation
Recent Memory Impairment
Diminished Reasoning
Sensory Indiscrimination

Although cases of brain syndrome usually include more than one of these core deficits, clinical detection of any of them constitutes presumptive evidence for an organic mental disorder and should commit the clinician to seeking further medical evaluation.

The clinician engaged in critical assessment, however, cannot be content with watching only for expressions of brain syndrome; there are other important clues to organic mental disorders. When found in association with psychiatric symptoms, these clinical clues provide additional evidence for organicity. In this book we have considered two levels of evidence: alerting clues and presumptive evidence. Alerting clues further sensitize the clinician to the possibility of an organic mental disorder. Presumptive evidence is even stronger in its clinical implications; if discovered, these factors, like elements of brain syndrome, must be considered indicative of organicity. In the presence of psychiatric symptoms, alerting clues include:

No History of Similar Symptoms
No Readily Identifiable Cause
Age 55 or Older
Coexistence of Chronic Disease
Excessive Use of Drugs

Presumptive factors are:

Head Injury
Change in Headache Pattern
Visual Disturbances
Speech Deficits
Abnormal Body Movements
Sustained Deviations in Vital Signs
Changes in Consciousness

Optionally, the clinician can employ three special tests, Write-a-Sentence, Draw-a-Clock, and Copy-a-Three-Dimensional-Figure, which can be quickly administered to provide supplemental information with respect to critical assessment.

The search for clues to organic mental disorders need not be intrusive or excessively time-consuming. Through the course of a normal interview, questions with reference to a number of items will be answered without resorting to special questions or observations. Questions that are not spontaneously answered can be inserted at appropriate points to complete the critical assessment.

Care should be taken to avoid clinical deceptions that account for a disproportionately large number of critical assessment errors. These misleading clinical traps are:

Mistaking Symptoms for Their Causes
Listening Without Fully Considering
Equating Psychosis with Schizophrenia
(or Functional Psychosis)
Relying on a Single Information Source

Brain tumors, particularly of the frontal and temporal lobes, brain seizures, and endocrine disorders are three kinds of organic conditions that well illustrate the range and subtlety of clinical manifestations of organic mental disorders.

Drug-induced mental disorders are on the rise, and the use of drugs (including medications) must always be suspect with respect to critical assessment. When given in sufficient amounts or in combination with various other substances, few medications are incapable of producing organic mental disorder. The very drugs used to treat psychiatric symptoms have become major producers of additional symptoms in the form of side effects. A vast array of over-the-counter preparations, available to anyone in whatever quantity is desired, are notorious for creating symptoms of brain syndrome and other mental disturbances. This is particularly true of the multitude of sleep medications, muscle relaxants, and cold preparations with powerful anticholinergic properties. Both drug intoxication and drug withdrawal from addicting substances can lead to bizarre psychiatric symptoms easily misconstrued as schizophrenia.

The translation of psychological conflicts into physical or somatic symptoms is called "somatization." This explanatory concept should be used with considerable caution, in that with time many cases thought to be somatization prove to be the reflection of an organic condition. Certain clinical features of conversion reactions, simple somatization, and Briquet's syndrome (hysteria) are so characteristic that when they are absent, the clinician should strongly resist the somatization hypothesis.

Old age does not imply senility and should *never* be used as an explanation for psychiatric symptoms. Although such diseases as Alzheimer's are not reversible, given our present state of knowledge, their accurate recognition helps prepare the person as well as his family for future problems that will inevitably arise. It also avoids inappropriate referrals for misdirected therapy. Of even greater importance, a number of conditions initially thought to be irreversible dementia prove correctable if recognized and properly treated in the early stages. This is why psychiatric symptoms first appearing in a person's later years should be completely evaluated medically. Medications must always be high on the list of suspects in older people. Sensory deficits, especially impaired hearing and decreased visual acuity, produce psychiatric symptoms; and accidental falls, for which older people are at risk, can cause subdural hematomas with a wide range of masquerading appearances.

With respect to children, any rapid change in personality or mood, especially if the child appears ill, should be interpreted as organic until a medical evaluation proves otherwise. Other important indicators of possible organicity include the appearance of psychotic symptoms or a substantial decline in school performance.

Like the aged, children may develop psychiatric symptoms as a reaction to sensory deficits. Vision and hearing should always be checked in a child initially seen for behavioral or psychological problems.

Finally, seizures and disorders of movement occur in children, which—with their associated psychiatric symptoms—can be mistaken for psychological reactions.

PUTTING IT TO THE TEST

I have selected ten case histories as a final exercise for the reader. Although most of these cases are instances of organic mental disorders masquerading as psychological reactions, some are not; it is left for you, the reader, to decide.

Your task is to review the brief case synopses, taking care to note any evidence that argues for the possibility of an organic mental disorder. When you have concluded your reading of each case, stop and consider the following questions:

What factors, if any, raise the suspicion of an organic mental disorder?
Is the evidence strong enough to merit further medical evaluation?
Based on the evidence you have, do you think this case is a psychological reaction or an organic mental disorder?

Once you have answered these questions to your satisfaction, continue reading and compare your answers with the facts of the case.

CASE HISTORY #1

THE TRANSFER

An aging woman in her early seventies was transferred from a nursing home to a hospital for treatment of symptoms of a urinary tract infection.

Initially, she was managed on a medical service, but within a short time, psychiatric consultation was sought because she was "disturbing the rest of the ward." The examining psychiatrist found her disoriented to time and place. In addition her general awareness widely fluctuated from one interview to another. At times she referred to objects and people in her hospital setting as though she were at home.

The patient had been taking several medications before coming to the hospital, one of which was the antipsychotic agent, chlorpromazine. When the psychiatric consultant was unwilling to increase this medication to control the woman's psychosis, the medical staff strongly urged that she be transferred to the psychiatric unit.[1]

DISCUSSION

CASE HISTORY #1

Here we have an *elderly* woman taking *medications,* who upon being examined is found to have at least one core manifestation of brain syndrome, *disorientation.* She also evidenced a *fluctuating level of consciousness.* The psychiatric consultant resisted the medical staff's insistence that the woman was schizophrenic requiring more medication.

After the woman was transferred to the psychiatric unit, all her medications were discontinued. Ten days later she was alert and fully oriented, stating that "she felt better than she had in years."

An interesting additional note: the woman left the hospital to live with her sister instead of returning to the nursing home where she had previously been living.

Medications are always suspect!

Condition: Drug-induced organic mental disorder.

CASE HISTORY #2

WORKAHOLIC

A highly successful businessman, age 45, with no previous history of psychiatric disorder, began to act different from his usual self. He seemed increasingly driven at work. His working hours gradually lengthened, until finally he was sleeping only 2 to 3 hours a night; the rest of the time he worked. He became irritable and engaged in uncharacteristic sprees of spending beyond his means.

Although he felt extremely productive and even claimed he was doing the work of five men, his boss felt otherwise. He was worried about the man's excessive preoccupation with work, having observed several recent examples of poor business decisions.

Finally, when the man complained of headaches, his boss insisted that he seek help before he returned to work again.[2]

DISCUSSION

CASE HISTORY #2

This patient had *no previous history* of similar psychiatric symptoms, and his poor business decisions could have indicated a *deterioration in simple problem-solving skills.* But the most compelling evidence for organicity is found in the emergence of *headaches* associated with a striking change in behavior.

When examined medically, the man was found to have severe papilledema (a sign of increased intracranial pressure detected through an ophthalmoscopic examination). Further investigation revealed four tumorous masses in his brain, presumably spread there from another site in the body. Eleven months later, he died of his cancer.

Condition: Organic mental disorder secondary to metastatic cancer of the brain.

CASE HISTORY #3

THE DESPONDENT LADY

Shortly after the announcement of the engagement of her only child, a 53-year-old married woman became irritable and began compulsively to overeat. Previously, she had been in good health, without history of trauma, alcoholism, or drug abuse.

As the wedding approached, the woman appeared more and more withdrawn and finally refused to have anything to do with the wedding preparations.

In subsequent months, she deteriorated mentally. Eventually, she lost her job due to her inability to concentrate. Her friends observed her obsessively counting out loud to herself on occasion. Later, she became extremely fearful of losing her life and had considerable difficulty sleeping.

She grew depressed and expressed thoughts of suicide, for which she was hospitalized in a psychiatric facility. Treatment with various psychiatric medications over a period of 6 months produced no change in her condition; in fact, she worsened. She had an episode of catatonia with mutism, after which she was disoriented. Her walking became increasingly unsteady, and she began to urinate on herself.[3]

DISCUSSION

CASE HISTORY #3

The stressful life situation is there: A mother losing her only child to marriage. She becomes depressed and due to her resulting apathy loses her job. Other findings, however, suggest that this psychological explanation might be highly misleading.

First, this is a 53-year-old woman with *no previous history of psychiatric problems.* Now, in addition to her depression, she *loses her ability to concentrate* and is fired from her job as a result. What is really happening to her cognitive ability? Perhaps there is more than a problem with concentration.

Time and treatment, which usually favorably alter the course of depression experienced as a psychological reaction, failed to benefit this woman.

The evidence for an organic mental disorder becomes overwhelming when she eventually experiences *catatonia, mutism, disorientation, and urinary incontinence.* Despite such evidence, this woman was treated with electroconvulsive therapy, during which she manifested additional neurological signs. A special neurological study (pneumoencephalogram) provided the diagnosis of normal pressure hydrocephalus. Neurosurgical shunting produced a gradual improvement, but residual symptoms—unsteadiness in walking, decreased spontaneous speech, and intermittent disorientation—persisted, presumably due to irreversible brain damage sustained prior to treatment.

A final note: this woman early in the course of her disease experienced a strong sense of impending death. Although certainly not a universal finding in organic diseases, this fear of imminent destruction often surfaces in association with organic mental disorders.

Condition: Organic mental disorder secondary to normal pressure hydrocephalus.

CASE HISTORY #4

"OUT OF THIS WORLD"

"What a curious feeling!" said Alice. "I must be shutting up like a telescope!"

And so it was indeed: she was now only ten inches high, and her face brightened up at the thought that she was now the right size for going through the little door into that lovely garden. First, however, she waited for a few minutes to see if she was going to shrink any further: she felt a little nervous about this; "for it might end, you know," said Alice to herself, "in my going out altogether, like a candle. I wonder what I should be like then?"

A while later . . .

"Curiouser and curiouser!" cried Alice. (She was so much surprised, that for the moment she quite forgot how to speak good English.) "Now I'm opening out like the largest telescope that ever was! Goodbye, feet!" (For when she looked down at her feet, they seemed to be almost out of sight, they were getting so far off.) "Oh, my poor little feet, I wonder who will put on your shoes and stockings for you now, dears? I'm sure I shan't be able! I shall be a great deal too far off to trouble myself about you: you must manage the best way you can"—"but I must be kind to them," thought Alice, "or perhaps they won't walk the way I want to go! Let me see. I'll give them a new pair of boots every Christmas."[4]

DISCUSSION

CASE HISTORY #4

Of course this is not an actual clinical case history, but rather a quote from Lewis Carroll's *Alice in Wonderland.* I have included it because of Alice's graphic description of some unusual perceptual experiences. She is suddenly gripped by *bizarre distortions in her vision,* alternating between seeing herself as extremely small and then as extremely large.

During this experience, a sense of fear comes over her, momentarily, and she has *difficulty speaking.*

This history of sudden *changes in consciousness,* if presented by a client, would constitute presumptive evidence for organicity. More specifically, Alice's problem smacks of temporal lobe epilepsy, particularly the perceptual changes often seen during the initial aura. Similar perceptual distortions also occur in rare forms of migraine, a condition suffered by Lewis Carroll, interestingly enough.

Condition: Organic mental disorder secondary to complex partial seizure(?)

CASE HISTORY #5

DOWNHILL

A 22-year-old male graduate student was referred to the student health service by a professor. Over the past semester, the student's grades had dramatically declined. He found himself unable to concentrate on his studies and had little initiative. He had difficulty falling asleep and felt "down." These symptoms had emerged shortly after he broke up with his male lover, who had then enrolled in college in another state.

Although the young man admitted to the passing thought of suicide, there was no evidence that this was a serious possibility. On examination, he was alert and showed no physical abnormalities with respect to speech, vision, or movement. He denied the use of medications or drugs other than weekend beer drinking. There was no history of serious injury or disease. His answers to questions revealed an intact, above-average intelligence.[5]

DISCUSSION
CASE HISTORY #5

This is a case of depression resulting from a significant personal loss, a psychological reaction. The student's decline in academic performance reflected his loss of initiative and interest, common accompaniments of feeling depressed, rather than a cognitive deficit. *No presumptive evidence for an organic mental disorder was found.* The absence of such findings in conjunction with an identifiable precipitating event strongly argued against an organic mental disorder.

The student was followed in psychotherapy for eight sessions during a period of 2 months. By that time he had worked through his personal loss and had resumed most of his social activities. His school performance returned to its previous level of achievement.

Condition: Psychological reactive depression.

CASE HISTORY #6

SUPERNATURAL

Suddenly, she would be "seized by a horrible feeling of terror." These spells came over this 44-year-old woman irrespective of what she was doing at the moment. After a minute or so she would sense a peculiar odor, "a horrible smell—not a real smell—somewhat like the smell of burning hedges". At times she felt she was choking on this unpleasant odor.

Although she rarely lost consciousness, on occasion she would dramatically sink to the floor. There for a short while she would be unable to respond but could follow the conversation going on around her. Sometimes she experienced hallucinations and felt an unusual sensation in her abdomen.[6]

DISCUSSION

CASE HISTORY #6

Episodic attacks involving a *shift in consciousness, olfactory hallucinations* (smell), and the *inability to speak momentarily* must be considered organic until proven otherwise.

When this woman was evaluated neurologically, she was found to be of normal intelligence without memory deficit or disorientation. Visual testing, however, revealed that she was functionally blind in her right eye and had lost the sense of smell in her right nostril. These findings, along with her clinical history, suggested the possibility of a tumor located in the right temporal and frontal areas; and, in fact, at surgery a sizable meningioma was removed from that area. Six months later the woman reported that she had not experienced any further attacks. It is important to note that the woman's vague awareness during her seizures could have created a misleading impression of hysteria.

Condition: Organic mental disorder secondary to a meningioma of the right frontal/temporal area.

CASE HISTORY #7

SATAN'S WORK

She was an active high school student, a competitive swimmer, in excellent health. Abruptly, she began to act unlike herself, taking copious notes on her family's conversations and on various television programs. She made comments no one else could understand, and at times her speech was jumbled. Three days later, having experienced chills at night and subsequently claiming that "satan is taking me over," she was driven to the hospital by her parents and treated with neuroleptic medication, but without improvement. Her speech became increasingly slurred, and then she stopped speaking altogether. Her temperature was measured at 102°F, and she was observed to have a limp. She was transferred to the psychiatric service of a university hospital.[7]

DISCUSSION

CASE HISTORY #7

A healthy high school student *abruptly becomes psychotic.* She rapidly develops a *speech deficit,* begins to *limp* and has a *fever of 102°F with chills.* The real question is why she was ever admitted to a psychiatric service. Her condition should have been readily recognized as neurological in nature.

Shortly after her admission, a spinal tap showed the presence of white cells, indicating an infection in the brain. An EEG also showed changes consistent with this diagnosis. It was presumed from the clinical picture that she had contracted herpes simplex encephalitis, a viral infection having a particular predilection for the limbic system.

Condition: Organic mental disorder secondary to herpes simplex encephalitis.

CASE HISTORY #8

SUSPICIONS

Despite 6 months of alleged sobriety, a 45-year-old woman required an admission to the hospital when she continued to deteriorate in her ability to care for herself. Although her husband claimed she had not resorted to her old alcohol habits, she seriously neglected her housework and had considerable difficulty moving about the house without falling over the furniture. She had lost her way in the neighborhood as well as being involved in several minor automobile accidents; nevertheless, she insisted on continuing to drive the family car.

While talking to the interviewer at the hospital, the woman claimed that her husband was trying to have her committed so that he could continue his affair with a neighbor's wife. When asked the date, she missed it by 10 days, and—although she was able to name the hospital—later, while on the hospital ward, she wandered away and was unable to find her way back. She made several errors in serially subtracting 7 from 100 and finally declined to continue. Her hands were tremulous. She was only able to recall one out of three objects after a 5-minute period.[8]

DISCUSSION

CASE HISTORY #8

Difficulty walking, combined with *a history of automobile accidents* and *losing her way in the neighborhood* make a psychological explanation for this woman's behavior highly unlikely. The argument for organicity is further strengthened by the clinical observations that she was *disoriented* and had a *severe deficiency in recent memory.*

After several days of hospitalization, this woman was found to have in her locker a large quantity of proprietary sedatives containing bromides. A blood test for bromide showed a level which fully accounted for her cognitive deficits. Several days later, once the bromide had been excreted from her system, she was bright and alert, back to her usual self.

Condition: Organic mental disorder secondary to drug intoxication (bromide).

CASE HISTORY #9

MYSTERY WOMAN

A middle-aged woman was discovered at night in a deserted parking lot by a policeman on routine patrol. She was untidy in appearance and had no possessions with her other than the clothes she wore. She offered no spontaneous conversation, but followed simple instructions and made some attempt to answer questions. She had no idea of who she was or where she was. She was taken to a hospital emergency room.[9]

DISCUSSION

CASE HISTORY #9

This woman was found in strange circumstances. She is *mute.* Her untidiness as well as the fact that she appears to be lost suggest *cognitive impairment* associated with brain syndrome. On this basis, the woman should receive a thorough medical examination.

Further investigation in this case, however, revealed no other evidence for organicity. The woman was suffering from a psychological reaction known as a dissociative disorder. Her inability to remember where or who she was proved to be a psychological defense against facing her actions of having run away. Evaluation showed that, in fact, she was not generally disoriented and her memory was intact. A further indicator of the psychological nature of this woman's problem was her disorientation to self. While disorientation to place and time is a hallmark of brain syndrome, disorientation to self is quite rare in organic conditions.

The principles of critical assessment should have led the reader to suspect *organicity* in this case. The fact that further evaluation showed this not to be true does not detract from the importance of suspecting this possibility. Critical assessment will inevitably produce some false positives.

Condition: Psychological reaction, dissociative disorder.

CASE HISTORY #10

STOPS AND STARTS

For 5 years, a middle-aged man underwent attacks of peculiar behavior. These episodes lasted from a few minutes to as long as several hours. Gradually, they increased in frequency until they were occurring four or five times a week. During these periods, the man's behavior was quite variable but always in striking contrast to his usual self.

On one occasion he wandered about the place where he worked for over 2 hours, appearing confused; eventually, he inappropriately removed his shirt and stared foolishly as various people tried to engage him in conversation. During another attack, he abruptly stopped chopping wood and walked about his neighborhood, glassy-eyed, with his ax held in a threatening manner. Finally, when he was taken to a hospital, he was observed to speak indistinctly and to exhibit grotesque, purposeless movements.

Usually, he had no recollection for these strange episodes, which most often occurred after excessive exertion or towards the end of the morning.[10]

DISCUSSION

CASE HISTORY #10

Unexplained *shifts in consciousness* with a related *memory disturbance,* plus the description, on at least one occasion, of *disturbed speech* and *abnormal body movements* add up to organicity. The tendency of these attacks to occur after excessive exertion and during the morning hours provides an important clue to the specific problem, hypoglycemia.

Eventually, a fellow employee, whom the patient threatened with a knife during one of these attacks, contributed a detailed description, having observed numerous episodes. He stated that the man was usually quite pale, unsteady on his feet, and sweated profusely.

Laboratory studies confirmed that these periods of behavioral changes were correlated with dramatic drops in the patient's blood sugar level. The attacks were the product of an insulin-producing tumor, a so-called insulinoma.

Condition: Organic mental disorder secondary to hypoglycemia resulting from an insulinoma.

LISTING OF ILLUSTRATIVE CASE HISTORIES

Chapter 1
brain tumor, frontal, p. 4
syphilitic brain disease, p. 7

Chapter 2
herpes simplex encephalitis (limbic encephalitis), pp. 20–21
Huntington's chorea, p. 23
paroxysmal atrial tachycardia (with mitral stenosis), pp. 24–25
small strokes, pp. 25–26
lung cancer, pp. 26–27

Chapter 3
marijuana intoxication, p. 33
water intoxication, pp. 33–34
birth control pill depression and psychosis, pp. 35–36
ulcerative colitis, p. 37
L-dopa intoxication, p. 38
pheochromocytoma, pp. 39–40
caffeine intoxication, pp. 40–41
hypothyroidism, p. 42
stroke, pp. 43–44
amphetamine psychosis, p. 47
organic fluoride intoxication, p. 50
subdural hematoma, pp. 51–52

Chapter 4
Parkinson's disease, pp. 55, 58, 61, 64–65, 68, 72
pneumonia, pp. 61–63
senile dementia (Alzheimer's disease), p. 67
pernicious anemia (vitamin B_{12} deficiency), p. 69
Korsakoff's syndrome, pp. 70–71

Chapter 5
brain tumor, frontal-temporal-parietal, p. 74
subdural hematoma (from an aneurysmal malformation), p. 75
viral hepatitis (with cirrhosis of the liver), p. 77
bromide intoxication, p. 78
meningoencephalitis, p. 81
brain tumor, frontal, p. 84
anticholinergic psychosis, pp. 86–87
temporal lobe epilepsy, p. 88
brain tumor, temporal, p. 89

Chapter 6
anticholinergic psychosis, p. 105
psychological reaction, marital problem, p. 107
viral encephalitis, p. 109

Chapter 7
brain tumor, frontal, pp. 114–115
brain tumor, frontal-parietal, pp. 115–116

LISTING OF ILLUSTRATIVE CASE HISTORIES (*continued*)

brain tumor, frontal, pp. 117–118
brain tumor, limbic, pp. 118–119
brain tumor, temporal, p. 119
complex partial seizure, pp. 123–124
temporal lobe epilepsy (complex partial seizure), p. 125
episodic dyscontrol, p. 126
hypoglycemia, retroperitoneal fibroma, pp. 129–130
hypoglycemia, reactive, pp. 130–131
hypothyroidism, p. 133
hypothyroidism ("myxedema madness"), p. 134
hyperthyroidism, pp. 135–136

Chapter 8

anticholinergic psychosis, p. 140
neuroleptic intoxication, p. 141
anticholinergic psychosis, p. 149
stimulant psychosis (diet pill), p. 151
delirium tremens (alcohol withdrawal syndrome), pp. 156–157

Chapter 9

parathyroid adenoma, p. 163
hyperventilation, p. 164
Briquet's syndrome, pp. 166–167
multiple sclerosis, p. 168
pancreatic cancer, pp. 170–171
conversion reaction, pp. 172–173
migraine, basilar type, p. 175
idiopathic torsion dystonia, p. 176

Chapter 10

sedative intoxication, p. 182
subdural hematoma, p. 183
normal pressure hydrocephalus, pp. 184–185
supraventricular tachycardia, p. 187
subacute sclerosing panencephalitis, p. 188
petit mal epilepsy, p. 190
Wilson's disease, p. 191

Chapter 11

drug intoxication
brain tumor, metastatic, p. 201
normal pressure hydrocephalus, p. 203
complex partial seizure, p. 207
psychological reaction, depression, p. 209
brain tumor, frontal-temporal, p. 211
herpes simplex encephalitis (limbic encephalitis), p. 213
bromide intoxication, p. 215
psychological reaction, dissociative disorder, p. 217
hypoglycemia (insulinoma), p. 219

ANNOTATED BIBLIOGRAPHY

Adams, James L.: *Conceptual Blockbusting: A Guide to Better Ideas,* San Francisco, W. H. Freeman and Company, 1974.

This is a concise, well-written book on creative problem-solving, with special emphasis on how to create a porous mental set conducive to perceptual blockbusting. "Conceptual blocks," says the author, "are mental walls which block the problem-solver from correctly perceiving a problem or conceiving its solution." The greatest barrier for the clinician in approaching critical assessment is premature closure: being unable to stave off the seduction of favorite clinical hypotheses in order to observe the actual facts of the case.

Ajax, E. J.: The Aphasic Patient (A Practical Review). *Diseases of the Nervous System,* 34: pp. 135–142, 1973.

The various faces of aphasia are reviewed in a clear and practical presentation. The article includes illustrative transcripts of aphasic speech as well as an example of writing produced by a patient with fluent aphasia. There is much useful information contained in this 8-page review.

Anonymous Author: Death of a Mind: A Study in Disintegration. *Lancet,* i: pp. 1012–1015, 1950.

I have quoted extensively from this article in Chapter 3. If I could recommend but one reference to give the clinician a feeling for the progressive emergence of brain syndrome, this would be it. Written by a sympathetic, personally involved yet keen observer, this presentation poignantly communicates the struggle of a deteriorating mind.

Baldessarini, Ross: *Chemotherapy in Psychiatry.* Cambridge: Harvard University Press, 1977.

A lucid guide to psychotropic drugs. The book includes chapters on antipsychotic agents, lithium, antidepressants and antianxiety medications as well as such special topics as geriatric and pediatric psychopharmacology. The author does a particularly good job of noting potential drug side effects, some of which can be misconstrued as psychological reactions. Given the extensive use of psychotropic drugs, it behooves all clinicians to have a working overview of these substances, their indications, actions, and side effects.

Benson, D. Frank: Amnesia. *Southern Medical Journal,* 71: pp. 1221–1227, 1978.

The author characterizes amnesia as the impaired ability to learn despite normal immediate and long-term memory and the preservation of other cognitive and personality traits. In reading this brief but fully packed article, the clinician will review the various presentations of defective recent memory.

Benson, D. Frank: Psychiatric Aspects of Aphasia. *British Journal of Psychiatry,* 123: pp. 555–566, 1973.

Written especially for the clinician, this article focuses on the assessment of impaired language. The author does an excellent job of delineating psychiatric disorders with which aphasia can be easily confused. A number of practical clinical tips are given for helping to distinguish aphasia from language changes found in psychological reactions. One section focuses specifically on how to distinguish schizophrenic language from aphasia.

Benson, D. Frank and Deitrich Blumer (Eds.): *Psychiatric Aspects of Neurological Disease.* New York: Grune & Stratton, 1975.

This is a compilation of chapters by different authors, covering such topics as mental concomitants of physical disease, dementia, disorders of verbal expression, personality changes with frontal and temporal lobe disorders, organic brain syndromes, temporal lobe epilepsy, and spontaneous and drug-induced movement disorders seen in psychotic patients. The opening chapter by Norman Geschwind entitled, "Some Common Misconceptions," serves as an excellent introduction to the subject of critical assessment. The final chapter includes a series of proven cases of "organic brain disease mistaken for psychiatric disorder."

Benson, D. Frank and Norman Geschwind: Psychiatric Conditions Associated with Focal Lesions of the Central Nervous System. *American Handbook of Psychiatry,* 4: pp. 208–243, 1975.

A comprehensive chapter on localized brain disorders which manifest as prominent behavioral and psychological changes. A variety of psychiatric symptoms are discussed, including paranoid reactions and visual hallucinations. Specific brain disorders are covered in some detail: head injury, brain tumors, syphilis, Huntington's chorea, normal pressure hydrocephalus, and temporal lobe epilepsy. The chapter is extensively referenced (193 inclusions). Although at certain junctures it may provide the human services professional with more detail than he wants, overall, it is an excellent resource.

Comfort, Alex: *Practice of Geriatric Psychiatry,* New York: Elsevier, 1980.
A well-written presentation of the psychiatric problems of the elderly. It includes chapters on the assessment of "senility" and "organic dementing processes." The first chapter is a must for all human service clinicians; the author does a masterful job in a few pages of introducing the subject of psychiatric symptoms among the aged, placing special emphasis on those resulting from various organic diseases. "Of all old people who present with a 'psychiatric' problem, between 10% and 30%, according to age, owe their illness to an undiagnosed medical condition, or to the effects of medication, or to both."

Duvoisin, Roger: Clinical Diagnosis of the Dyskinesias, *Medical Clinics of North America,* 56: pp. 1321–1341, 1972.
This is a review of various movement aberrations found in neurological diseases. Despite the fact that it is somewhat technical, written for clinical neurologists, I would encourage the nonmedical clinician to read this article. Woven through it are quite a number of little gems of clinical observation appropriate for all human service clinicians.

Gelenberg, Alan J.: The Catatonic Syndrome, *Lancet,* 1: pp. 1339–1341, 1976.
A short, but well-documented presentation of the dangers of falling into the clinical trap of always explaining "psychological" symptoms psychologically. The author describes cases of catatonia resulting from Parkinson's disease, viral encephalitis, brain tumors, epilepsy (petit mal), diabetes, psychoactive drug intoxication as well as schizophrenia.

Lawall, John: Psychiatric Presentations of Seizure Disorders, *American Journal of Psychiatry,* 133: pp. 321–323, 1976.
A discussion of the various ways that seizure disorders are mistaken for psychological reactions. The author comments on temporal lobe epilepsy as well as grand mal and petit mal seizures and provides three illustrative case histories that "demonstrate some of the principles to keep in mind in diagnosing epilepsy with predominantly psychiatric symptoms."

Lewin, Roger: *The Nervous System,* Garden City, Anchor Press/Doubleday, 1974.
This slim volume is an entertaining and informative presentation of the design of the nervous system. It provides the reader with a relatively painless means of reviewing the neurological underpinnings of organic mental disorders. The author is a superb translator of technical information into readable prose.

Lishman, William: *Organic Psychiatry: The Psychological Consequences of Cerebral Disorder,* Oxford, Blackwell Scientific Publications, 1978.
The most comprehensive single volume on organic mental disorders: an encyclopedic presentation. This is an excellent resource for the clinician wishing to review in detail specific diseases that give rise to organic mental disorders. It is filled with case examples and provides numerous references to additional literature. The 14 chapters are: Cardinal Psychological Features of Cerebral Disorder; Symptoms and Syndromes with Regional Affiliations; Clinical Assessment; Differential Diagnosis; Head Injury; Cerebral Tumors; Epilepsy; Intracranial Infections; Cerebrovascular Disease; Senile Dementia, Presenile Dementia and Pseudodementia; Endocrine Diseases

and Metabolic Disorders; Vitamin Deficiencies; Toxic Disorders; and Other Disorders Affecting the Nervous System. Although not exactly a volume for bedtime reading, this is a one-of-a-kind resource for the clinician in need of detailed material about organic mental disorder.

Maletzky, Barry: The Episodic Dyscontrol Syndrome, *Disease of the Nervous System,* 34: pp. 178–185, 1973.
Relying heavily on his clinical study of 22 persons with episodic dyscontrol, the author discusses this somewhat controversial syndrome of periodic violence. Two illustrative case histories are included.

Pincus, Jonathan H. and Gary J. Tucker: *Behavioral Neurology,* Second Edition, New York: Oxford University Press, 1978.
Although technical in places, this is a useful reference on selected topics essential to the practice of critical assessment. Chapter 4, "Disorders of Intellectual Functioning," considers several organic conditions seen among children, including autism, minimal brain damage, and nutritional disorders. The concluding chapter, "Distinguishing Neurological and Psychiatric Disorders," contains information on hyperventilation, headache, and hysteria.

Restak, Richard: *The Brain: The Last Frontier,* New York: Warner Brooks, 1979.
An extremely well-written, entertaining, and up-to-date discussion of the brain. For the clinician interested in an informative overview of the neurological substrate of organic mental disorders, this book is essential reading. Although written for a popular audience, it includes the most recent findings in brain research and is amply documented. At well-chosen points, the author confronts the reader with provocative philosophical speculations that further add to the book's overall appeal. It is a treat to read.

Rossman, Phillip L.: Organic Diseases Resembling Functional Disorders, *Hospital Medicine,* 5: pp. 72–76, 1969.
A discussion based on a study of 130 patients whose initial symptoms led to a variety of such psychiatric diagnoses as psychoneurosis and conversion reaction, but who subsequently were all found to have organic diseases. The author discusses the futility of trying to match psychiatric symptoms to certain organic diseases. For example, in his study he found that hyperthyroidism manifested as four entirely different symptoms: anxiety, psychoneurosis, personality disorder, and depressive reaction. This article highlights the need for an *approach to critical assessment based on certain general principles* rather than a cookbook method that assumes that certain psychiatric symptoms will always be associated with specific organic diseases.

Saravay, Stephen and Lorrin Koran: Organic Disease Mistakenly Diagnosed as Psychiatric, *Psychosomatics,* 18, pp. 6–11, 1977.
The authors discuss their clinical experience on a psychiatric consultation service, where 4% of all referrals were found to be instances of organic illness masquerading as psychological reactions. Although 4% may seem like a low figure, it is impressive when you consider that these referrals

were being made by physicians. The article contains four illustrative case histories.

Strub, Richard L. and William F. Black: *The Mental Status Examination in Neurology,* Philadelphia, F.A. Davis Company, 1977.
This book goes into considerable detail about many of the clinical factors considered in critical assessment. It is a how-to-do-it book that covers some finer points relative to the assessment of such mental functions as attending, memory, language, and level of consciousness. Parts of the book are technical and are probably more appropriate for the medically trained professional; nevertheless, overall, the book is a useful guide for the human service clinician who wishes to expand his working knowledge of the nitty-gritty aspects of critical assessment.

Swonger, Alvin K. and Larry L. Constantine: *Drugs and Therapy, A Psychotherapist's Handbook of Psychotropic Drugs,* Boston, Little, Brown and Company, 1976.
This spiral-bound paperback is a practical and yet relatively comprehensive reference on psychotropic drugs, written for the practicing psychotherapist. The authors are not content with making a rote presentation of the actions and side effects of various drugs; rather, they present the reader with a useful context derived from selected elements of neuroanatomy, neurochemistry and pharmacology. Don't let these formidable topics scare you away from this book. The authors consistently show a feeling for the everyday needs of the practicing clinician. Several helpful appendices are included: a listing of the most commonly prescribed psychotropic drugs with trade name, generic name, and drug action; a guide to adverse drug reactions; and a drug index that provides a quick referencing system for additional information on specific medications. This is a solid book for the clinician interested in obtaining an introduction to psychotropic drugs.

Waugh, Evelyn: *The Ordeal of Gilbert Pinfold,* Boston, Little, Brown and Company, 1957.
A semi-autobiographical, fictional account of a successful but nerve-racked, middle-aged novelist who sets out on a recuperative trip to Ceylon. As a result of his overindulgence in self-prescribed medications, the gentleman soon finds himself entering a terrifying world of strange sounds—wild jazz bands, barking dogs, and loud revival meetings—as well as unfamiliar human voices talking about him in threatening ways. The reader sees the world through the eyes of a man caught up in the throes of the paranoid confusion of organic brain syndrome, unaware of the true nature of his problem. Good reading.

Woodruff, Robert, Donald Goodwin, and Samuel Guze: *Psychiatric Diagnosis,* New York, Oxford University Press, 1974.
A "no-nonsense," "just-the-facts" treatment of the major psychiatric diagnoses. This book provides excellent discussions of Briquet's syndrome (hysteria), schizophrenia, affective disorders, and brain syndrome. In a time when many psychiatric texts have become voluminous and often extraneous, this "little" volume remains an excellent practical reference.

REFERENCES

CHAPTER 1: THE PROBLEM BEFORE US

1. Rubert, Shirley and Frederick Remington: Why patients with brain tumors come to a psychiatric hospital: A 30-year survey, *American Journal of Psychiatry,* 119: pp. 256–257, 1962.
2. Hall, Richard, Michael Popkin, R. A. DeVaul, Louis Faillace, and Sondra Stickey: Physical illness presenting as psychiatric disease, *Archives of General Psychiatry,* 35: pp. 1315–1320, 1978.
3. Koranyi, Erwin: Morbidity and rate of undiagnosed physical illnesses in a psychiatric clinic population, *Archives of General Psychiatry,* 36: pp. 414–419, 1979.
4. Hall, Richard, Earl Gardner, Sondra Stickney, August LeCann, and Michael Popkin: Physical illness manifesting as psychiatric disease II: Analysis of a state hospital inpatient population, *Archives of General Psychiatry,* 37: pp. 989–995, 1980.
5. Tissenbaum, Morris, Harry Harter, and Arnold Friedman: Organic neurological syndrome diagnosed as functional disorders, *JAMA,* 147: pp. 1519–1521, 1951.
6. Spark, Richard, Robert White, and R. B. Connolly: Impotence is not always psychogenic, *JAMA,* 243: pp. 750–755, 1980.
7. Slater, Eliot: Diagnosis of "hysteria," *British Medical Journal,* 1: pp. 1395–1399, 1965.
8. Hofling, Charles: *Textbook of Psychiatry for Medical Practice,* 2nd Ed., Philadelphia, J.B. Lippincott Co., pp. 292–298, 1968.

9. Abercrombie, M. D. Johnson: *The Anatomy of Judgement,* New York, Basic Books, 1960.
10. Chesteron, G. K.: "The Invisible Man" in *Selected Stories,* London, Kingsley Amis, 1972.
11. Rosenhan, David: On being sane in insane places, *Science,* 179: pp. 250–258, 1973.

CHAPTER 2: DESIGN OF THE NERVOUS SYSTEM

1. Omenn, Gilbert: Neurochemistry and behavior in man, *Western Journal of Medicine,* 125: pp. 434–451, 1976.
2. Heilman, Kenneth: Exploring the enigmas of frontal lobe dysfunction, *Geriatrics,* December, 1979, pp. 81–87.
3. Benson, D. Frank and Norman Geschwind: Psychiatric conditions associated with focal lesions of the central nervous system in *American Handbook of Psychiatry,* 4: pp. 208–243, 1975.
4. MacLean, Paul: Man and his animal brains, *Modern Medicine,* 3: pp. 95–106, 1964.
5. MacLean, Paul: Contrasting functions of limbic and neocortical systems of the brain and their relevance to psychophysiological aspects of medicine, *American Journal of Medicine,* 25: pp. 611–626, 1958.
6. Kluver, H. and P. C. Bucy: Psychic blindness and other symptoms following bilateral temporal lobectomy in Rhesus monkeys, *American Journal of Physiology,* 119: pp. 353–363, 1937.
7. Wilson, Lawrence: Viral encephalopathy mimicking functional psychosis, *American Journal of Psychiatry,* 133: pp. 165–170, 1976.
8. Dewhurst, K.: Personality disorder in Huntington's disease, *Psychiatrica Clinica,* 3: pp. 221–229, 1970.
9. Simeons, Albert: *Man's Presumptious Brain,* London, Longmans, 1960.
10. Shulman, Ralph: Psychogenic illness with physical manifestations and the other side of the coin, *Lancet,* i: pp. 524–526, 1977.
11. Alvarez, Walter: *Little Strokes,* Philadelphia, J.B. Lippincott Company, pp. 84–85, 1966.
12. Charaton, F. B. and J. B. Brierley: Mental disorder associated with primary lung carcinoma, *British Medical Journal,* 2: pp. 765–768, 1956.
13. Koranyi, Erwin: Morbidity and rate of undiagnosed physical illnesses in a psychiatric clinic population, *Archives of General Psychiatry,* 36: pp. 414–419, 1979.

CHAPTER 3: CLINICAL DECEPTIONS

1. Torrey, E. Fuller: *The Mind Game: Witchdoctors and Psychiatrists,* New York, Emerson, 1972.
2. Erikson, Eric: *Childhood and Society,* New York, Norton, 1963.
3. Talbott, J. and J. Teague: Marijuana psychosis, *JAMA,* 210: pp. 299–302, 1969.

4. Rosenbaum, Jerroid, Jonathon Tothman, and George Murray: Psychosis and water intoxication, *Journal of Clinical Psychiatry,* 40: pp. 287–291, 1979.
5. Gallant, Donald and George Simpson (Eds.): *Depression,* New York, Spectrum Publishing, 1976.
6. Daley, Robert, Francis Kane, and John Ewing: Psychosis associated with the use of sequential oral contraceptive, Lancet ii: pp. 444–445, 1967.
7. Shulman, Ralph: Psychogenic illness with physical manifestations and the other side of the coin, *Lancet,* i: pp. 524–526, 1977.
8. Ryback, Ralph and Robert Schwab: Manic response to levodopa therapy, report of a case, *New England Journal of Medicine,* 285: pp. 788–789, 1971.
9. Doust, Brewster: Anxiety as a manifestation of pheochromocytoma, *Archives of Internal Medicine,* 102: pp. 811–815, 1958.
10. Greden, John: Anxiety or caffeinism: a diagnostic dilemma, *American Journal of Psychiatry,* 131: pp. 1089–1092, 1974.
11. Greden, John: ibid.
12. Hall, Richard, Michael Popkin, Richard Devaul, Louis Faillace, and Sondra Stickney: Physical illness presenting as psychiatric disease, *Archives of General Psychiatry,* 35: pp. 1315–1320, 1978.
13. Jefferson, James: Lithium carbonate-induced hypothyroidism, its many faces, *JAMA,* 242: pp. 271–272, 1979.
14. Weissberg, Michael: Emergency room medical clearance: an educational problem, *American Journal of Psychiatry,* 136: pp. 787–790, 1979.
15. Bell, D. S.: Comparison of amphetamine psychosis and schizophrenia, *British Journal of Psychiatry,* III: pp. 701–707, 1965.
16. Golden, Joshua, et al.: Toxic and functional psychoses, *Annals of Internal Medicine,* 66: pp. 989–1007, 1967.
17. Taylor, Robert, John Maurer, and Jared Jinklenberg: Management of "bad trips" in an evolving drug scene, *JAMA,* 213, pp. 422–425, 1970.
18. Galenberg, Alan J.: The catatonic syndrome, *Lancet,* i: pp. 1339–1341, 1976.
19. Schwab, John and Mark Barrow: A reaction to organic fluorides simulating classical catatonia, *American Journal of Psychiatry,* 120: pp. 1196–1197, 1964.
20. Cadoret, Remi and Lucy King: *Psychiatry and Primary Care,* St. Louis, The C. V. Mosby Company, p. 201, 1974.

CHAPTER 4: A FIRST STEP TOWARD CRITICAL ASSESSMENT: RECOGNITION OF BRAIN SYNDROME

1. Selzer, Benjamin and Ira Sherwin: Organic brain syndromes: an empirical study and critical review, *American Journal of Psychiatry,* 135: pp. 13–21, 1978.
2. Wells, Charles: Chronic brain disease: an overview, *American Journal of Psychiatry,* 135: pp. 1–12, 1978.
3. Williamson, J., I. H. Stokoe, S. Gray, et al.: Old people at home: their unreported needs, *Lancet,* i: pp. 1117–1120, 1964.
4. Anonymous Author: Death of a mind: a study in disintegration, *Lancet,* i: pp. 1012–1015, 1950.

5. Lishman, William: *Organic Psychiatry,* London, Blackwell Scientific Publications, 1978.
6. Farber, Irving: Acute brain syndrome, *Diseases of the Nervous System,* 20: pp. 296–299, 1959.
7. Sakles, G. J. and George Ballis: Acute brain syndromes, in *Clinical Psychopathology,* (Ed.) George Balis, Boston, Butterworth Publishers, Inc., pp. 65–86, 1978.
8. Wolff, Harold G. and Desmond Curran: Nature of delirium and allied states, *Archives of Neurology and Psychiatry,* 33: pp. 1175–1215, 1935.
9. Lipowski, Z. J.: Delirium, clouding of consciousness and confusion, *Journal of Nervous and Mental Disease,* 145: pp. 227–255, 1967.
10. Horvath, Thomas: Organic brain syndromes, in *Psychiatry for the Primary Care Physician,* (Eds.) Arthur Freeman, Robert Sack and Philip Berger, Baltimore, Williams and Wilkins Company, pp. 215–245, 1979.
11. Freeman, Frank: Evaluation of patients with progressive intellectual deterioration, *Archives of Neurology,* 33: pp. 658–659, 1967.
12. Strachen, R.W. and J.G. Henderson: Psychiatric syndrome due to avitaminosis B_{12} with normal bone marrow, *Quarterly Journal of Medicine,* 34: pp. 303–317, 1965.
13. Benson, Frank: Amnesia, *Southern Medical Journal,* 71: pp. 1221–1228, 1978.
14. Lidz, Theodore: The amnestic syndrome, *Archives of Neurology and Psychiatry,* 47: pp. 588–605, 1942.

CHAPTER 5: FURTHER CLUES TO ORGANIC MENTAL DISORDERS

1. Waggoner, R. W. and B. W. Bagohi: Initial masking of organic brain changes by psychic symptoms, *American Journal of Psychiatry,* 110: pp. 904–910, 1954.
2. Carlson, Richard: Frontal lobe lesions masquerading as psychiatric disturbances, *Canadian Psychiatric Association Journal,* 22: pp. 315–318, 1977.
3. Weissberg, Michael: Emergency room medical clearance: an educational problem, *American Journal of Psychiatry,* 136: pp. 787–790, 1979.
4. Sayed, Joseph: Mania and bromism: a case report and a look at the future, *American Journal of Psychiatry,* 133: pp. 228–229, 1976.
5. Sandler, N.: A case of meningitis admitted as schizophrenia, *Journal of the Kentucky Medical Association,* 73: pp. 25–26, 1975.
6. Geschwind, Norman: Current concepts: aphasia, *New England Journal of Medicine,* 284: pp. 654–657, 1971.
7. Mark, Vernon and Frank Ervin: *Violence in the Brain,* New York, Harper and Row Publishers, pp. 58–59, 1970.
8. Grancher, Robert and Ross Baldessarini: Physostigmine, *Archives of General Psychiatry,* 32: pp. 375–380, 1975.
9. Lawall, John: Psychiatric presentations of seizure disorders, *American Journal of Psychiatry,* 133: pp. 321–323, 1976.
10. Geschwind, Norman: The borderland of neurology and psychiatry: some

common misconceptions, in *Psychiatric Aspects of Neurological Disease,* (Eds.) F. Benson and D. Blumer, New York, Grune and Stratton, p. 7, 1975.

11. Chidru, F. and N. Geschwind: Writing disturbances in acute confusional states, *Neuropsychologica,* 10: pp. 343–353, 1972.
12. Robbins, Edwin and Marvin Stern: Assessment of psychiatric emergencies in *Psychiatric Emergencies,* (Eds.) R. Glick, A. Meyerson, E. Robbins and J. Talbott, New York, Grune and Stratton, pp. 9–48, 1976.

CHAPTER 6: PUTTING CRITICAL ASSESSMENT TO WORK

1. Greiner, Theodore: A case of "psychosis" from drugs, *Texas State Journal of Medicine,* 60: pp. 659–660, 1964.
2. Taylor, Robert: Extracted from private clinical files.
3. Penn, Henry, John Racy, Lowell Lapham, Michael Mandel, and John Sandt: Catatonic behavior, viral encephalopathy and death, *Archives of General Psychiatry,* 27: pp. 758–761, 1972.

CHAPTER 7: THREE MASQUERADERS

1. Waggoner, R.: Brain syndromes associated with intracranial neoplasm in *Comprehensive Textbook of Psychiatry,* (Eds.) A. Freedman and H. Kaplan, Baltimore, The Williams & Wilkins Co, pp. 786–791, 1967.
2. Rushton, J. and E. Rooke: Brain tumor headache, *Headache,* 2: p. 147, 1962.
3. Gilroy, J. and J. Meyer: *Medical Neurology* (3rd Ed.), New York, Macmillan Publishing Co., 1973.
4. Waggoner, R., ibid.
5. Soniat, T.: Psychiatric symptoms associated with intracranial neoplasm, *American Journal of Psychiatry,* 106: pp. 19–22, 1951.
6. Kanakaratnam, G. and M. Direkze: Aspects of primary tumors of the frontal lobe, *British Journal of Clinical Practice,* 30: pp. 220–221, 1976.
7. Carlson, B.: Frontal lobe lesions masquerading as psychiatric disturbances, *Canadian Psychiatric Association Journal,* 22: pp. 315–318, 1977.
8. Oppler, W.: Manic psychosis in a case of parasagittal meningioma, *Archives of Neurology and Psychiatry,* 64: pp. 417–430, 1950.
9. Hunter, R, W. Blackwood and J. Bull: Three cases of frontal meningiomas presenting psychiatrically, *British Medical Journal,* 3: pp. 9–16, 1968.
10. MacLean, P.: Man and his animal brains, *Modern Medicine,* 3: pp. 95–106, 1964.
11. Malamud, N.: Psychiatric disorder with intracranial tumors of limbic system, *Archives of Neurology,* 17: pp. 113–123, 1967.
12. Johnson, J.: Sexual impotence and the limbic system, *British Journal of Psychiatry,* III: pp. 300–303, 1965.
13. Adebimpe, V.: Complex partial seizures simulating schizophrenia, *Journal of the American Medical Association,* 237: pp. 1339–1341, 1977.

14. Hooshmand, H. and B. Brawley: Temporal lobe seizures and exhibitionism, *Neurology,* 19: pp. 1119–1124, 1959.
15. Bach-y-Rita, G., J. Lion, C. Climent, and F. Ervin: Episodic dyscontrol: a study of 130 violent patients, *American Journal of Psychiatry,* 127: pp. 49–54, 1971.
16. Maletzky, B.: The episodic dyscontrol syndrome, *Diseases of the Nervous System,* 34: pp. 178–185, 1973.
17. Smith, C., J. Barish, J. Correa, and R. Williams: Psychiatric disturbances in endocrinologic disease, *Psychosomatic Medicine,* 34: pp. 69–86, 1972.
18. Laurent, J., G. Debry, and J. Floguet: *Hypoglycemic Tumors,* Amsterdam, Excerpta Medica, 1971.
19. Silvis, R. and D. Simon: Marked hypoglycemia associated with nonpancreatic tumors, *New England Journal of Medicine,* 254: pp. 14–17, 1956.
20. Bovill, Diana: A case of functional hypoglycemia—a medico-legal problem, *British Journal of Psychiatry,* 123: pp. 353–358, 1973.
21. Martin, J. J.: Physical diseases manifesting as psychiatric disorders in *Psychiatry in General Medical Practice,* (Eds.) Gene Usden and Jerry Lewis, New York, McGraw-Hill, pp. 337–351, 1979.
22. Oivarius, B. and E. Roder: Reversible psychosis and dementia in myxedema, *Acta Psychiatrica Scandinavia,* 46: pp. 1–13, 1970.

CHAPTER 8: DRUG-INDUCED ORGANIC MENTAL DISORDERS

1. Fadiman, James: Ground rules for integral medicine, *Holistic Health Review,* 3: pp. 20–36, 1979.
2. Hall, R. C. W., M. K. Popkin, S. K. Stickney, and D. R. Gardner: Covert outpatient drug abuse: incidence and therapist recognition, *Journal of Nervous and Mental Disease,* 1661: pp. 343–348, 1978.
3. Ban, Thomas: Drug interactions with psychoactive drugs, *Diseases of the Nervous System,* 36: pp. 164–166, 1976.
4. Granacher, Robert and Ross Baldessarini: Physostigmine, *Archives of General Psychiatry,* 32: pp. 375–380, 1975.
5. Gelenberg, Alan and Michael Mandel: Catatonic reactions to high-potency neuroleptic drugs, *Archives of General Psychiatry,* 34: pp. 947–950, 1977.
6. Goodwin, F.K.: Psychiatric side effects of levodopa in man, *JAMA,* 218: pp. 1915–1920, 1971.
7. Shader, Richard and David Greenblatt: Uses and toxicity of belladonna alkaloids in synthetic anticholinergics, *Seminars in Psychiatry,* 3: pp. 449–476, 1971.
8. German, Elaine and Mural Siddiqui: Atropine toxicity from eyedrops, *New England Journal of Medicine,* 282: p. 689, 1970.
9. Taylor, Robert, John Maurer, and Jared Tinklinberg: Management of "bad trips" in an evolving drug scene, *JAMA,* 213: pp. 422–425, 1970.
10. Hoffman, Brian: Diet pill psychosis (letter), *Canadian Medical Journal,* 116: pp. 351–355, 1977.
11. Taylor, Robert: Extracted from private clinical files.

CHAPTER 9: THE OTHER SIDE OF THINGS

1. *American Psychiatric Association Diagnostic and Statistical Manual of Mental Disorders* (3rd Ed.), pp. 241–252, 1980.
2. Martin, M. J.: Physical disease manifesting as psychiatric disorders, in *Psychiatry in General Medical Practice,* (Eds.) Gene Usdin and Jerry Lewis, New York, McGraw-Hill Book Company, pp. 337–351, 1979.
3. Dubousky, Steven and Michael Weissberg: *Clinical Psychiatry in Primary Care,* Baltimore, Williams and Wilkins Company, p. 203, 1978.
4. Pincus, Jonathan and Gary Tucker: *Behavioral Neurology,* New York, Oxford University Press, pp. 183–187, 1974.
5. Woodruff, Robert, Donald Goodwin, and Samuel Guse: *Psychiatric Diagnosis,* New York, Oxford University Press, pp. 58–74, 1974.
6. Kaminsky, Michael and Philip Slavney: Methodology and personality in Briquet's syndrome: a reappraisal, *American Journal of Psychiatry,* 133: pp. 58–88, 1976.
7. Fuller, David, M.D., Professor of Psychiatry, University of Texas at San Antonio Medical School: personal communication.
8. Feinglass, Edward, Frank Arnett, Carole Porsch, Thomas Zizic, and Mary Steverns: Neuropsychiatric manifestations of systemic lupus erythematosus: diagnosis, clinical spectrum and relationship to other features of the disease, *Medicine,* 55: pp. 323–339, 1976.
9. Yaskin, Joseph: Nervous symptoms as earliest manifestations of carcinoma of the pancreas, *JAMA,* 96: pp. 1664–1668, 1931.
10. Kolb, Lawrence C.: *Modern Clinical Psychiatry,* Philadelphia, W.B. Saunders Company, p. 520, 1977.
11. LaWall, John and Kalarickal Ooommen: Basilar artery migraine presenting as conversion hysteria, *Journal of Nervous and Mental Disease,* 166: pp. 809–811, 1978.
12. Friedman, A. P. and S. H. Frazier: Critique of the psychiatric treatment of chronic headache patients, in *Proceedings of the 5th World Congress of Psychiatrists,* New York, American Elsevier, 1973.
13. Lesser, Ronald and Stanley Fann: Dystonia: a disorder often misdiagnosed as a conversion reaction, *American Journal of Psychiatry,* 135: pp. 349–352, 1978.

CHAPTER 10: THE OLD AND THE YOUNG

1. Fox, Jacob, Jordan Topel, and Michael Huckman: Dementia in the elderly —a search for treatable illnesses, *Journal of Gerontology,* 30: pp. 557–564, 1975.
2. Comfort, Alex: *Practice of Geriatric Psychiatry,* New York, Elsevier, 1980.
3. Cummings, Jeffrey, Frank Benson, and Stephen LoVerne: Reversible dementia, *JAMA,* 243: pp. 2434–2439, 1980.
4. National Institute on Aging: Safe use of medications by older people, "Age Page," U.S. Department of Health and Human Services, November, 1980.
5. Comfort, op. cit.
6. Stuteville, Peter and Keasley Welch: Subdural hematoma in the elderly, *JAMA,* 168: pp. 1445–1449, 1958.

7. Pygott, F. and D. F. Street: Unsuspected treatable organic dementia, *Lancet,* i: p. 1371, 1950.
8. Raskind, Robert and Benjamin Glover: Chronic subdural hematoma in the elderly: a challenge in diagnosis and treatment, *Journal of the American Geriatric Society,* 20: pp. 330–334, 1972.
9. Price, Trevor and Gary Tucker: Psychiatric and behavioral manifestations of normal pressure hydrocephalus, *Journal of Nervous and Mental Disease,* 164: pp. 51–55, 1977.
10. Eisdorfer, Carl: Paranoia and schizophrenic disorders in later life, in *Handbook of Geriatric Psychiatry,* (Eds.) Ewald Busse and Dan Blazer, New York, Van Nostrand Reinhold Co., pp. 329–337, 1980.
11. Clark, A. N. G.: Ectopic tachycardias in the elderly, *Gerontologica Clinica,* 12: pp. 203–212, 1970.
12. Mark, Stewart and Ann Gath: *Psychological Disorders of Children,* Baltimore, Williams and Wilkins Co., p. 32, 1978.
13. Laufer, Maurice and Shetty Taranath: Acute and chronic brain syndromes, in *Basic Handbook of Child Psychiatry,* Vol. 2 (Ed.) Joseph Noshpitz, New York, Basic Books, Inc., pp. 381–402, 1979.
14. Ornitz, Edward and Edward Ritvo: The syndrome of autism: a critical review, *American Journal of Psychiatry,* 133: pp. 609–621, 1976.
15. Livingston, Samuel, Lydia Pauli, and Irving Bruce: Neurological evaluation of the child, in *Comprehensive Textbook of Psychiatry/III,* (Eds.) Harold Kaplan, Alfred Freedman, and Benjamin Sadock, Baltimore, Williams and Wilkins, pp. 2461–2473, 1980.
16. Bearn, A.G.: Wilson's disease, in *The Metabolic Basis of Inherited Disease,* 3rd Ed., (Eds.) J. B. Stanberry, J. B. Wyngaarden, and D. S. Fredrickson, New York, McGraw-Hill, Chapter 43, 1972.
17. Malamud, Nathan: Organic brain disease mistaken for psychiatric disorder: a clinicopathologic study, in *Psychiatric Aspects of Neurological Disease,* (Eds.) D. Frank Benson and Dietrich Blumer, New York, Grune & Stratton, pp. 287–307, 1975.
18. Golder, Gerald: Tourette syndrome, *American Journal of Diseases of Children,* 131: pp. 531–534, 1977.
19. Varga, James: The hyperactive child, should we be paying more attention, *American Journal of Diseases of Children,* 133: pp. 413–418, 1979.

CHAPTER 11: A SUMMING UP

1. DeVaul, R. A.: Acute organic brain syndrome: clinical considerations, *Texas Medicine,* 72, pp. 51–54, 1976.
2. Jamieson, Robert and Charles Wells: Manic psychosis in a patient with multiple metastatic brain tumors, *Journal of Clinical Psychiatry,* 40: pp. 280–283, 1979.
3. Rosen, Harold and Mary Swigar: Depression and normal pressure hydrocephalus, *Journal of Nervous and Mental Disease,* 163: pp. 35–40, 1976.
4. Carroll, Lewis: *Alice in Wonderland and Other Favorites,* New York, Washington Square Press, pp. 8–11, 1951.
5. Taylor, Robert: Extracted from private clinical files.

6. MacRae, Donald: Isolated fear: a temporal lobe aura, *Neurology,* 4: pp. 497–505, 1954.
7. Wilson, Lawrence: Viral encephalopathy mimicking functional psychosis, *American Journal of Psychiatry,* 133: pp. 165–170, 1976.
8. Horvath, Thomas: Organic brain syndromes, in *Psychiatry for the Primary Care Physician,* (Eds.) Freeman, Arthur, Robert Sack, and Philip Berger, Baltimore, Williams and Wilkins Company, p. 228, 1979.
9. Gregory, Ian: *Fundamentals of Psychiatry* (2nd Ed.), Philadelphia, W. B. Saunders Co., pp. 352–358, 1968.
10. Romano, J. and G. P. Coon: Physiologic and psychologic studies in spontaneous hypoglycemia, *Psychosomatic Medicine,* 4: pp. 283–300, 1942.

INDEX

ABOUT THE AUTHOR

Robert L. Taylor, M.D., is clinical assistant professor of family, community, and preventive medicine at Stanford University and consulting psychiatrist to the California Department of Mental Health. In addition, he is the author of numerous journal articles and conducts intensive seminar workshops for human service professionals on the clinical recognition of organic mental disorders. Dr. Taylor is a graduate of Baylor University Medical School.

HURRAH FOR HUMANS

HURRAH FOR HUMANS
Volume One

Inspiring stories of kindness and courage

Annemarie Eveland

Library of Congress
Cataloging-in-Publication Data.

Eveland, A. 2020.

Inspirational Stories.

ISBN-13-979-8554485893

HURRAH FOR HUMANS

Cover design by Victoria Davies at
www.vcbookcovers.com

First Edition.

Published by Hurrah for Humans, LLC.
AnnemarieEveland.writer@gmail.com

HURRAH FOR YOU!
OTHER BOOKS BY ANNEMARIE EVELAND

At First Glance: What Faces Reveal

Keesha and the Rainbow Parrot Guide

The Guidebook for Children's Book Keesha

Echoes from the Rim an Anthology

Be the Ripple

Real Women Don't Wear Glass Slippers

An Uncommon Sense of Self

Hurrah for Humans

<u>SMALL POETRY BOOKS</u>

Reaching for the Sun

Wisdom of the Heart

Journeys of a Soul

Turns in the Roads

Hurrah for Humans

DEDICATION

To those kindred souls who have inspired me, enriched me, and shared their love with me. I have been abundantly blessed.

To those human beings who awakened strength and courage in me from lessons in my live challenges. They helped me grow.

CONTENTS

ACKNOWLEDGMENTS

I deeply appreciate the encouragement I received from family and friends to write these stories.

I thank my two friends, Connie Cockrell, Author, for her valuable help in the formatting of this book and Carole Matthewson, Author, who did some editing of my stories.

Thank you to Artists Don Harmon, and Willy Whitefeather; and Photographer D.J. Craig for their contributions.

INTRODUCTION

These stories stem from my life and the lives of people I have met, from whom I learned important truths, experienced awakenings, or shared divine blessings.

No one touches us without leaving something of themselves. And, in turn, we leave something of ourselves with them.

These stories celebrate our human spirit—that almost unnamed strength which lies within us. When we are challenged by life's unexpected hardships, it restores our faith in ourselves and in our fellow human beings.

Hurrah for Humans demonstrates an open heart and by remembering our true, intrinsic, and eternal Soul Self, we are able to overcome any obstacles.

Hurrah for Humans!

HOW TO USE THIS BOOK

This book is comprised of a series of stories in which you are invited to allow your feelings to emerge as you read. At the end of each story, you might examine your life and determine whether there is an event therein that evoked similar feelings.

When you read that which you have written, explore how you might change your way of handling the situation; or congratulate yourself for a job well done, and, too, give yourself a "hurrah for humans" cheer.

Chapter One

THE GOATS AND THE GUYS

"I always prefer to believe the best of everybody—it saves so much trouble."

Rudyard Kipling

This story shows that if we don't judge our fellow humans, there may be time enough left to appreciate them. I found this to be quite accurate and made me feel glad to respect those less fortunate than myself.

The Goats and the Guys

In our mountain country, we are always vigilant about being fire wise concerning our properties, especially as the spring/summer fire season arrives.

My mountainside Bed and Breakfast was nestled overlooking the beautiful Pine Valley. The natural landscape surroundings had become overgrown for many years and our fire department was concerned that it was prime fuel for hazardous wildfires.

Mike was in charge of the Wildfire Prevention project, and he approached me to cooperatively work on my two-and-a-half-acre property to make it more fire wise. I had thought some of his crew would be coming out to trim the bushes and trees. I was very wrong concerning that guess.

He explained that they would bring in goats. The goats would trim down the overgrown landscape. They would be fenced in areas and then moved to the next adjoining area when they finished. I thought it was a modestly practical approach.

The goats arrived. I mean, lots of goats

were shuttled in. My property became a massive munching ground. I couldn't even count the number of goats in this huge herd that seemed to endlessly arrive. They bleated gleefully as they munched the tender greenery, the twigs, the brittle bushes, the low hanging trees. They clearly found bark tasty.

They climbed upon my picnic tables to reach the higher morsels, and they nibbled at the table edges. They seemed to find everything edible. They were relentless in their munching.

The goat herd protector dog, Patrick, along with his female mate arrived. Their sole responsibility was to guard the goats. We were in a wilderness area, so mountain lions have been known to find goat dinner very tasty. Patrick and his pregnant bride were huge, white, beautiful sheep dogs. All seemed to settle into their proper roles for an unknown duration.

My Bed and Breakfast guests found the activity to be fascinating and some would sit on the front covered deck with binoculars and view the entire production as excellent guest entertainment.

I had a differing opinion, listening

constantly, as I did, to the great munching going on. I wondered if there would be any vestige of anything green when the munchers were moved to the next section of my land.

When dark of nighttime fell softly upon us, the guests went to bed, I finished my work, and I decided to have one last look at the goat-brigade. I was surprised to see two white dogs lying on my chaise loungers *outside* the securely fenced in goat-eating arena. Evidently, even pregnant dogs can jump fences. I put them both back inside the fenced area. I hushed them and headed back inside.

I couldn't have been inside long, when I heard Patrick howling loudly. Was Patrick howling his romantic song to his female mate? Surely sounded passionate to me. I rushed outside and earnestly and intently told Patrick to shush! Shush! He obediently stopped, wagged his tail as if proud of his song.

I tiptoed back into the home. I listened for a while, hoping not to hear Patrick howling again. It was quiet. I sighed with relief and went to sleep.

But the next morning I found why it was quiet. Patrick and his lady had again jumped the fence and were found lying comfortably stretched out on my chaise loungers outside the fenced goats.

I was even more amused when I saw the two goat herders driving up the road in their rattle-trap truck, to check on everything. As though on cue, Patrick and wife jumped off the loungers and leaped over the fence. They stood as if they had been guarding the goats throughout the night.

I never told on them! They kept quiet at nights. It was a good trade off.

###

Soon, the land looked bare. I called Mike. He said, "We'll have them move the goats to the next part and bring in the prisoners."

"What?" I exclaimed. "What prisoners?"

"Oh, they'll bring them from Globe. The guards come with them. They have shotguns," he said assuredly with a slight hidden smile.

I hadn't heard about that part before.

The next morning, when my guests checked out, I decided not to book any guests while the rest of the fire-wise fervor was finishing, not knowing how guests might view my grounds being covered with flaming orange colors.

Then a reporter from the newspaper arrived to do a story about the program. That same day, the correctional officers, in tan dress, and the inmates in blaze orange and yellow hard hats, gloves and protective eye wear arrived early in the morning to start work.

There was a huge chipper truck, equipment truck, and the guards with shotguns. All the prisoners exited their transport bus and seemed to know exactly what work had to be done. They quickly began, moving the water tank, chopping at brush stubble, cutting tree limbs, and dragging brush to the chipper.

Sadly, many of my ponderosa pines had to be cut down due to the bark beetle infestation, when our long drought weakened the trees and left them vulnerable to the huge swarms of bark beetles, which devoured the pines.

The sounds of dueling chain saws roared in the air all day. I heard they had to work several days, and they went back to Globe prison at night.

Occasionally, I heard a laugh or two, but these guys worked hard. When they were allowed a break, they talked among themselves, and they walked over to give Patrick and his mate a pat or two. I liked the gentle affection they showered upon the two recalcitrant "guard dogs."

The article on the fire wise prevention project with the use of prisoners came out in the newspaper. I showed it to the guys when they had a break. They said they really wanted a copy but weren't allowed to receive anything like that. But could I send it to mothers, girlfriends, etc. Sure, I would and did.

###

While the project was being completed, I had an idea that I shared with Mike. Recently my dear friend had died, and we had a funeral service and Celebration of Life service at my

Bed and Breakfast. Someone supplied huge racks of steak meat and much was still frozen.

I asked if I could cook the meat for "the boys" when they were finished.

Mike said, "They're gonna' love you forever!" He added that he had been to meat cutter school, had his own seasonings and knives, and that he would slice them into nice steaks, and he'd get our fire chief to come over and barbeque the steaks.

"Wow!" I said, "Then I will prepare a big picnic for them, and a celebration cake. And I decided to get our local well-known fiddler to come and play music for them. Also, a guitarist I knew. All agreed to participate.

Then a troubling thought occurred to me. I wondered if it would be a good idea for me to give those prisoners sharp steak knives. Would that be a problem? I asked Mike, and he laughed loudly.

"Annemarie, these guys have chainsaws, hatchets, and much more. And you're worried about a little steak knife! No, they'll be fine." He chuckled again.

So, the day they finished their work, I laid

out the entire banquet, our Fire Chief arrived and barbequed their steaks to order. The young men lined up respectfully and loaded up on the banquet offerings.

During that afternoon, I got a chance to talk with some of them. *Nice fellows*, I thought. *How did they end up in prison?* I was touched by some of their comments to me.

One said, "When we go out on these types of jobs, many times the owners will hide inside their homes and never come out, close their shades, and lock their doors."

Another said, "We get to go into different restaurants, and we can order anything we want off the menu. But this has been the best meal we have ever had. Thank you!"

And they all took turns coming up to me, shook my hand and sincerely thanked me, not only for the lavish, unexpected, and delicious food, but for something else that touched me greatly

One prisoner said, "We are thankful that you gave us a great meal, but more than that, you gave us back our dignity by the way you have treated us." I swallowed hard.

The inmate's words took me by surprise as I was just thinking of sharing *my* appreciation to them for all the work they did on my property to make it fire-wise.

I smiled softly and thought, *hurrah for all of us humans that can kindly appreciate each other.*

What about you?

When in your life did you have a project to do and the person helping you was by society's standards labeled negatively. But you found something to appreciate about them?

Insight from your life:

Insight from *the Goats and the Guys*

____

____

____

____

____

____

____

____

____

____

____

____

HURRAH FOR YOU!

Chapter Two

IN A TWINKLING MOMENT

My Life Changed in the Twinkling of His Eyes

"Love is simply the joy of being fully what we are meant to be."

Robert Muller

Once when I was traveling in England and feeling dispirited, a stranger's joyful countenance touched me just for a moment, yet, had a lasting change in me that I still remember today. It reminded me of the power of being a fully radiant human.

In a Twinkling Moment

England can be dreary, even in summertime. The summer in question was especially chilling and dispiriting. My beloved husband had died. I was attempting to find meaning again in life by journeying abroad.

The quest was providing limited success. The historic sites, the sacred rituals, and the studies in esoteric knowledge each sliced a tiny bit off the heaviness that I could not shake. But still I carried the heavy weight of grief.

I stood at England's Stonehenge; the giant solid granite figures too awesome to describe. They seemingly magnified the weight in my heart, the heaviness in my soul.

It was late afternoon, the sunlight, though cold, trickled slowly down the faces of the granite monoliths.

I shivered. A core cold feeling flooded my entire body. *Can I ever feel warm again?* I thought. I longed for something I knew would never return.

It was not possible for me to escape the chilling feelings within me. They had remained with me since leaving the gravesite of my beloved.

I forced myself to straighten up my body and with effort took a deep breath in. Strangely, the numbness persisted.

With a deep, sad pain in my heart, I gazed out across the bleak landscape. The chilling wind added its howling messages of mourning. In the distance of the deep green landscape, I saw a slender arched shadow-figure briskly striding towards me. My breathing increased rapidly as I waited for my eyes to reveal the truth.

The shadow grew into the size of a man. An elderly man by outside appearances, yet he seemed vibrant and energetic. He was moving straight towards me. I gasped and tightened my grip on the stone centurion.

No! I thought, *He must be headed for the village behind me. I couldn't deny the panic I felt for no apparent reason.*

I felt frozen in the long few minutes that stretched between us. I was startled by this unexpected feeling.

His pace quickened, matching my pounding heartbeat. Suddenly he was beside me, and as he strode past, I felt his magnetic intensity. His brilliantly, blue twinkling eyes peered deeply into my soul.

His radiant sunshine smile shone forth. I heard him say with the kind, soft, clear yet energetic voice, "Enjoy your day!" Then, he was gone.

His warmth lingered much like a soft fuzzy cloak warming my shoulders and heart.

"Enjoy your day?" How could that common greeting be so profound? Yet, I could not deny I was changed by his words. That which he left with me was far more impressive than the historic site of the giants to which I tenaciously clung.

In passing by me, the gentleman's twinkling eyes, and sunny message warmed my heart that changed my life forever. That glance, genuine and caring, provided purpose for my soul. It was as though my entire journey shifted from that defining moment.

As we journey through life, we find a variety of defining moments. They may come from trusted friends and power-filled experiences within our homes, or they may make their mark in a moment from a stranger.

The next time you think that taking a moment to share your sunshine heart with a stranger will not matter, will not make a difference in someone's life, remember the warming experience of my life, and take the chance that you can make a dramatic change in someone's life. Mine was changed by the twinkling of the man's eyes.

He was definitely a hurrah for humans.

What About You?

Have you experienced a heartfelt change within you in just a moment's exchange with a stranger?

INSIGHT from your life:

Insight from *A Twinkling Moment*

____
____
____
____
____
____
____
____
____
____
____
____
____
____

HURRAH FOR YOU!

Chapter Three

ANGEL IN THE AISLE

"It is love that asks, that seeks, that knocks, that finds, and that is faithful to what it finds."

Saint Augustine

If we pay attention, we can find our spiritual uplifting moments, even in a rustic small grocery store in a mountain village town. I just had to walk down a certain aisle, and there was an angel smiling at me!

Angel in the Aisle

Her genuine "Hello!" along with an enthusiastic nod of her head, caught my attention. It was a small gesture, a normal salute, in the little local country grocery store which stocked only essentials. But her greeting was backed with such vibrancy and enthusiasm.

What I first noticed was her beaming sunny smile, then I noticed she had no teeth. Her mouth gaped open unabashedly. There were definitely NO teeth.

She must have sensed my shock, though I felt I showed none. Her mouth pursed down into a tiny rosebud. I felt uncomfortable in her presence. Had I rejected a slice of heaven's true joy, without permission or understanding? Uneasiness stirred within me.

Her eyes, however, clearly viewed my discomfort, shining like her previous smile. This tiny, ragged lady, unafraid that her smile would be unwelcomed, had an abundance of true joy to share with me.

I was humbled beyond words; frozen in a moment that seemed to stretch endlessly on.

In one brief moment, an immensely great lady showed me how I still clung to the “right form” before I could receive her joy.

###

Despite my numerous teachings, journeys, counseling, awakenings, I found I was still hiding a part of myself that did not automatically greet her wholeheartedly with my genuine caring. Yet, from her eyes, I saw only joy and love, not reservation.

I don’t know where this lady next went to share her smile of sunshine, an authentic reminder of how-to live-in joy and share the joy every day with everyone.

As I stood between the cans of Campbell’s soup and Texas Habanero chili, I received a priceless gift from this ragged, richly blessed lady.

My moment of true awakening came from when I realized she *was* an angel in the aisle.

I realized that this woman shared noticeable radiance. She knew how to be a truly loving person. I salute her as a genuine hurrah for humans.

What about you?

When have you found that someone who was imperfectly formed showed you unconditional love?

INSIGHT from your life:

Insight from *Angel in the Aisle*

____

____

____

____

____

____

____

____

____

____

____

____

____

HURRAH FOR YOU!

Chapter Four

AUNTIE ANN HELPS LITTLE GIRL

"When you act upon something you feel you're called to do, you feel inspired."

Author Unknown

In this story we see how a moment of perceptivity can help a young person begin to feel whole again.

"Auntie Ann" Helps Little Girl

Kings Canyon National Park in California boasts of the largest grove of Sequoias in the world. It is awesome and spectacular. My gal friend and I stood there admiring the great sequoia forest around us. While most of it is wilderness with some easily traversed trails, there are some areas of the park areas that offer gentle recreation for visitors.

We had traveled from Arizona with our backpacks with the anticipation of camping in these giant redwoods.

As we surveyed our options, we noticed a school bus which had brought young students on a field trip to become educated concerning these magnificent giants. We viewed them now getting back on the bus to leave.

My eyes were quickly drawn to a distant tree with a little girl leaning against it. She was vomiting.

I immediately rushed over to her and saw her little body shaking. I put my arms around her and held her. She began crying. I then picked her up and held her as though I would a baby. She snuggled deeper into my arms.

Then slowly she stopped shaking.

"What is wrong?" I asked her gently.

"I'm afraid to get on the bus because those boys are mean to me," she said between sniffles.

"What is your name?" I asked.

"Kayla," she stated in a whimper.

Kayla is from the current generation who are given modern names like that, I thought. My name is simpler.

"Well, why don't you and I get on that bus together and you can find a friend who you feel good about to sit with. Would that be okay?" I said warmly.

"Yes," she replied, "I wish you were my mother." She sounded sad again. I wondered if she didn't get much nurturing at home.

"Well," I said, "Why don't I be your Auntie Ann for today? Would you like that?"

Her big, blue eyes shone, and a little smile appeared at the edges of her mouth.

I wiped her tears, patted her gently on the cheek as I let her down. As promised, like a caring aunt, I placed her hand in mine and we both walked to the bus.

After entering the bus, we passed several rows of seated students, and then she saw a friend and called to her. I ushered the little child to that seat and when she was tucked in, I kissed her goodbye.

Her friend said, “Who is that?”

“Oh, that’s my aunt,” Kayla said. There was enthusiastic pride in her voice.

###

I left the bus and walked back to my friend.

“How did you happen to see that little girl way over there? Jenny asked puzzled.

My response was, “I don’t really understand it myself. Something just calls out to me, like someone tugging at my heart with a need. I don’t know how it happens, but such things have happened most of my life. That’s how I know who and how to help.”

With that, we hiked back to our campgrounds, and began preparing dinner.

I thought about Kayla and sent a blessing to the little girl who had stood beside the giant sequoia tree trembling.

Hurrah for our little fragile human beings that give us an opportunity to bring about a change for their situations.

What about you?

When have you been drawn intuitively to reach out and help someone without thinking of yourself?

INSIGHT from your life:

Insight from *Auntie Ann Helps Little Girl*

____

____

____

____

____

____

____

____

____

____

____

____

____

____

HURRAH FOR YOU!

Chapter Five

CABIN EXPERIENCE TEACHES COMPASSION

"The ultimate lesson all of us have to learn is unconditional love, which includes not only others but ourselves as well."

Elizabeth Kubler-Ross

In all our lives, there are hard lessons at times. How we react to these lessons and what we take away from them as a powerful truth to help us live better lives is a benchmark for us. It tells us whether we are evolving on our spiritual path or retreating. This lesson was a powerful one for me.

Cabin Experience Teaches Compassion

The giant redwood trees of the Santa Cruz Mountains in California have always given me a feeling that they provide healing.

I worked in San Francisco at Xerox Corporation, but still longed to spend time in the forests.

So, I found a little cabin to rent for weekends and vacations in the small village of Brookdale, inland from Santa Cruz. I loved the tall, majestic redwood trees.

Each weekend I eagerly drove south down the Pacific Coast highway to my safe, serene sanctuary. I looked forward to my weekly trips and I decided at one point to invite my new boyfriend to join me.

Unfortunately, Jeff was of a different temperament than I. I discovered he had outbursts of sparking, unpredictable anger. However, I assured myself that in time, his soul would become one of peace, his words kind and caring and that we would grow into "happily ever-after." I was Cinderella's sister.

I convinced myself that he needed more love. However, he claimed I caused his explosive anger. So, I tried to be nicer, kinder, more attentive to his every wish, and tiptoed gently around him. His verbal abuse grew into physical abuse.

On several occasions, I was hospitalized with significant injuries. I lied to the treating physicians, with flimsy stories to protect Jeff. I thought he would be appreciative and that he would change his ways. However, he did not.

One hellish weekend in my "heavenly cabin," he constantly ridiculed my thoughts and berated my feelings. When I did not react, he began enraged beatings.

Bloodied, bruised, and stripped of some of my clothing, my survival instincts finally took hold. I bolted from my cozy cabin, running blindly down a country dirt road, where to I did not know. All I knew was that I had to get away from his abusive actions.

Although barefoot, shredded clothing and without outer protection in cold drizzling rain, I ran for my life.

I did not feel the sharp rocks cutting my feet, the thorny bushes scraping my arms nor the mud splattering up from the road on my bare legs. My head pounded loudly. Each breath became a labored gasp. I didn't notice the blood streaming down my arms and dripping on the road as I stumbled blindly forward. Numb from shock and the freezing rains, I felt nothing.

Finally, exhausted and shaking uncontrollably, I sank to the ground. Excruciating pain emanated from my head. Frightening thoughts raced through my mind. My heart pounded wildly under the darkening night sky. I shook desperately as though releasing all my hopeful dreams about waiting for "the guy in my life to become the love of my life."

Time stretched endlessly, although it was probably only a few minutes. Dark rain clouds gathered overhead, and the forest became strange with eerie nighttime sounds that I barely noticed.

Huddled on the roadside of the forest, I grasped my knees to stop them from shaking violently. My teeth clattered against each other.

I tried to think of a safe place to go. I was too humiliated to seek any friend, wanting to protect them from his wild raging. My own cabin was unsafe. I could not think of anywhere to go.

Then I saw headlights in the distance coming up the road. A terrifying thought came to me. What if he used my car to search for me? He might kill me.

All my energy drained from me. I hid in nearby bushes until I saw that it was a sleek black Cadillac coming up the road. I leaped up and ran into the headlights, frantically waving my bloody arms and shouting, “Help me! Help me, please!”

The black Cadillac stopped. The electric windows rolled down. I rushed closer. To the well-dressed woman in the passenger seat, I pleaded, “Please, help me! Take me to a hospital!”

The woman passenger’s mouth gaped open. Her eyes widened with horror. I saw her face suddenly pale with shock and fear as she quickly blurted out, “We can’t get involved with domestic quarrels!” The electric windows quickly rolled up.

As the car sped away, I still remember my

face reflected in the window—beaten, blood-soaked, and swollen beyond recognition. But I *never* forgot her words. They haunted me for many years.

A while later, another car came along, and those good Samaritans took me to a hospital.

While they stitched me up in the emergency room, I told myself, "That woman taught me a great lesson today. I'm afraid of what happened to me, but that woman's fear was hidden so great, she would not consider helping another human being."

I silently vowed to myself, "I will never ignore someone in need of help. I will find a way to help them." And I have kept that promise.

I came to realize that I couldn't change anyone else. I realized I wasn't responsible for someone else's behavior. I learned healthier boundaries and created more loving support for myself. Those steps of self-protection drew more loving people into my life and have given me strength to take care of myself.

I thank the woman who gave me that

strident powerful lesson. I am grateful for that moment in the rain and for seeing the reflection of my face in that window. It has helped me in my commitment to be of loving service to others.

Many times, in ordinary days, a woman will ask to talk to me and bare her injured soul without even knowing my experience. I can easily be a caring, genuine, and supportive listener, and provide good referral places to help her make positive changes in her life.

It takes courage to make these changes. Even more important it takes incredible strength and resolve to master the fears that hold us prisoners in our minds.

To such incredible women who find the strength and resolve to make life sustaining changes I give my wholehearted support and am privileged to know them and honor them.

Although that night in the drizzling rain was a hard lesson for me, I realize that everything in our life has a blessing or a learning that will make us stronger and more loving if we are able to see our experiences as such.

I still say, “Hurrah for humans who teach us powerful lessons that help us be more caring human beings.”

What about you?

Has there been a trauma or hardship in your life and from it you became a wiser and stronger person?

INSIGHT from your life:

Insight from *Cabin Experience Teaches Compassion*

____

____

____

____

____

____

____

____

____

____

____

____

____

HURRAH FOR YOU!

Chapter Six

BED AND BREAKFAST MINISTRY

"Those who bring sunshine to the lives of others cannot keep it from themselves."

Sir James Barrie

Sometimes in life when we do not think we are doing our life's true purpose, though we may think we want to change our occupation, it may prove far better for us to change our attitude about our current role.

Bed and Breakfast Ministry

When I became an ordained minister, I was certain I had finally found my niche.

During most of my life, I was helping people and rendering caring suggestions to empower them.

Now, I had a sanction, a certification with the ordination and the tools to properly address humanity's situations.

It didn't last long, however. As I found myself without a home in which to live, the breakup with a long-time mate, without funds with which to take care of myself, and a bleak future concerning what would be happening to me.

I prayed in earnest that my path, in some way, would be made clear to me, and that in some way, I would be able to take care of myself.

Friends suggested that I move to my place in the mountains up north which had been a getaway and a place in which to hold retreats.

Since I had to make a living, they

encouraged me to turn it into a Bed and Breakfast. I reasoned that the idea might provide me with an expedient way to have a place to live, and it would be a safe: it would be a serene: and it would be a lovely place for travelers to take their vacations while providing a much-needed source of income for my living expenses.

But what troubled me was the picture I had of myself as I would be doing all the work myself. I had no funds to hire help. That would mean handling everything, including maintenance of the property. I was glad I was raised in a contractor's family and familiar with a lot of repairs. I also would be doing all the yard work, the marketing and promo output, taking all the calls, handling all the correspondences and office related work, responding to all booking requests, setting up the website, shopping for all supplies, all the laundry for guests, the daily food preparations, the guest services what would be a myriad of different needs and desires, and clean up from meals, and the cleaning of guest rooms as well as the main area.

And there was bound to be all the unexpected things that I would need to attend to in the solo running of the business. Considering all the negative work, I proceeded with the plan.

After four months of inspections, and bringing everything up to codes, creating a website, joining an association and stocking up on what would be guests' services and food supplies, I said my prayers that my new business would be successful.

I was completely married to the Bed and Breakfast. There was no time for holidays, time off, or personal time to restore my energy. At times people were checking in and out, back to back. At such times, I sprang into action and did double duty and somehow when I greeted new guests, I tried to make it look like I was leisurely waiting for hours just for their arrival between 4pm and 7pm like our brochure said. But often it was late evening when guests often arrived. So, I had to be flexible and understanding.

Two months passed by, and I asked in my prayers, what good did it do to get my ministerial degree if I was to be just a charwoman? I prayed that I could do my sacred work, which I had prepared to do.

Then something very special happened. I didn't really talk about it, but in my silent prayers I said that my heart's desire was to provide an important, loving service to the hearts, minds, and souls of people.

The message I received as a result of praying was that I should bless that which I was doing, and that all would be manifested. So, I changed my attitude and began to feel that what I was doing was important work—that being holding sacred space at my Bed and Breakfast for travelers to feel safe, comforted, and relaxed and able to enjoy their stay and the beauty of our magnificent mountain rim country. And to see myself being a kind, caring hostess. That became my important mission.

It happened almost immediately—visitors began sharing with me deep emotional pains and joys and inviting me into their hearts to share very personal thoughts and feelings.

My heart was delighted, and that is how I came to know that the spiritual work I was trained to do, came in the form of surroundings that made it easy and possible to feel comfortable. Guests felt at home in my place and felt blessed in the confidential things they safely shared with me.

I believe my slogan for the business was a good one. "Come as guests, stay as friends and return as family."

Hurrah for those travelers who felt my loving energy, in a safe space, to share of themselves in very personal and private ways.

Hurrah for me that I learned I could do my spiritual work anywhere I was, as long as my heart was open. I felt truly blessed.

What about you?

Have you ever felt that your job wasn't fulfilling your life purpose, and then discovered it was doable in your job?

INSIGHT from your life:

Insight from *Bed and Breakfast Ministry*

____

____

____

____

____

____

____

____

____

____

____

____

____

____

HURRAH FOR YOU!

Chapter Seven

CAMPER SAVED BY A DEER

"When we show our respect for other living things, they respond with respect for us."

Arapaho Indian saying

Often, when we need help, we don't often think about the animals on our planet coming to help us. This was a time when I was helped by an animal.

Camper Saved by a Deer

I pride myself on my ability to be comfortable in the outdoors. I could solo backpack in the wilderness, canoe alone in the lakes of Arizona, and thanks to my wilderness training, I could handle a seven-day trek in the Arizona mountains without fears or trepidation. I drew the line at rappelling alone, though, for dangling from a rope without hope of touching the ground safely kept me from venturing out by myself.

My solo trip through the Utah mountains, with a stop in a campsite wilderness area did not bother me in the least. I even found it a bit too civilized for my personal taste. I would rather choose the environmental wilderness areas where one never saw another human or a touch of trash or other leavings, nor a fire ring for campfires.

The environmental campsites were basic, without tables, hookups, or fire pits. That was fine for me, but still there were the "arranged" spots.

Oh well, one must make some concessions for the city slickers who like condo camping when traveling! I mused silently.

I settled for the last campsite—secluded and backing up to the forest. No one around, at least when I arrived.

"Good enough for me," I mumbled as I got out of my van and began pulling out my tent, and gear and set up my camp.

Soon, I had everything arranged "properly." I always set out an extra camp chair with jacket and hat on it—the old standby to make it appear as though there were two of us. Most likely, the public would figure it was a guy and not just myself.

The reddening sun began to slip behind the mountain ridge, the night folded into a jet-black backdrop with glittering diamond stars. My campfire died out, and I rolled into my sleeping bag. So lovely was the feeling of a down mummy bag. I slept soundly.

The next morning, I stoked the fire and beside its hot welcoming flames, I sipped my hot steaming coffee. While I dined on cold muesli with apple juice, I planned my activities for the day.

I wanted to explore down towards a lake some distance away but thought I would first take a jaunt up the mountain to the ridge, for an overview look. I would only be gone a half hour.

So, after dowsing my fire, I bounded out, leaving everything behind me. It crossed my mind about my Ten Essential daypack I always had ready for emergencies –but I thought I was only going to be gone a few minutes. *Not to worry,* I thought softly to myself.

The ridge rose sharply, and I had to bushwhack around several outcroppings as I wound my way around the stubborn rock facings.

Finally, I stood on top of the mountain to survey the landscape below. However, it was densely covered with barbed brush and thick trees. I could not see anything that might help me identify my location. Clearly my sense of direction was lost. I began to feel uneasy.

I started to walk fast, first in one direction, then the other direction. But all I accomplished was disappointment. By that time, it was almost late afternoon. Daylight was beginning to fade. A good portion of the day was spent in trying to get to the top; not to mention my futile attempts to determine exactly where I was.

I walked ever faster at that point. The cool late afternoon air made me shiver and I wished I had taken my jacket with me. The daylight was fading quickly, and long shadows prevented me from seeing any distance.

I panicked and began to rush through the trees. After a while, I became aware of my own footprints on the ground. I groaned. I had been going in circles.

My mind was clamoring, *it is getting dark. You must get back to camp now. It will be freezing tonight! Hurry! Hurry! Get going! But, where? I don't really know which direction to go.*

Then I recalled that one *must* sit down and still the mind when lost. I looked for a place to sit down in order to calm my racing thoughts and the stern accusations I was hurling against myself. I was feeling both foolish and scared.

I saw a log. I slumped down on it, closed my eyes, and I took a deep breath. Then I took another deeper breath. A feeling of calm filled me, then I slowly opened my eyes.

I was surprised to see a deer standing in a clearing, in front of a grouping of pine trees. I looked at the deer still somewhat stunned and said aloud, “Well, you are not lost. Clearly, you know where you are.”

Strangely, those words amused me. I gazed at the beauty of the deer. She was both magnificent and powerful. As we looked at each other, I sat still, and she stood motionless. Moments ticked past. I felt suspended in time.

Then, as though she had read my mind, she turned and slowly began angling down the side of the mountain.

I thought, *why not follow the deer?* The deer turned and looked back at me. I imagined it saying, “Why NOT follow me? I know where I am going.”

I followed the deer, down, down, down the mountainside. The deer did not run away but kept a distance from me that encouraged me to walk faster and follow at a respectful pace.

It was growing dark and cold by then. Night would soon be here. Soon, the sounds of gurgling water awakened my senses. It became increasingly louder as we approached the stream. The deer remained in front of me until she reached the stream.

Then she turned, looked back at me as if to say, "You're all right now." I could barely recognize her outlined body as she effortlessly jumped the stream and disappeared into a thicket.

I stooped down, drank a few handfuls of water from the stream and reassured myself that all streams lead downward. So, if I followed the stream, I should eventually come to something and it most likely would be the highway into the campsite.

I followed the stream in the dimming twilight, increasing my pace as fast as I could without danger of tripping. Finally, as night was falling, I saw the highway, and I breathed a sigh of relief. When my feet hit the asphalt, my heart silently leaped with joy.

Soon a car approached, and I flagged it down. It was a sheriff's car. I was thankful to see them, and I asked the shiny badges to give me a ride. I did not notice the seriousness in their faces as they queried why I was afoot in the area.

"I just need a lift, to get back to my campsite," I told them. Then I added a bit sheepishly, "I misjudged my day walk direction."

"Not today," said the heavy-set one with a rounded Santa Claus-style face. He huffed a bit as he continued to speak, "It's too dangerous. No one is allowed in. The area is sealed off. We are evacuating everyone."

I felt amused and thought it was a kind of mistaken power struggle. *What had happened? A deer got loose or something?* I amused myself with the thought.

He continued, "There's a prisoner from the state prison. We think he is in this area."

"Oh, please!" I pleaded. "I must get to my campsite. Can't you let me get my van and camp stuff?" I did not think anything serious could happen in such a beautiful, serene mountain paradise area. *The suspect probably had been arrested for petty theft or some such minor infraction of the law, but I said nothing aloud.*

The men agreed to escort me to my

campsite, but they told me to make it quick, and they drove speedily to my campsite. The campsite appeared as I had left it, but I said nothing as we got out and I started collecting my camping gear.

"Hey, look here," the lean and tall one said. "Tracks. He's been here." He reached in the car for his radio and another gun.

Suddenly I felt fear racing through me. The hairs on the back of my neck stood up and a cold chill ran down my spine. I shoved everything into my van as fast as I could, without care or thinking where anything was going.

"What did he do?" I shouted. My teeth were chattering.

"He is up for murder," came the reply from the rotund man with a badge.

I couldn't move fast enough to suit myself. My legs were wobbly, and my hands shook as they grabbed whatever they could find. The thought of being murdered in my campsite dashed my idea of having security by way of putting a second chair out at the firepit, gave me no hint of security.

The sheriff's deputy helped me load my camping things. In a few minutes which seemed to last hours, we finally had my things packed ready to go. One of the men offered to drive me out. I humbly and gratefully accepted the offer.

I probably couldn't have focused on the winding road anyway. Besides, my legs would not stop shaking. It didn't really matter, as my hands were shaking too.

We got to the highway in whirlwind time. I was driven to a small town nearby. I was relieved to have them with me, or more accurately, me with them and back into a more civilized environment.

That night, I stayed in a local motel, grateful for the city surroundings. I would not say I slept soundly, but I did think a lot about how I took the walk that got me lost, how the deer led me down to the stream, which the stream led me to the highway and the sheriff. If I hadn't left camp for that little walk, would I have been at my campsite when the prisoner came through the area? I shuddered!

Sometimes when we feel we are doomed; we are possibly being saved from something far more devastating.

I was thankful for my unexpected angelic care. And this time, it was possible that my angel was disguised as a deer. But, most certainly, it showed me hurrah for humans who save me from harm, in this case, the hurrah came in the form of a deer. Even our animal friends offer help as a hurrah for lost humans!

What about you?

Was there a time when you saw an animal in the wild and you felt it was communicating something to you or that its presence was a gift to you?

<u>INSIGHT from your life:</u>

Insight from *Camper Saved by a Deer*

____

____

____

____

____

____

____

____

____

____

____

____

____

HURRAH FOR YOU!

Chapter Eight

GRANDFATHER DAVID HOPI ELDER

"No act of kindness, no matter how small, is ever wasted."

Aesop

I have revered our Native Traditional people, their way of life, their philosophy, their prayerful ways, and especially their respect for Mother Earth.

This story shows how easy it is to misconstrue things, even with the best of intentions and kindness of heart.

Grandfather David, Hopi Elder

The Hopi village in northern Arizona, on the reservation, is a sacred place. I was privileged to meet the Hopi Elder, Grandfather David, when I visited Second Mesa with my Cherokee Medicine Man friend.

I took with me grapefruit from our trees. The occasion was in the wintertime when the Hopi Land didn't receive much fruit. Also, I was told this Hopi Elder liked parrot feathers. I had a collection of them, and I took some with us. I'm from the old school that dictates when visiting someone, we should take a gift.

The modest way in which these Native Traditional people live is simple, and yet inspiring.

Upon arriving, we sat on their earthen floor with my Indian friend and he began to talk about the Old Ways. I recognized that respect was being shared among them, and I listened quietly as they talked about earth signs and the needs of their people.

It was a memorable visit, imprinting in my mind the joyful children, the meager dwellings, and the preparations they were making for the next traditional plaza dance. "White eyes" (which referred to us, the white man) could attend such dances, but not many of the other dances that were sacred only to members of their clan.

During our visit, I was allowed to record on tape some of the songs that Grandfather David sang to us. Apparently, they were not the sacred Kiva songs they sang only among themselves.

Following my return home, I became busy with daily matters, and the trip to Hopi land and Grandfather David became a historical memory.

One day, a friend called and asked, "Did you hear that Grandfather David died?"

I was in shock. "We just saw him a few months ago, and he looked well. How do you know he died?" I asked.

My friend replied, "Well, we were just up there, and during our visit we talked to his wife. She told us about his passing."

I couldn't believe it. He was such a revered Elder*! His wife should know if he isn't still alive,* I reasoned.

Then I wondered what I could do to honor his memory. I began an ardent campaign and I contacted everyone I knew who might have known about him or that would appreciate being informed concerning his death. I gave the tape to a couple who owned a bookstore, and they made copies and sold them to all those customers who wanted to listen to "The Last Songs of Grandfather David."

We all began to send prayers up to Hopi Land, honoring Grandfather David.

About three weeks later, another friend telephoned me and said, "Hey, I thought you told us that Grandfather David was dead. Well, we were up on Second Mesa and visited their village and saw him walking around. He is just fine. He is NOT dead!"

I was stunned. How could this be? I telephoned my first friends who told me about his demise, and I asked them about the latest revelation. "I said, "You told me my friend Grandfather David Palheco, died, didn't you?"

There was a silence on the phone. Then slowly she replied, "No, we meant Grandfather David Mononge."

"What!" I choked out. "This is incredible. I thought there was only one Grandfather David at Second Mesa."

"Well," said my friend, "That is probably true now that there is only one Grandfather David."

My heart sank. What had I done! Immediately I began contacting the long list of people I had called formerly. To my heartfelt relief, all them were most delighted and thanked me for the updated good news.

Only one couple was upset to learn the news of his death was not true—the couple who ran the store, and who had sold many copies of the "Last Songs of Grandfather David." It had been one of their best sellers!

My mate at the time said, "Don't worry. By the time you get this "Grandfather David is dead" message all straightened out, it probably WILL be true.

This story is to honor our native elder people who live on Second Mesa in Hopi Land. The Hopi traditional ways honor Mother Earth and all human beings.

Hurrah for these traditional humans,

they inspire us to honor our elders, whether they are alive or in spirit form.

What about you?

Can you think of a time when you wholeheartedly shared information you thought was correct, then learned it was not, and tried to correct the situation?

INSIGHT from your life:

Insight from *Grandfather David, Hopi Elder*

____

____

____

____

____

____

____

____

____

____

____

____

____

HURRAH FOR YOU!

Chapter Nine

IN PLAIN SIGHT

"Nothing is impossible to a willing heart."

John Heywood

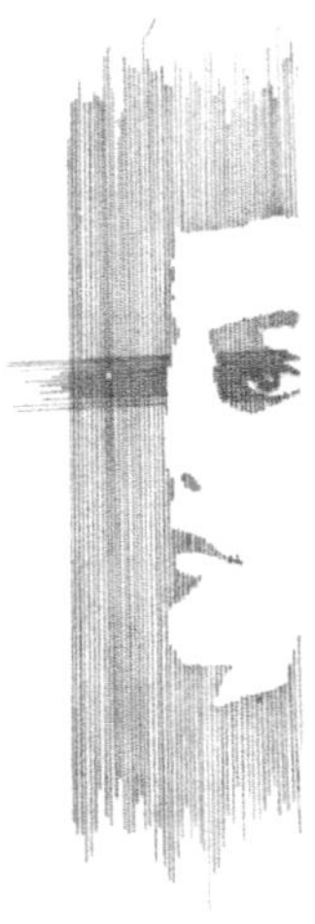

There are times in our lives when we are blinded by our own perceptions of how things are. This story taught me that I did not see what was directly in front of me. And it helped me appreciate another person's way of life

In Plain Sight

It is said that if you want to hide something, hide it in plain sight. I think this story demonstrates that quite nicely.

My friend Cheryl invited me to join her for lunch at her friend Patti's home. I understood Patti was a talented pianist and that she would play an arrangement for us.

I have always admired musical talent, and I looked forward to meeting her friend Patti.

We arrived at Patti's home and in silence, I mentally admired her beautiful front yard. It was landscaped with so many varieties of stunning flowers, rich in colors and design. Amidst the flower arrangements were edible salad fixings. I considered it a nice combination.

From the earth-hugging pansies and the sturdy sky-reaching pink and white stalks of hollyhocks, everything was as though Better Homes and Gardens had used her property for a magazine cover. The walk up to her front door was magical.

Cheryl turned and whispered to me, "She

does all the gardening herself. I can't imagine where she finds the time."

Patti welcomed us warmly with a beaming smile and a warm-hearted hug.

As we followed her into the dining area, I noticed everything was so perfectly placed. Nothing was out of place. Except for things arranged on the walls, the room appeared quite bare. It seemed rather sterile for my taste. I wondered if she was one of the perfectionists who always avoided mislaying things. No room for loose flexibility? I wondered.

We sat in the dining room, with large picture windows that looked out on an equally cared for back yard. How does she keep it so nice? I wondered.

Sipping freshly made lemonade, we waited for Patti to serve our lunch. She insisted she had everything under control.

She had prepared homemade soup, garden gathered salad fixings and a chicken Kiev. Dessert was cherry cobbler. Patti surely had a talent. She had made everything from scratch.

After dinner, we retired to the living room, where stood a gleaming baby grand piano. Patti glided effortlessly onto the piano bench and began to play. I felt I was in the presence of a master pianist. She rivaled many of the professional concert pianists who I had been privileged to hear perform. Our private concert lasted an hour.

As we left, I thanked our hostess for a delightful afternoon. When Cheryl and I reached the car, I spoke about my puzzlement.

"Cheryl, Patti seems to be a lovely lady, but why is everything so restrictive, and almost bare in most of the rooms, and lined up as they are in a row?"

Cheryl looked very surprised and replied, "You mean you couldn't tell?"

"Couldn't tell what?" I said with a hint of defensiveness in my tone.

"Well, Annemarie, Patti is blind. Still, she is an accomplished pianist, a great gardener, a perfect entertainer, and best of all, one of my best friends."

I gasped, partly from the realization that I had not detected she was blind. She had hidden it so well. And there was my insensitivity in not noticing what one noble person did to make her environment workable- to live and share her beauty–inside and outside.

I thought, hurrah for this blind beautiful human being who showed me how to see more clearly things in plain sight!

What About You?

Was there a time when you thought someone was a certain way, and then you discovered that person had a handicap you had not been aware of when you met them?

INSIGHT from your life:

Insight from *In Plain Sight*

HURRAH FOR YOU!

Chapter Ten

COTTONWOOD TREE HEART

"Nobody has ever measured, not even poets, how much the heart can hold."

Zelda Fitzgerald

Nature has its own brand of beauty, but this was a time, it went far beyond my expectations of enjoying its natural beauty. It held a secret that I discovered.

The Cottonwood Tree with a Heart

I stood beside a busy two-lane highway as semi-trucks roared past and streams of vehicles followed in a hurry. The rushing traffic was matched with a high decibel barrage of noise.

My friend and I had driven north from Arizona Rim Country and stopped at Ash Springs, a little roadside stop along Highway 93, near the National Wildlife Refuge Pahranagat in Nevada. The Refuge, settled mostly by ranchers, got its name from the water source, which is believed to be part of a vast aquifer underlying much of eastern Nevada.

The fuel at the little convenience store/gas station was high—but the RV overnight rate was most reasonable—with electric, water and sewer. Adjacent pastures with grazing cattle, felt very bucolic.

Beside the store stood a giant old cottonwood tree. How can one determine its age? I know one can tell by the number of rings of its trunk. In a good growth year, the rings are far apart; in trying years, the rings are close together. One local said it takes several people linking hands to surround the tree.

The tree was a masterful piece of growth, in modest surroundings. It had stood the test of time. Its massive trunk and outstretched limbs, reaching to the sky, fascinated me. It was too large to hug, too big to photograph from top to bottom. It had a huge hollow in its trunk.

At dusk, I walked towards it to get a closer look.

To my surprise, there was a heart shaped rock in its hollow. I almost felt I invaded its personal space. But my curiosity got the best of me, and I picked up the rock and to my amazement, there lay an envelope with clear printing on it, "*To My Beloved.*"

My head began to spin. Who would write such a letter? Was this the secret spot where two lovers exchanged communications? Were they old or young? How long had this been going on? How long had it been in this tree?

Although I admit I was *very* curious, I restrained myself and did not open the envelope. I gently put the stone back, turned and walked towards the little convenience store.

Inside the tiny store, crowded with many snack and sundry items for hurried travelers, I found Sandy, who has lived there many years and knows a bit about the area.

She said Ash Spring has hot mineral springs, but not "the kind that is stinky." The Native Americans who used to live in the area used the springs. She told me the old cottonwood tree is at least 500 years old and that the owners of the little store were going to cut it down because they wanted to build a another structure there and it was in the way.

She also said Las Vegas was after the area around the springs for water and she wasn't happy about giving "them water for who knows what silly use."

It seems that years ago, the swimming hole at Ash Springs was closed by the BLM Land and not open to public due to safety concerns.

My heart felt pangs of sadness. This tree had endured for many years, and now to bite the dirt for another building? I felt a sad longing, too, for the lovers that left notes to each other under the rock in the "heart of this tree."

This hot spring was an oasis for both prehistoric and historic travelers. Petroglyphs (prehistoric rock art) were carved on over sixty boulders in this area. The most common animals depicted on these historic rocks are bighorn sheep, coyotes or dogs and snakes.

Native Americans used it intensively as a camp during the last 1,000 years spring and summer.

Also, there were other archaeological remains and artifacts that revealed the daily life of the ancient ones who lived near this hot spring.

I shuddered. What a historic piece in this dusty, dry desert land. But there are many cottonwood trees in the area; and from my wilderness training, I know when backpacking, cottonwood trees are a sure sign of water source. If you camp overnight though, it's best not to sleep under these trees. They store water in their limbs and sometimes become water-logged and drop their limbs.

Hopefully, you will not be sleeping under such limb! And if you need to start a fire to keep warm, the cottonwood is good material for the bow and drill fire-making materials.

Cottonwood is a soft wood but its bright green leaves in the hot summertime show you there is water nearby. They have some unique and helpful properties. Since they grow very quickly, they make great windbreak tree lines.

Their trunk hollows provide shelter for small animals and twigs and bark provide food. Initially, their soft wood burns hot and quickly. They have heart-shaped leaves that arrange in an alternate pattern on the branches. The buds are covered with a sticky antimicrobial resin, protecting the tree.

The buds tend to grow through the winter and turn into leaves in early spring, grow into green fruit and in May, flood the landscape with their "look alike" winter snowstorm. Their name was derived from the white fluffy "cotton balls" that float in the air.

They produce male and female parts on separate trees. Female trees produce tiny red blooms in Springtime, then create masses of seeds with a cotton like covering, which provide a delightful fragrance for several days.

Cottonwoods have lustrous, bright green foliage in summer which turns to brilliant yellow in the fall. They are members of the poplar family.

Settlers and early Americans used them for lightweight construction material and tools. Native American used all parts of them. Trunks made dugout canoes; bark fed horses and made medicinal tea. The Omaha Indians made a dye from the leaf buds and made their Sacred Pole from trunks. Both humans and animal ate their sprouts and inner bark. The Apaches considered it a symbol of the sun. Some northern Mexican tribes thought cottonwoods dealt with the afterlife, and they used the boughs in funeral rituals. Traditionally, cottonwood was used by Cherokees for rheumatism, sores, colic, tooth aches and more. Iroquois used the bark to kill worms, for arthritis, skin sores, and as laxative.

In Arizona, we are familiar with the hand carved Kachina dolls, masks, and ceremonial objects created by the Hopi, Pueblo and Navajo tribes. The Plains Indians made their sacred poles from Cottonwood branches and trunks.

As a healing agent, Cottonwoods have many uses. One favorite one is to soak them in oil to make salves. This salve has a fragrant aroma and used to relieve sore muscles, joint pain, bruised limb and good for minor cuts and bug bites. Salves can last for a very long time as a preservative without becoming rancid. A tincture of this makes a good expectorant for mucus from bronchial infections. The tree is of the Salicaceae family along with willow and aspen. They reduce arthritic pain.

When you are in the Southwest, take time to admire this beautiful and useful tree. And who knows, maybe you will find a little note tucked in its hollow for you too.

This old Cottonwood tree brought two special people many messages of love. The stories that this tree could tell might be a legacy of love.

It was truly a special spot that celebrated hurrah for humans!

What about you?

Have you come across something shared by two lovers and felt you had intruded upon their privacy? Did it touch you? Did you leave it there out of respect for the lovers?

INSIGHT from your life:

Insight from *Cottonwood Tree Heart*

HURRAH FOR YOU!

Chapter Eleven

LEARNING TO BE AMERICAN AGAIN

"The supreme happiness of life is the conviction that we are loved; loved for ourselves, or rather loved in spite of ourselves."

Victor Hugo

This story shows how when we humans are prejudiced against a group of people, we cannot see their good qualities. When the disfavor is against us, we may act in regretful ways. Luckily, I had a chance to turn that label on 'Americans' around.

Learning to be American Again

Traveling in Italy while on my honeymoon, I wanted a place in which to enjoy dinner off the beaten tourist roads—something more authentic—where the *real* locals gathered. That was during a time when "The Ugly American" image was not easy to hide. We were not appreciated by many European people.

My new husband and I hesitantly got into one of the infamous Italian taxi cabs. Italians are known for their bravado as drivers. Our snappy cab driver assured us he had "just the place," and we brashly jetted through the cobblestone streets in high gear.

As we arrived at this "locals only know this place," he let us out "for the evening," he said. I didn't think it would take five hours for us to eat a dinner, but dismissed my trepidation telling myself that I needed to go with the flow—be a local Italian who took time to appreciate a dinner.

Night was falling and the sky was turning dark. I felt I was "in the dark about this adventure" and pretty much stayed in the dark the whole evening.

Our cabbie dropped us off at what looked like impressive ancient stone walls and tiled roof. The entry was overgrown with tenacious climbing vines and dark forest-green leaves.

I wrestled with the heavy wood planked door, which groaned as I opened it revealing a dimly lit room filled with laughter and music. The sound of excited foreign conversations filled the air. Definitely "*Italian only*" spoken here!

As our eyes became accustomed to the change in light, I noticed the walls were lined with little cave-like spaces, and people sat on roughhewn heavy plank benches with a single candle burning dimly in a wine bottle dripping colored wax over many other candles that had burned in the bottles. The uncovered sturdy wooden tables were filled with brown bag lunches, and many bottles of wine along with bread and cheeses.

All eyes glanced up and their conversations fell to low murmurs as we were ushered down a seemingly endless corridor. I could feel their eyes boring into me. Some people pointed at us, some just stared. We were obviously out of our element. Their hushed voices followed us. "English. English!"

was the only phrase I could interpret.

I sighed with relief at being considered "English" and not "American." I silently chided myself for hiding my secret embarrassment for forsaking my nationality and hiding behind another one they considered more agreeable.

There was a certain false pride smiling inside me in that I had been thought of as English, but even as I breathed deeply and stood a little straighter, I still stung from the unnoticed label "Ugly American."

We settled down at one of the empty tables, and immediately a bottle of wine was placed on our table. As we had not brought a "sack dinner," we began to sip our wine.

Suddenly, several other diners came by and put breads, cheeses, and fruits on our table and energetically extoled blessings upon us before retiring back to their own space. We nodded our thanks.

Somehow during that evening, we were able to learn that we were at some old catacombs which had been converted into useable space for locals to come and enjoy time together.

I sat there in surprising cloudy comfort. There was the part of being in another subculture and being accepted somehow (albeit through a little deception on my part—illusion on theirs); and the flavors surrounding the Italians, warm and charming and energetically passionate.

Thankfully, when we had finished all the wine and food we could eat, we were able to tell someone we wanted a cab, to return home. Surprisingly, the same cabbie came and picked us up. How did he know? I guessed those Italians had one big family that knew everyone.

Arriving home, I thought about my reticence in admitting I was an American and of my silent delight at being thought to be English. I did not feel very good about myself for hiding who I was, who I am.

That feeling stayed with me many years until I returned to Europe on another trip after my husband's death.

At that time, I was backpacking around Europe and stopped at a Gast Haus in Germany for a snack and one of their famous beers. Drinking in Germany is a very respectable pastime.

As luck would have it, I managed to pick a place that was a hangout for the locals of that village. As I entered, I suddenly became aware that I was *again* the "only American." Everyone else was very German. I approached the bar with reticence and dread, quietly ordering, "Ein bier," and stole a quick glance at the other patrons.

We stared at each other, the Germans and me. They spoke no English, I spoke only "Ein bier!" We offered the perfunctory nod and then retreated to our tiny personal spaces in front of us.

After what seemed an interminable time (probably only five minutes,) the door opened and in walked a Frenchman, who we all discovered, spoke perfect English *and* perfect German!

Hooray, I thought. I asked him to interpret for me and I turned to the Germans seated closest to me and asked, "What do you think of Americans now?"

Several responded vehemently. French relayed to me, "Bah! Rich Americans. They can afford to do anything they want! They buy everything they desire; they travel anywhere they want, and they have plenty of money to do everything."

I was stunned. I thought for a moment and then asked, "How much does the average German make a year?"

In response, Frenchy interpreted for me, "How much do YOU make per year?" They weren't giving an inch. I truthfully revealed my year's earnings. And to my surprise, their faces revealed shock with disdain.

"Bah, we do not work for that!" they exclaimed, through my French interpreter.

This was now my segue. I explained that in America, you could own a baby grand piano and live in a studio apartment. You could own an expensive home and never travel. Or you could do what I was doing and spend your money traveling modestly so you could experience other cultures.

I explained that we didn't have a certain social status to attain before we made our choices. I heard that in Germany they were very socio-economic status conscious, and you wouldn't be owning a piano unless you had an appropriate home in which to display it, etc.

An enthusiastic barrage of questions and chatter began roaring in the room. They insisted that I have one more beer. I protested. They ordered. Soon, there were ten beers lined up before me. I had barely finished my first.

We continued to exchange "real-people thoughts and ideas" and to dissipate illusions we had about each other. The conversations we shared that day dissolved preconceived stereotyped ideas of what Americans are-and are not.

On that day I made friendships that went beyond borders. On that day, I was pleased to show others of the freedom we have in America to make choices. On that day I was *proud* I chose to call myself an *American.*

I exclaimed, "Hurrah for us humans—of many different cultures!"

What about you?

Was there a time when you didn't acknowledge your nationality and later found a way to tell others you were proud of your nationality? How did you feel?

INSIGHT from your life:

Insight from Learning to be American Again

HURRAH FOR YOU!

Chapter Twelve

A GIFT GREATER THAN WATER

"The less effort, the faster and more powerful you will be."

Bruce Lee

Signing up for a seven-day trek into the wilderness was one leap of confidence for me. I was the only woman, and I wondered about my ability to keep up the pace set by our leader. But I was to discover an unexpected gift from taking the risk to go on the trek. Gifts usually come as a by-product of what our intended purpose is. I found this to be true.

A Gift Greater Than Water

I stood beside the gurgling Campaign Creek in the Superstition Wilderness, near an 1800s pioneer homestead which is now a survival school. I had risked signing up for their seven-day survival trek.

I breathed in deeply and thought to myself, *just take one moment at a time, you will be fine. Don't worry. You will survive. You survived the accident and the traumatic brain injury. You survived metastasized cancer. You survived your mates. You many betrayals. You survived your life –so far! So, be here now!*

I eyed my blue Jansport external frame backpack. It bulged with the essentials for this seven-day survival trek in the Arizona Superstition Mountains, led by renowned wilderness instructor Peter Bigfoot. I had taken some trainings earlier on wilderness plants and doctoring that year, however, I wondered what survival challenges I would face. Fear and excitement raced through me.

Reevis Mountain Survival School was nestled in a valley 14 rugged miles off the main road from Roosevelt Lake. Reevis Mountain operated off the grid with 100 fruit trees, lush organic garden, solar cells, stone shower house, and hand-built teepees, "yurpees" (a hybrid design of Yurt and Teepee) and cabins.

Ten eager trekkers lined up their packs on the ground outside the house for inspection. Leader Peter Bigfoot systematically sorted through each pack, tossing out what he deemed "nonessentials." The nine men passed, although piles of miscellaneous items now lay discarded on the ground before them.

The last pack was mine, the token female. Amused, Bigfoot quickly tossed my toothpaste, deodorant, fingernail file and first-aid kit. I humbly conceded they *might* pollute the earth's rivers. But when he seized my Tampax, I cried out in alarm.

"Oh, all right," he chuckled with sly amusement. "I'll give you this one. Now get repacked and let's move out. You're allowed one quart of water and one pound of food. The rest you'll forage for."

Some of the classes I attended earlier that year were to prepare for this trek focused on using edible plants as medicine and food. The Wilderness Doctoring class I took in case my car broke down and I got stranded someday.

But *this* adventure felt different. This put classroom instruction on the line for seven days and seven nights. It sounded daunting. But I reminded myself I had known daunting before.

The other male hikers easily shifted their backpacks and fell in line behind the lanky leader who strode off effortlessly down the trail.

I slung my now lighter pack over my back and scurried to catch up. Peter Bigfoot's size fourteen feet along with his long leg, posed a challenge.

Bigfoot made his own leather shoes with Pirelli tire treads for soles. A self-made mountain man, he also had a penchant for gentle healing practices and innovative survival ideas. And he gained his nickname Bigfoot from the size fourteen shoes.

I saw the other men's facial expressions as we left Reevis Mountain Community house, an original pioneer homesteaded structure. I imagined they thought, *she's going to slow us down. We will probably end up carrying her. Why did she join us?*

I felt uncomfortable, but said nothing, determined to keep up. I commended myself that I had signed up for this challenge.

We picked up the trail leading out of Reevis Mountain on a bright Arizona day. Sunlight streamed through the yellow-green sycamore trees. The creek babbled alongside the marked trail. Birds chirped noisily. We followed Peter in single file. I brought up the rear.

How to keep up with them, I puzzled. Then I experimented. I pulled my hat down around my eyes and focused only on the boots of the man in front of me and my own steps taken behind him. Soon I lost track of all else except my small world of two feet in step. I fell into a very hypnotic, easy cadence, and time passed quickly. Soon I heard “Break stop!”

We slid our packs off our backs and shed our hiking boots in order to dangle our feet in the icy cold stream. A few men teased me about tagging along. Our break was short.

Soon, we climbed up a steep hill. There were no comments then concerning my having lagged behind. Very little conversation ensued for most of the day. I was grateful for the silence, as multiple conversations hurt my head. I still couldn't easily sort background and foreground sounds, a residual from the traumatic brain injury.

For several hours we kept a steady pace along a high ridge. The vast mountain range vistas were breathtaking. Then, we dropped down into a valley with lush thick brush.

When we reached a shady spot for an afternoon break, I noticed grape vines winding up in the trees. I pulled off a few leaves and layered them in my socks. They felt cool and soothing against my skin. Several men tried it also. I gathered more grape leaves to use later in a salad.

Peter commented, "Good, Annie. Glad you remembered." I realized then how impressionable I felt with people in authority. How, historically, I sometimes gave them more power than deserved—my parents, the priests, and nuns of early years; my mate, the Buddhist monk; the list was endless. Now I admired his knowledge of the wilderness. Something to explore about my thinking, like peeling the many layers of an onion.

We saw watercress and cattails. *Yummy*, I

thought. Soon we harvested them for dinner. Earlier in the day, we stopped and culled wild oats from the hillsides for hot cereal in mornings. Tea made of inner bark of a willow tree quickly cured my headache.

I noticed how our landscape took care of our needs. It was a comforting feeling to realize that nature could provide our needs, and it was true that as we made friends with our environment, we could know its natural uses for our own use.

Several days later, we plodded along the lower desert range. The sun seemed to beat down on us mercilessly. Our water supply was very low. In Arizona, dehydration sets in fast. We needed to reach the next water source soon.

I was thinking about what my mate said before I left home, “I wish I could do something to make sure you’re safe, but I’m not a hiker nor an outdoors person.”

“Don’t worry about me,” I said, with assurance. “We’ve got the best leader in the west. I’ll be fine.”

When our group sat down for a break, I

noticed a glint of something shiny out of the corner of my eye, in a distant Palo Verde tree. I walked over to investigate. To my astonishment, I spied a large canteen wedged in between the branches near the trunk.

It was the old-fashioned kind, metal canteen with fabric side liners with a wide webbed strap. I pulled it out and shook it. More than half full of water! I brought it back to our group to share. As I opened the canteen, a chill ran up my spine. On the side of the canteen, my mate's surname was printed in bold block-style lettering! It stunned me. I could not explain the surprising appearance of the canteen in that tree, way out there in the middle of the desert and the fact that I saw it when we were a low on drinking water. And to add to the mystery, his name was on the side of the canteen.

But I often receive help in mysterious ways, and now it has happened in a remote desert. I then thought about the miracle of my own recovery from a very bleak life prognosis and how I had received help from many different people and in surprising circumstances.

My personal experiences reinforced a

deeper knowledge that we have everything needed to take care of our needs. We just need not to worry nor hurry. Just trust the process. Take one step at a time and believe what is set before me will strengthen me and enlighten my life. Bring it on!

Like the I-Ching says, Change has two symbols Danger and Opportunity. I chose opportunity. That was the day that danger of low water brought an opportunity to remind me that there is a greater power providing us with unseen help. It is another beautiful story of hurrah for humans.

What about you?

Can you recall a time when you were in dire need and unexplainable help came in an unexpected way? What did you learn from that?

INSIGHT from your life:

Insight from *The Trek—A Gift Greater than Water*

HURRAH FOR YOU!

Chapter Thirteen

EARTH ANGELS

"Love cures people-
both the ones who give it
and the ones who receive it."

Karl Menninger

This story is about receiving generous help that is offered from humans that care greatly. Usually I was the person offering help to others. But this experience gave me a greater understanding and appreciation of receiving help for myself.

Earth Angels

They are lurking in the edges of night. They travel in the bright of day. So, how will we recognize these messengers of the divine, since we don't notice their fluttering wings and the horns that loudly proclaim their arrivals. They do not come in bands, swooshing their feathers audibly. They forget to let their feet float above the ground. And they do not leave bushes burning, nor even a thin slice of waters parting. We cannot recognize them from whispered life-changing pronouncements and the revelations that make us shiver.

No, these earth angels are more grounded in the place we walk upon. They hide their true extraordinary identity in the ordinary day. You will have to trust your feelings more than your eyes, except for the acts by which you will recognize beyond the shadows of your doubt, that they truly come from the divine. You will have to stop your own racing thoughts if but for a moment to catch them in the act of being divine.

There is a way you can easily identify these bundles of blessings. Just look around your everyday places. That is where you will find them. And without any heavenly fanfare music, they bring the sounds of helpfulness and healing into the circumstances of your day.

These earth angels are the ones responsible for making your day a little lighter, a little brighter because of what they do.

Perhaps you are having a few tough "earth days." Perhaps your friend down your road just died from a sudden heart attack, and another dear friend accidently drove into a tree killing her; then maybe the next day you receive word from your family that your beloved brother took his own life, and you can't understand that, since you have loved life so much that you spent two and a half years healing your own cancer. And neither can your other brothers and sisters. None have resolved the death of your father and your other sister.

But the day gets even tougher. The same day your heart-buddy is standing in front of you and he goes into a seizure/stroke, something undeterminable to your untrained medical eyes. The color of gray on his face propels you to call 911 emergency; and the paramedics come and take him to the hospital, where he has spent his time in the critical care unit. You are dazed but keep numbly focused on the urgent matters for your friend and running your business.

However, now your family is calling, and a few minutes later, you stuff some clothes in a bag and head out for another state for your brother's funeral, returning a few days later to pick up some of the pieces of your life. Your life seems to be in pieces, and not at peace. It is a whirlwind of sadness and tragedy.

Now, this is where the earth angels appear. Because they are pragmatic, you will see them reach out and give you a hug. Then they say something—not the usual platitudes that we other humans give when we don't know what to say to people who are in trouble.

They say something that has meaning. However, you are not sure what since you are still dazed; but your soul body instantly greets their words with a sigh of relief. Relief because it knows real help is finally present.

Earth angels spring into action! Yes, I said action. They do not sit about and radiate their beauty. Yes, they *can* radiate their splendor making you feel better; but they are much more practical than just "lilting around."

You will recognize these earth angels because they will be on your floor, scrubbing it. They will be in your kitchen cleaning it. Or that toilet and shower you couldn't even stand to get near. Yes, there they are bravely, boldly and beautifully sanding it back down to its initial structure, layer by layer.

They will be talking to the other people in your everyday life on your behalf, just to give you a break, so that you can begin to restore your own inner core. They will be taking out your garbage, doing your laundry and shopping to give you a break and support. They know intuitively what practical things will make your ordinary day with its most extraordinary challenges feel a bit safer from the unreal events that just took place.

They come as a reminder that we are never alone. Even more than the "heart-home" feeling they bring with their love—in-action deeds; they bring that comforting feeling that things will be all right, and that we are going to be all right too.

They may add a mix of stories or a slice of laughter, to keep a portion of our resource center open and viable. But, most of all, they take their divine hands and put them to work for us. Seemingly insurmountable tasks that we perform everyday are taken over by them.

They seem to know the secret concerning our giving them permission to help nurture our reserves, so that we can take back our life, in whatever condition it might be. They know that we will be able to rebuild, in whatever fashion the great divine has in store for us.

Oddly enough, they do not preach any religion, any creed or doctrine to which they might like to convert us. They do not expect payment or credit. They are selfless and incredibly powerful in their determination to help. Not rescue us but help us. With their wizard eyes, they can see beyond the current circumstances and within the heart of us.

They provide us with insights concerning our own intrinsic beauty and magnificence without it sounding like flattery. Their genuine remarks register deep in our heart where we thought only we could go. That which we feel with them is beyond blessings. It is an odd mixture of a human halo and the hand of God.

Others may try to convince us that these earth angels are not real. But no one can take from us the knowing of how our heart felt when they arrived to make our life safer, more beautiful and peaceful as a result of their loving actions.

Wild horses cannot drive from our minds the memory of how they turned our extraordinary circumstances into a reasonable and ordinary restored and peaceful day.

And when they turn to go, you may then notice that subtle but powerful glow that comes from their smiling eyes, as their gaze falls upon you, a little slice of their light, to stay and keep you company. It is a hint that you were right to recognize them as an earth angel.

So, when you have an extremely extraordinary and challenging event in your life, take a moment to look around, as you will most likely find that an earth angel has suddenly appeared near you.

And, who knows, maybe that earth angel will be the same one who came to help me. Hurrah for our earth angels disguised as humans!

What about you?

Was there a time in your life when things were going very wrong and you were overwhelmed? Then suddenly help came to you in many ways, and it felt incredible? How gracious were you in receiving help from others?

INSIGHT from your life:

Insight from *Earth Angels*

HURRAH FOR YOU!

Chapter Fourteen

THE TRUCKER ACCIDENT

"When I dare to be powerful—
to use my strength in the service of my vision,
then it becomes less and less important
whether I am afraid."

Andre Lorde

In our everyday living, we may come upon an opportunity to take a risk and do something for a stranger that will change his life forever and your life will be blessed. Take the risk and follow your heart.

The Trucker Accident

A misty rain was falling as I drove north on the two-lane highway to the Arizona Rim Country from Phoenix, Arizona. I usually enjoyed that drive because the elevation of the landscape changed from flat desert to juniper and pinion pines and then to the ponderosa pine trees.

About an hour into the drive, I came upon a long line of vehicles at a standstill. After waiting for a short time, I got out of my car and walked up the road to see what was causing the holdup problem. Cars were backed up for what seemed to be a good part of a mile in length.

When I got to the front of the line, it was clear there was a large truck that had overturned and was blocking traffic in both directions across the highway. A large crowd of onlookers was standing around and talking, while eating snacks and drinking sodas. Some of their comments ranged from mild irritation to ballistic anger at being delayed for so long.

How long, I inquired. I was told over a half hour at the time, with no movement in sight. I asked where the driver of the truck was. No one seemed to have checked on him.

I started across the highway towards the overturned truck which was on a slope, and a lady from the crowd shouted at me, "Don't go there. You can't touch anything or else you may be liable. If you do anything, you could be sued." Her voice was edgy, and she sounded fearful.

"I feel that someone needs to be with the trucker until help comes," I replied calmly, while trembling inside me.

She screamed back at me, "Well, you can be sued for interfering!"

As I walked towards the truck, I found him lying motionless on his back under a part of the truck.

I was shocked! I felt compelled to do something for the poor man. He was all alone and no one had gone up to talk to him or stay with him.

I shook inwardly but proceeded to go towards the victim. I looked at his face and saw that his eyes were rolled back. He appeared white and he was not moving.

I began to talk to him, as though he could

hear me. I thought he was unconscious, as there was no response to my words as I was trying to rouse him by shaking him gently. One of his leg was turned backwards, and one hand appeared folded sidewise. I took off my jacket and covered his chest area in the hope of providing him some warmth.

I recalled in the natural healing courses that I had taken, there were trigger points to help people out of unconsciousness. I felt an urging to use my training. I placed my hands under his head, on those points, and I began talking to him. I explained what appeared to have happened, how he was now under his truck, and that I was there to stay with him until the help arrived to take him to a hospital where they could help him.

I told him that I would not leave him alone. I promised I would stay with him until help arrived.

Something stirred inside me, and I found myself saying something that I did not think out. “You have a choice. You can go, or you can choose to stay here on earth and continue to live your life.”

As my hands continued to hold the man’s

head, his eyes rolled back down and looked at me. They appeared glazed. But something very powerful happened. As he gazed at me, a tear rolled down the side of his face.

I took that to mean that he had heard me and that he was thankful someone had come to be with him.

Finally, when a helicopter circled and landed, paramedics from the helicopter came to him. His eyes stared at me again. It was a moment in which I felt we strongly connected, and I recognized his look of appreciation as he was lifted onto the stretcher.

As the paramedics carried the stretcher past me, the injured man said to one of the paramedics, “Did you see that beautiful angel? She stayed with me until you came to get me. Where did the angel go?”

I began to get up, but found my legs to be shaky, and I felt a bit queasy. My heart was beating a little faster, and I felt humbled by the way divine intervention helps those in need.

I wobbled past the bystanders and the same woman who had screamed at me earlier. She exclaimed, “Good thing there was a professional nurse on the scene!"

I could only murmur to her as I walked past, "Lady, I am not a professional. I am just a person who cares about people."

Hurrah for all of us humans who care about our fellow human beings!

What about you?

Was there a time in your life when you took the challenge to help someone despite outside negative feedback? How did it feel to follow your heart?

INSIGHT from your life:

Insight from *The Trucker Accident*

____

____

____

____

____

____

____

____

____

____

____

____

____

HURRAH FOR YOU!

Chapter Fifteen

WHEELCHAIR CAUSES HEALING

"Determination gives you the resolve to keep going in spite of the roadblocks that lay before you."

Denis Waitley

Some people when required to use a wheelchair, resist not only the use of it, but they resent the fact they *must* use it. My husband, John, was different. He used the wheelchair when he had to, and then he thought he'd give me the chance to see what it was like viewing life from that seated level. It sounded like a good idea initially, but what happened was a shocking surprise.

Wheelchair Causes Healing

At times, my husband brought about changes through his sense of humor and kindness. On our visit to a museum, I was surprised by his ability to make unexpected changes in me, as well as in two other women simultaneously.

My husband, John, and I were visiting the Phoenix Art Museum on one sunny day. As a result of having been injured by a tiger (another story), his right foot had a high built-up orthopedic shoe. Often, it was necessary that he sit in a wheelchair and be pushed about. I learned how to manage the chair on curbs, rough terrain, and many tenuous areas.

But nothing taught me how to manage the wheelchair at the time of the incident during our museum visit. After visiting various museum exhibitions, he got tired of sitting in the wheelchair and he suggested that I sit in it and he would push me around for a while, to give his back a rest. I agreed. The elevated leg rests made sitting in the very restful for me. And it provided me an opportunity to recognize how someone in a wheelchair would see things from that seated level rather than from my accustomed standing position.

It was a nice break from my always working to maneuver the wheelchair and watching objects that might cause an accident.

The exhibits at the museum were most interesting, and we spent a good portion of the day enjoying our visit. As we made our way around the various rooms, we came to one room that displayed vintage period paintings.

It was empty except for two very elderly women seated on the museum bench. Their faces were scrunched up like two pale, dried, and wrinkled prunes. Their deeply furrowed frowns announced they were not experiencing any joy. They stared ahead at nothing, but their eyes were piercing and their mouths downturned. Their backs were hunched over, and their hands were tightly clenched in their laps.

I said, “Oh, please, let’s not go into that room! They are a very unfriendly energy.”

My husband replied, “Oh, they’re just having a bad day. They won’t disturb us. There’s some really nice art to see here.”

In resistance, I sighed. Nothing could be

worth getting closer to the grouchy expressions on their faces, but my husband had a way about him that could convince me of almost anything.

As he rolled the wheelchair into the room, however, John quickly pushed me straight in front of the two women and stopped.

I was shocked and very nervous but unaware of what was to happen next. My uneasiness was not unfounded.

With the eyes of the women upon him, John looked upward and shouted out loudly, “I know you can do it! I know you can do it, Ann. Just trust in the Lord, and you can be healed!”

I was embarrassed, flustered, and confused. I leaped from the chair and ran out of the room, only to hear John shout loudly, “Hallelujah! Hallelujah! I knew you could do it! You believed and you are healed. Praise be!”

As I glanced back, the two women, stunned out of their chiseled frowns, could only sit with their mouths gaping open and their eyes wide with shock.

John turned towards the women and as he pushed the empty wheelchair past them and out of the room, he exclaimed, “It’s a miracle, sisters! It’s a miracle, and you witnessed it, too. Hallelujah!”

I do not know if those women were ever the same after that. I know I wasn’t. But John certainly brought a change in their day. And as always, he changed mine too.

Sometimes, a bit of storytelling emphatically presented helps jolt us out of our hum drum living. I can only imagine those two ladies had a lot to talk about for a very long time, because my husband decided that they could use a ‘hurrah for human’ change.

What about you?

Can you recall a time when humor and surprise helped get a point across and shock someone out of their static old life patterns? What impact did it have on you?

INSIGHT from your life:

Insight from *Wheelchair Causes Healing*

HURRAH FOR YOU!

Chapter Sixteen

DOLCE VITA SONG

"A life isn't significant except for its impact on other lives."

Jackie Robinson

Through this story experience, I learned the power of love expressed in song by a father who loved his daughter.

Italian Wedding

Ribbons of red, white, and yellow flowers gracefully danced before our eyes. We sat with about one hundred other guests at long banquet tables covered with thickly woven white cotton linens which were stiffly starched.

Long tables were heavily laden from an array of unlimited foods of bright colors and shapes. The aromas that wafted from the freshly prepared foods smelled sumptuous and delicious.

Spirited music charged the air, energizing and uplifting the gaiety. The most fun wedding I had attended for quite some time.

As the time came for toasts to be made, the father of the bride stood up, raised his champagne glass high, and suddenly, without warning and to our amazement, he broke into song.

Well, his song was a far distant cry from melodious, as he sang mercilessly off key. The sounds were so piercing and so badly off key that guests became uncomfortable and felt embarrassed to the point that they could not look in his direction.

All eyes avoided connecting with another's eyes. Many tried to muffle their under-breath nervous chuckles. It was a most awkward situation for such a momentous occasion.

I, too, was so taken back by this interruptive spontaneous outburst, that I stared, unblinking, into my food. I must have tunneled into my plate for about three painful minutes.

Then something most unexpected happened. I realized that the bride's father was so overjoyed with this precious moment when he was giving his daughter away, that he could do nothing else but open his mouth and let his heart bellow out his love. His heart bubbled over with happiness for his daughter!

The moment I realized this; the vocal sounds he was making truly sounded beautiful to my ears. I smiled eagerly and raised my champagne glass, caught the eyes of guests, and enthusiastically nodded my approval.

Soon, others were looking up and smiling. When the father had finished his "song" everyone stood up and cheered. Now caught up in the same endearing enthusiasm, they shouted “Bravo! Bravo!”

All of us then felt connected with the true message of his love, the real meaning of the celebration.

It was that Italian father, on his daughter’s wedding day, who reminded me that if I speak truth from my heart, my message (my song) will always sound beautiful to those who listen with open hearts.

Dolce vita! Hurrah for that Italian human who reminded me of the power of genuine love.

What about you?

On happy occasions in our lives, we can still learn about a deeper truth shared by someone who cares deeply. If you have experienced this, how did it change you?

INSIGHT from your life:

Insight from *Dolce Vita Song*

HURRAH FOR YOU!

Chapter Seventeen

DEAD ENGINE COMES ALIVE

"Life is really very simple, but
we insist on making it complicated."

Confucius

When I got married, my new husband and I traveled throughout the United States, Canada and Mexico. It was to be a little honeymoon trip that lasted about two years. Often, we would take the back roads and see the little towns of America and the countryside. His famous saying was always, "It'll be an easy and simple solution to any wrinkle in our road trips." Usually our travels worked out well, but this time it was different, and I admit I was much younger and impatient too.

Dead Engine Comes Alive Again

My husband John and I traveled together for some time on road trips throughout the United States, Canada, and Mexico. We hauled a travel trailer behind his Cadillac. It was going to be an extended vacation honeymoon trip. It lasted two and a half years. We had many experiences, which I could not explain in ordinary terms, such as this one.

On one occasion, we broke down on a dusty road in a very remote town somewhere in the back hills of Middle America. I was young and did not glide easily with unexpected mishaps. I complained to John about the inconvenience when the news from "the backyard repair shop" mechanics indicated, that due to the holiday, it would be one week before the parts could be shipped by bus to rebuild the engine. Evidently, the connecting rod hit the engine and ruined it completely. Causing, in one "mechanics" terms, to be "dead in the water." And that replaced engine had a whopping price tag!

I suspected they saw us "vacationers" coming and knew we were in a tight spot. I sighed heavily, imagining how it had cut into our "extended honeymoon vacation." Forlornly,

I imagined how we would be stranded for a long time in what seemed to be less than a village with only one main street. Maybe I shouldn't have wanted to explore those "blue back roads" in our United States. I felt all was bleak.

I had come to know that my husband had some uncanny ways about him, with certain abilities that I did not possess, nor did I have expectations to develop such esoteric talents.

Sometimes he helped people in a very different way. For example, it was my responsibility to "buddy-sit" his body as his spirit left his body from time to time to appear and help people in trouble. At first, I didn't know if what was happening was real or not. It was all very mystical and intriguing. He would leave, then I would hear what was going on from his side of the experience through his verbal conversations. Then he would "return" and give me the whole story about the situation and how he was able to help people in various situations.

I will admit, at first, I was doubtful. I thought maybe it was just imagination talking. However, there were several occasions later, in which I learned from other people that indeed a "mysterious man" appeared and helped them or did something to intervene in their trying situations. One was with my own family member.

My brother and his wife were traveling from Tucson to Phoenix on the main highway. She fell asleep, and in a dream, she said to me later, that she saw a kind looking man holding out to her the biggest, most delicious ice cream sundae with oozing hot chocolate topping she'd ever seen. She loved ice cream. It woke her up.

Her mouth watered and she felt compelled to stop at the halfway mark in a roadside restaurant/store and get one of those sundaes. My brother wanted to continue and get back to Phoenix as soon as possible. Speeding along a little above the speed limit, he was making good time and didn't want to waste it on such a frivolous whim.

She managed to whine, beg and then she insisted they stop. My brother finally acquiesced, with reluctance to appease his wife, and have some peace and quiet. He turned off for the stop.

Later, we learned that there was a traumatic, many car pile-up accident that involved closing the highway. It happened just a couple of minutes after they exited. It delayed them getting back, but in effect saved their lives. They would have been in that accident which caused a number of deaths.

John told me before I learned about the details of the accident, that he created the image of that dessert in her dream to help them get off the highway to safety.

However, that was "those people and circumstances."

So, when our car broke down in the "middle of nowhere," I imagined the worst possible enduring time we would spend waiting for the needed parts to arrive by camel through the forsaken farmlands. And I did not have a problem in voicing my disgruntlement at such an inconvenience.

John looked at me with such compassion that I almost felt guilty for my "childish" disappointment and unhappiness. Then, quietly, he said, "Is it *that* important to you, my darling? You wish to be on the road right now?"

"Yes," I retorted. I could hear the

defensiveness in the tone of my voice. I was not sufficiently embarrassed, however, to say 'no.'

He took my hand and as he walked me over to his Cadillac, he just said softly to me, "Get in the car."

I began to protest against his wanting me to sit in a vehicle which the mechanics had already told us we had a broken-down engine. It made no sense at all! I wanted to question why he would say that, and then I thought better of it.

I obediently slid into the passenger seat, and watched John put the key in the ignition and turn it.

To my amazement, the engine started easily and smoothly. I stared at John in disbelief as we drove out of the garage. The mechanics also watched in disbelief, with their jaws dropped open. They, too, couldn't believe it! They had just examined that engine!

As we drove back to the trailer park where our trailer was parked, I sat speechless. After a long silence, John calmly said, "It is not good to use your powers for your own needs.

Use it to help others."

I believe that I grew out of the childlike part of myself that day. John helped me by demonstrating the power he had, and the fact that he would use it only to help others—myself in this instance. And he taught me while sharing in a loving way with me.

What a powerful combination—witnessing such powerful happening with John and growing myself up a bit!

What a hurrah for humans!

What about you?

Did something happen in your life that you cannot explain with logical thinking, but you know for certain it happened? How did you feel by trusting your own experience to be true?

INSIGHT from your life:

Insight from *Dead Engine Comes Alive*

____

____

____

____

____

____

____

____

____

____

____

____

HURRAH FOR YOU!

Chapter Eighteen

SERVICE VS. SERVITUDE

"My true desire is to relieve others of their pain though I myself may fall into hell."

Bassui

There are times in our lives when we give without taking the time to assess if our actions will deplete us of our time, energy and money so much that we will have no ability to take care of ourselves. It is a humbling and awakening realization.

Service vs. Servitude

I was reared very religious, and I grew up believing that my life was to be one of loving service to humanity. Even as an adult, I constantly volunteered for projects, taking care of the wishes of friends, family and strangers; often I found myself exhausted, to the point of not accomplishing personal matters, and not taking care of my own physical body.

At the time of this story, it had become a lifestyle beyond a growing habit. My mate at the time had a son who was in jail. Appearing at our front door one day was the son's wife and two small children. She wondered if they could stay with us a couple weeks. until her husband was released from jail. They were without a car, a job, or a home since they were evicted from their apartment.

I was on an intense natural therapy for advanced cancer. But what is one to do? Their need was apparent, and to add to the intensity of the situation, they were family. So, we wholeheartedly said yes to her request for help.

So, began the lesson of service vs. servitude. Since their lives were disrupted and exposed to a new home and lifestyle, the young children behaved badly, crying, screaming, and whining excessively. Their mother tried her best to keep them quieter and neater, but it was to no avail.

They had to be shuttled everywhere, and we had to purchase their groceries, clothing, and many needed services, as she had no monies available to her. Literally, it felt as though we had adopted a brood of our own children. I was not accustomed to the wailing and whining. I was very ill with cancer and had limited energy and very little emotional reserves to deal with them. I cared deeply for them, but I was overwhelmed.

Finally, their Mother was able to secure a job, and we found a day-care place to take the children while she worked. We supplied the transportation, food, and cost of care for the children while she worked. We also encouraged the mother to save her money so she could eventually hunt for an apartment for herself and her children. We pledged that we would also pay for her living place, and for the day care of her children.

Because of the legal issues with her husband, she had to go to court. We went with her. When the judge learned that they were living with us, he felt that the stable environment of our home was better for her children and he ordered that they remain in our home, despite our explanation that she now had a job, the children were in day care and most importantly that I was on intense cancer therapy regime. That didn't matter. The Judge's ruling held. Our appeal did nothing to change his ruling. Disappointment and frustration followed.

We were all unhappy with the decision of the Court. It made living together even more trying and noisy. And that lasted more than two years, before she was able to have the order changed. The situation took a toll on my success in cancer therapy. After the situation got settled down, and they had their own place, I had time to think about the whole experience, how it started, how it ended, and what lesson was I to glean from it on a spiritual level.

Finally, a wise friend asked me, "If a stranger knocked on your door one day with two tiny children and asked you to let them stay with you for two years, and could you feed them, clothe them and transport them everywhere and be happy about the situation, would you have done so?"

I was stunned into silence as I thought about her question. It made me realize that I would not have done that to our home, or in order to heal, my need for peace and quiet to recover from cancer. I WOULD have helped them, but I would have found an agency and resources that would provide them help.

That awareness reminded me that I needed to begin giving to others from my abundance (of time, energy, and money) instead of depleting all of them for the sake of helping others and forgetting myself and my dire needs. It also made me realize that I can help people without sacrificing my life.

The image my friend gave me—if they were strangers, what would I do to help—was a turning point in my realizing how to balance helping others while helping oneself.

My friend said one other thing that remained with me. She added, "You gave to their need, not to them. And the mother, though grateful, likely began to resent you for it as it showed the mother that she was not capable of providing things to sustain her family." In hindsight, I regretfully conceded that my friend was correct.

That was a powerful lesson for me- the realization that there are many layers to giving and receiving. And when it is honorable, both parties feel that it is uplifting and not demeaning. That learning took me over two years to acquire! I feel sure that for another person it might have been a gentle quick lesson to remember that giving of your abundance will keep you healthy and keep the person you help feeling respected. Good for you, and good for the receiver. It becomes a sharing and a winning for both of you.

Hurrah for healthy humans who give in honorable ways without sacrificing themselves!

What About You?

Was there a time in your life when you gave of your time, energy, and money much more than you could afford to give? Looking back, what did you learn?

INSIGHT from your life:

Insight from *Service vs. Servitude*

____

____

____

____

____

____

____

____

____

____

____

____

____

HURRAH FOR YOU!

Chapter Nineteen

THE TIGER AND THE TRAINER

"You must watch my life, how I live, eat, sit, talk, behave in general. The sum total of all those in me is my religion."

Gandhi

He was one of those people you didn't forget. Not because he was married to me. But because he was his own sterling, unique, charismatic, brilliant, and kind soul. Many times during our life together, I saw him do unbelievable things and take risks to help others in danger. This story tells how helping a young man caused him permanent injury for the rest of his life, but he never complained.

The Tiger and the Trainer

My husband had a built-up right shoe. His right leg was considerably shorter than the left one due to a surgery resulting from a tiger attack. John was a wild animal trainer, who dealt with big cats and apes. His traumatic accident was due to a hired young man who was teasing the tiger.

The limited use of one leg never phased him in the least. If we were at the zoo, he would call out to youngsters who were looking at the odd shaped orthopedic shoe, “Come on over. Would you like to hear the story of how my leg became shorter?” Of course, they would.

Soon there would be a small crowd around him, and he would begin to tell the story of the tiger and how it carried him around in the ring, and of the tiger’s powerful jaws that crushed his hip, so that he didn’t have any hip bone left. He had to undergo surgery, and the surgeon inserted a steel plate to support his leg. It was the best medical science offered at the time. The special ball-and-socket surgery was not yet available in the United States.

John always told his story with color, and the youngsters were amazed. Their attentive bright eyes and their open mouths were a testament to that. And he emphasized that it was not the tiger's fault.

The young man, newly hired by him to care for the animals, was teasing the tiger by raising the cage door a bit and then slamming it down as the tiger went to put his paw under it to push it up. Finally, the tiger got his paw under the cage door and dashed into the ring.

The young man was terrified, and when John heard the commotion, he entered the ring and kept the tiger distracted with a chair prop. He wrapped a rope around the boy's leg and told side standers outside the cage to pull him out. Rather than pulling the young man out slowly, they jerked him out quickly, and the tiger leaped for the boy. I learned earlier from John that the moment the tiger leaps, he is unaware of anything else.

John stepped between the tiger, Saba, and the boy, to save the boy's life. The tiger's jaws then clamped down on John's right hip, picked him up and, in a daze, began walking around the arena. The tiger, Saba, didn't want John for he was invincible in the area.

Normally, tigers could swipe their paws at John; the chair, or other props, and he wasn't phased in the least. As far as the animals were concerned, John was the most powerful animal in the ring. He could "out psyche" them every time. When in the ring, he always watched the eyes of the animal facing him, and he knew instantly what the animal behind him was thinking.

The tiger, Saba, didn't want to harm John. He was, however, bewildered as to how he got into his mouth! Finally, after 50 some minutes, a security man got a head shot at Saba, and the 650-pound magnificent animal was killed.

John cursed a lot, even in shock, saying, "It cost me $5,000 to get him, and I spent six months training that animal!"

As a consolation prize, John was given one of Saba's claws on a gold chain while in the hospital. He was told, "Better that you wear him than that he wears you."

I recall times when we were visiting the zoo and kids were teasing the animals by throwing little rocks or lighted cigarettes at them. I would become very upset.

John would say, “Don’t worry. It’ll be fine. We can help them learn something valuable.”

Then he would begin making the animal sounds of the zoo animal exhibit we were visiting. He always amazed me that he could imitate the sounds of the animals so distinctly.

Soon, the animals came over to the fence where John was, and he began his talk about them. At first it was as though he was talking to me, then his talk expanded to include the youngsters who had gathered around him, and then eventually, parents joined us. The parents came to see what the kids were listening too. Soon, without any effort, he had a captive audience and he talked about the animals, from his wise caring trainer point of view.

John provided wonderful insights into the animals that the young audience and the adults too had not known. They always left with a greater appreciation for the wonderment of the animal kingdom.

I always marveled at John’s ability to invite questions and to educate without lecturing. All ages learned to respect the animals because of John’s “cage side sharing.”

And of course, he included in the story of how he got the tiger claw that he always wore.

John consistently demonstrated the ability to help people understand animals and to appreciate their contribution to our world.

Hurrah for him and for the tigers he trained. Hurrah also for the young people who learned a new way of understanding and relating to the animals.

What about you?

Have you witnessed the injury of someone because of the careless actions of another? How did that impact you?

INSIGHT from your life:

Insight from *The Tiger and the Trainer*

____

____

____

____

____

____

____

____

____

____

____

____

____

____

HURRAH FOR YOU!

Chapter Twenty

LE PICNIC WHIRLWIND

"There is more to life than increasing its speed."

Gandhi

There are times in life when we know we should be acting, but we want to rest a while; and that could easily be our undoing. This is such a whirlwind story.

Le Picnic Whirlwind

Picnics have always held magical moments for me. I have viewed them as special adventures that required kodak moments.

Some years ago, I had a friend who was so seriously ill that it was likely she would not survive the summer.

I asked Mary to share with me her fondest childhood memory. A happy smile covered her face.

"I remember picnics," she said fondly. I helped Mom prepare them. We always went to the park."

That was all it took for me to want to do something for my friend.

I began scouring our city in search of an upscale picnic basket and accoutrements.

Dissatisfied with what I was finding, I bought calico, quilting, lots of yardage, trim and many different sizes of baskets, and service ware that would provide a special occasion. Then I designed a special basket ensemble, which I sewed myself. And everything matched. Cozy tops for the wine glasses, napkin rings and napkins- every little container had a matching cover. There were more than two dozen special serving containers.

I even had ants in a small container with matching ruffles (to keep the picnic civil, I said). I set about hand calligraphing a special menu that listed the familiar basic picnic fare in French, with English subtitles.

I decided to bring music—my autoharp to play and soothing background music from a boombox.

The more special creative touches I thought of, the more enthusiastic I got became about doing more. I bought a bottle of champagne, soaked the labels off and created special hand painted labels with her name, the celebration wishes and date. And I had the wood candelabras made special to hold the long white taper candles.

I cooked everything from scratch. Nothing was too good for this one-time event of her lifetime. I brought my camera to take pictures of the layout I decided to serve her picnic on her front lawn overlooking a gentle green ravine.

###

The sky was a brilliant blue the day I served her picnic. The soft gentle breezes added ambiance. When I had everything in place, donned in my long blue skirt and bright yellow long-sleeved blouse with a ruffled calico apron and floppy brimmed hat with matching trim, I rang her doorbell.

I carried Mary outside and gently sat her down on the matching thick comfortable quilt. She was astounded. She loved the matching floppy brimmed hat I ceremonially placed on her head.

The celebration then began. I had written a song for Mary, which I played and sang.

And then began the posh picnic service. Each course became another elegant adventure for her.

When we were finished, Mary said, "That is the best picnic I have ever had in my whole life! You have gone to an incredible amount of work to make this happen for me. I will never forget this day, Annie."

I brought Mary the photos a couple of days later in an album, and of course the album cover was of the matching calico fabric of the items I had sewed for her picnic.

Mary's family told me that she talked about that one picnic every day and showed the photos to everyone who came to visit her.

I am pleased that the event provided such a happy memory for Mary. It was only a few weeks later that she died.

I believe that when she was leaving, her spirit was dancing in the memory of her most favorite picnic.

Hurrah for Mary, a human who truly treasured her one magical picnic.

###

I put all the picnic stuff away, with gratitude and sadness in my heart. I sadly missed my friend.

One day another friend saw the picnic

materials in my closet. It had been there for many months. She asked me to do an anniversary picnic for her husband and her. I said sure. I liked creating magic any day.

So began the moccasin trail referrals. I did it for the joy of seeing friends delight in the special attention and spangles and trappings.

Then one day, because of Mary's picnic, I began my picnic offerings to the public. Picnics went anywhere—homes, board meetings, parks, airplanes, wine cellars, nursing homes, back yards, front yards, deserts, mountain peaks, honeymoons, ladies' tea parties, seminars, boats, newly purchased empty homes, office buildings and more.

My brochure said, "My picnics come wherever you are." I hired a driver with a Rolls Royce to pick people up and take them to the Le Picnic adventure, and a minstrel if needed.

Somehow the magic of picnics got coverage from TV news coverages, talk shows, newspapers, and magazines; media coverage enough that I never had to advertise.

Picnics ranged from the romantic two-person picnics to one large, 126-people picnic for a law firm. That was a creative challenge for a couple of reasons. I had hired help, directed all the food preparations and transfer of everything to the picnic site, and I laid it out in one of our lovely local parks.

For the youngsters, I designed a special "Color-your-own-Cookie" eight-foot banquet table, with large cookies and many containers of frostings, and edible decorations to tantalize any child. I was amazed at how much "stuff" the kids piled onto one cookie!

The adult guests came back for seconds at the buffet picnic which was good. Then we cleared their tables. I told my staff that we should break down the food line setting. They quietly groaned and begged me to let them rest for another ten minutes.

My acquiescing was a big mistake. Suddenly, a huge, dusty whirlwind raced through the park, much like a tornado. It leveled everything in its path.

When it came to my 32 feet of picnic layouts on the serving line, it swept everything into the sky in a moment, rather like Dorothy's escapade in the Wizard of Oz.

There was nothing to stop it. My picnic remains, carried away in the winds, was never to be seen again.

All we could do was to stand with our mouths gaping open and our eyes fixed upon the fast disappearing disaster in the sky. The guests blinked in disbelief.

When the dust finally settled, and calm had settled back on the park, one guest said, "I guess you'll never know where all your things landed. They could be miles away. But the good news is, if you need an attorney to settle a claim for all the stuff that landed elsewhere, you are in good shape, as there is an entire firm of lawyers here!"

And one staff member chortled, "This is what I call an easy cleanup for us!"

Well, I thought, this picnic was successful, but it definitely ended up out of control.

I reframed my thinking and said, "hurrah for those humans who enjoyed the magic of my picnic while it lasted; and to those who can laugh at the "unpredictable" of this day!"

What about you?

Have you ever had a perfectly wonderful event, and then nature suddenly changed everything? How did you react to the sudden change?

INSIGHT from your life:

Insight from *Le Picnic Whirlwind*

____

____

____

____

____

____

____

____

____

____

____

____

____

HURRAH FOR YOU!

Chapter Twenty-One

COASTAL DRIVE REVEALS FACE OF CHRIST

"Life is what happens to us while we are making other plans."

Thomas La Mance

This story is about my realization that we may make our daily plans, but that sometimes, our intended day plans are changed in the whisper of a moment. We are given a chance to realize that a force much greater than us is at work and is truly orchestrating a most wondrous job despite us!

Coastal Drive Reveals Face of Christ

For one summer, I lived at a pottery-teaching facility called Big Creek Pottery Ranch near Santa Cruz, California on the Pacific Coast. I enrolled in classes that taught wheel throwing to make clay objects such as mugs, vases, plates, bowls and platters, using a kick-wheel. We didn't have the use of electric kick-wheel-only the use of our legs to kick the large, circular slab of concrete around to use for throwing our pots.

The result was that by the end of summer, I no longer able to fit my right leg into my jeans. I had to cut the right pant leg up the side in order to wear my jeans, but I was happy with the objects I had created from clay class.

To supplement the cost of my class and resident expenses, I was making pillows of many shapes, sizes, fabrics and designs. I stuffed them with foam crumbs, which required that I purchase the bulk foam in large burlap bags from a wholesaler of fabrics in Santa Rosa. During our weekend break, I decided to make a trip there and obtain need stock for my pillow-making business.

I left the Ranch at the crack of dawn and drove up to Santa Rosa. Pleased with my purchases, I loaded my convertible so full, that it was necessary for the top of my convertible to remain down in order to fit everything inside the car. Then I headed back down the coast on my return trip to the Ranch.

The ocean lay below, and the windy cliffs of the Pacific Coast Highway was beautiful. However, I hadn't much sleep and soon the sun, wind, and glittering ocean water caused sleepiness. I fought the fatigue with images of new pillow designs, playing loud music, and allowing the wind to whip through my hair. However, that method didn't last long.

Soon, all went dark. Fast asleep, I did not realize that my car had veered off the proper lane and was at the edge of the cliff and headed towards the ocean below. Suddenly, I jerked awake only to see the ocean far below me and my car directed straight towards the water.

At that moment, I felt a rush of panic, then, the face of Christ appeared to me. I still cannot explain how and why. Although I was reared very Catholic, I had not practiced the religion for some time.

What I saw was the kindest, most loving eyes along with radiant soft golden light, that gave me a most luminous feeling I have ever experienced. All I remember feeling is, "I'm home!" I felt great peace and safety, and I eagerly surrendered all parts of myself to the moment. I have never felt such love either before or after that moment.

It seemed like my experience was to last "forever" and was suspended out of time. However, it was probably a split second in earth time.

The next thing I remember is hearing a tremendous thud and my head violently jerked forward and struck the steering wheel. When my eyes became focused, I saw that strangely enough, I was on the opposite side of the highway. My car had not only turned away from the ocean, but it had crossed the road to the other side and had gone into a ravine. All was still, except for the people who soon rushed down the hillside to see what had happened—later I learned, to determine if I was alive.

I stepped out of the car and surveyed the damage. I could see that the front fender on the driver's side had been severely crushed.

Aside from that, there was no damage.

"Darn!" I said aloud, with irritation in my voice. "Now I am going to have to get that repaired and I have no insurance! Shucks!" While I was still fuming over the expense of the fender, a Highway Patrol car arrived.

The patrolman insisted that I go to a hospital, which angered me. I had no medical insurance. Despite my resistance, I was taken to a hospital. My car, driven by another officer, followed me.

"I am just fine. I don't need any attention!" I repeated over and over. But no one listened to me. Even after the doctor and x-rays showed me to be just fine, but they said they had to conduct an examination and run tests to make sure everything was okay.

It wasn't until much later that I had time to consider the face of Christ which had appeared to me at the time of the accident. I realized only then that I had escaped death and it impacted me of how the kindness of Christ also visited me.

I carry that image in my heart, and each time I think of it, I feel chills up my spine and down my arms. It still affects me, these many years later.

That experience showed me I am never left alone, and that there is nothing here more important than remembering that moment in time which seemed to last forever.

I know it was truly for me divine intervention, and a sacred moment of hurrah for humans.

What about you?

Was there a time when you encountered a deep spiritual experience which you know is true, even though others found it difficult to accept?

INSIGHT from your life:

Insight: from *Coastal Drive Reveals Face of Christ*

HURRAH FOR YOU

Chapter Twenty-Two

EVERYONE IS A SUSPECT

"Where there is great love, there are always miracles."

Willa Cather

It is a simple, ordinary happening. But, the timing of it and the mysteriousness of the giver gave me a tender feeling that someone cared for me, and that I was not all alone in my current hardship.

Everyone is a Suspect.

When I can't find who is responsible for what happens to me. I suspect everyone. I can't help it! I am always taken by surprise, though it should be considered normal by now.

I often see that people are wonderful, kind and caring. It isn't because I am a "Pollyanna", seeing the world through rose-colored glasses. More likely, it says more about them than about me.

Years ago, I was in dire straits financially. I didn't have enough money to pay my monthly utility bill. I worked two jobs to pay off my late husband's medical bills. His tragic death consumed me. He had survived the tiger attack but died from serum hepatitis in the blood transfusions during surgery. Life appeared bleak. I felt overwhelmed and sad most of the time. My life was devoted to paying the medical bills.

One day I trudged to my mailbox, hoping there would be no more bills. Among the usual advertisements and third-class mail was a white envelope with simply my name printed on it.

As I ripped it open, partly with curiosity but mostly bewilderment, out fell a fifty-dollar bill. I was stunned. There was no note, no person's return address—only my name on the front of the envelope, with no clues of whom I might thank.

So, what did I do? I suspected everyone. With my suspicion growing, the dark cloud which hung over my head began to lighten and somewhat dissipate. Clearly, someone cared. It seemed to me to be a sign that things would get better. I began to see everyone through eyes of gratitude, just in case they were the kind culprit that secretly left the surprise of cash for me.

A few days after the mysterious money arrived, I saw an ad for home typing. I took the extra work. That same day I sold two of my nature photographs for a good amount of money. And one medical provider called me and said, "We don't want to add to your hardship right now, so we are writing off your obligation with us." I could not believe my good fortune. I knelt down and prayed with gratitude for my blessings.

Then I was hooked. I joined the many anonymous givers that look for ways to give without people having to ask for help. I have delighted in opportunities to give secretly from that day forward. Each time I secretly help someone, my spirits are lifted too.

I have used the "white envelope" caper many times since I first received mine. White symbolized to me the purity of the giving—no return address and no name, no loss of dignity, no expected gratitude. Such gifts are given for the pure joy of helping another human being.

Opportunities to help are everywhere, every day. It is hard to go through one day without seeing where our kindness could be appreciated. It could be simply a genuine caring smile we generously give to someone when we see them.

Yesterday, I went into Walgreen's store. In the checkout line, before me a tattered young man was trying to use his credit card to get a jug of water. It was a hot sweltering day. His card was rejected. His shoulders slumped.

"Wait a moment. You're going to need water today," I said.

To the cashier I said, "Please add two water jugs to my bill." He looked surprised and left murmuring his thanks.

The cashier said, "Wow! That was very kind of you!" Then two other customers in line added their acknowledgements of the good deed. I only saw an opportunity in my day to quietly extend help to another human being.

Later when I shared my story, a friend said, "Yes, but none of the *other* people offered to help him." I didn't see it that way. I chose to think "those two customers who did nothing" really did something. They felt uplifted by witnessing a simple act of kindness and verbalized their appreciation of the thoughtful act. It touched not only the receiver (the young man) but the effect extended to the cashier and two other customers; not to mention my own personal feelings of joy.

That same day I went to a pet store to buy treats for my dog. I thought *his tail will be wagging happily as he tastes these meaty-like morsels.*

The elderly lady in front of me in line was checking out; her old sad-eyed basset hound was at her side. Isn't it wonderful that you can take your pet inside a store?

She purchased bags of vittles and some non-essentials for "Bruno." He stood patiently waiting to leave. The clerk said, "Would you like some help out? She replied, "Yes. Please."

I mentioned I was going out to the parking lot myself. I could easily carry her purchases to her car for her. She beamed with appreciation. Bruno's big brown eyes looked up as if to say, "Good I will be getting my treats sooner."

The young clerk said, "How kind of you. Thanks a lot. I'm not charging you for your treats." Another unexpected kindly gesture. Two patrons in line also commented on the kindness in action.

It doesn't take much, I thought. One simple act of kindness made all of us happier. At her car, I loaded her purchases, reached into my bag, and gave Bruno a treat before leaving. I can't be sure, but I think he was smiling too.

Tomorrow, perhaps you'll see someone who needs a smile, which wouldn't cost you anything but a moment of your time. If you can take a few minutes to give something of yourself, even to a perfect stranger, your day will change, and so will theirs.

Kindness is contagious, ever expanding. And each time it happens, it is a hurrah for caring humans. Besides, it just feels good!

What about you?

Recall a time in your life when you received a surprise and you had no idea where it came from. Did your heart become happier that it could be anyone?

INSIGHT from your life:

Insight from *Everyone is a Suspect*

HURRAH FOR YOU!

Chapter Twenty-three

FISHING THE EASY WAY

"Imagination is more important than knowledge."

Albert Einstein

Imagination was the perfect solution for my Bed and Breakfast guests who didn't get to go fishing in our mountain country streams because they found such comfort in my B&B's amenities and relaxing atmosphere. I "imagined" a fishing adventure that was memorable for them.

Fishing the Easy Way

My mountainside Bed and Breakfast was a popular destination for travelers from around the world. I was honored to greet such special people and to create happy memories that they took home with them. As I built my business, people from all over the world found their way to my Bed and Breakfast.

In fact, the slogan for my B&B was, "Come as guests, Stay as friends, Return as family." Many guests commented that they truly felt their stay reflected our slogan.

On one occasion when a couple came to visit, they had plans to go fishing during their visit. The husband felt sure that his wife would enjoy learning how to fish. His enthusiasm for fishing was ardent.

However, they became so comfortable relaxing at my B&B that time slipped away and suddenly they were to check out the next morning. He had intended to bring back "big fish" stories when they returned home.

I could tell he was a bit disappointed he did not get to go fishing. He had also wanted to teach his wife to fish.

The day they were to depart, I had an idea. On my property I had a waterfall and small pond with a mechanical fish that could move around in the pond to entertain guests.

Real fish wouldn't survive very long because of visiting wildlife that would consider fish tasty dinners.

I dug out my fishing gear and whispered to my guests to come down to the pond. As I staged them reeling in of my mechanical fish from the pond, I snapped a photo for them as a gift.

That did the trick, and happily the couple departed with cheerful smiles. They could hardly wait to get back home to share their creative fishing expedition story with friends.

I got an email from them a couple weeks after they got home which said they had so much fun entertaining friends with their crazy fish story, while eating, of course, a fish dinner.

I commented to myself, "hurrah for humans that just want to have fun and have a fishing story to share from their vacation."

What about you?

When you were entertaining friends or family, did your creative thinking create a happy memory from a disappointment?

INSIGHT from your life:

Insight from *Fishing the Easy Way*

____

____

____

____

____

____

____

____

____

____

____

____

____

____

HURRAH FOR YOU!

Chapter Twenty-four

MAGGIE'S MAGIC

"The heart has its reasons which reason knows nothing of."

Blaise Pascal

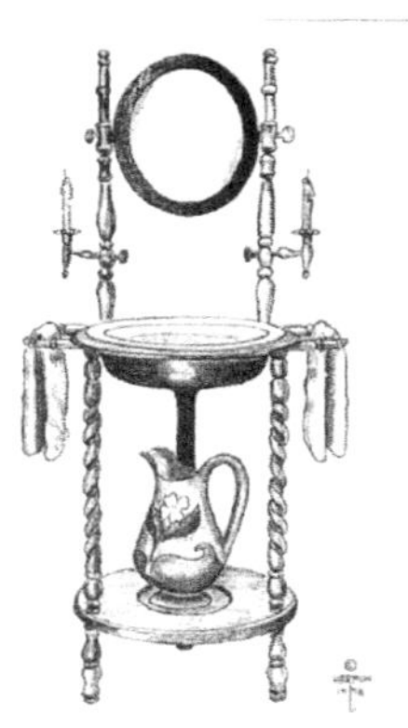

In this story I learned that sharing my appreciation came back to me tenfold and more. It was an unexpected joy that kept on giving.

Maggie's Magic

I met Maggie—vivacious, energetic, laughing Maggie—on an archaeological dig in Northern Arizona. When we disbanded from the site work, I wrote her a card in which I shared my appreciation for becoming acquainted with her. I told her what I liked about her.

Years passed without our having stayed in touch. Although from time to time, I recalled with fondness our time shared on the Archaeological Dig.

One day, I received a call. It was concerning Maggie, who had recently passed away. I was surprised and saddened. And I was stunned when her family told me what she had done. Maggie had taped my card and message on her mirror, and that she had read it every single day of her life since receiving it from me.

She explained to her family that it reminded her that she was special and loved, and it made a difference in her life.

I was speechless. I had no idea it impacted her to that extent. I merely wrote truthfully concerning what I felt about her.

Although her family felt that I had given her a wonderful lasting gift through my heartfelt words, I felt it was Maggie who gave *me* a gift on that day.

She reminded me that any small gesture of caring or sharing can profoundly affect the recipient's life. We may never realize the depth at which another person might treasure your words of kindness.

Each day we have an opportunity to share with someone that the person means a great deal to us. Let us not miss any opportunity to share our compliments.

We may never know how long our gift of words might be cherished, and what a profound impact a small gesture of genuine kindness might make upon a life that may be treasured for their lifetime.

Learning how much my words meant to Maggie was a true sign of Hurrah for humans!

What about you?

Has there been a time when you wrote an appreciation note to someone and later found out that it meant a great deal to them and they treasured it?

<u>INSIGHT from your life:</u>

Insight from *Maggie's Magic*

____

____

____

____

____

____

____

____

____

____

____

____

____

HURRAH FOR YOU!

Chapter Twenty-Five

THE CHACO CHALLENGE

"Life only demands from you the strength you possess."

Dag Hammarskjold

There are times when the forces of nature bring out in us our undiscovered power within. When faced with challenges, often these times help us discover a new level of strength. I found my additional strength from the challenges that came from my New Mexico Chaco Canyon trek.

The Chaco Challenge

It sounded like a fun trip—that of an archeological group going to New Mexico for a trek to an ancient site and camping in the canyon. Why not participate? I was once an avid backpacker. This couldn't be that challenging for me.

I had recently moved and at this time I made my home in a mountain village in Arizona. I was still recovering from a breakup of a seven and half-year relationship and was sorting through a myriad of personal belongings which I had hauled to my new mountain home.

I had not realized, however, that between the unexpected breakup and the arduous move, I was greatly stressed—to the point I was breaking out in large patches of rash. Later, it was diagnosed as a severe case of hives.

On the night before departing on my ten-day trek to Chaco Canyon, I was writhing in severe pain as the rashes covered most of the torso. I could neither sit nor lie down. The situation became so unbearable, I checked myself into hospital emergency room. I was concerned as to how I might tell my travel companions I had to bow out because my many holistic remedies I tried didn't heal the severity of the problem.

I had doubts about how long I would be at ER, with visions of hours of waiting. However, the doctor who was on call, came in to see me rather quickly. I started to show him cell phone pictures of how the large blotches repeatedly moved about. He replied that he wasn't interested in my photos! He knew instantly what my problem was. He quickly wrote five prescriptions and began writing his report. I was stunned.

He said, "You have a severe case of hives." His eyes were piercing as he asked me, "Under any stress?"

Instead of discussing my relationship breakup, my recent move, and mounting bills, I told him about my scheduled early morning departure the next day, for a road trip to New Mexico.

He replied, with a cautionary note, "Don't do anything strenuous. Rest a lot and be certain to take all those meds exactly as I have prescribed them. I really think you shouldn't be going, but if you promise to do nothing to exert yourself, and someone else is driving, you may be all right."

I couldn't imagine myself being unable to handle everything, so I ignored the possibility of any problem, and assured the attending physician that I would take it easy.

Only 30 minutes later, I had all the prescriptions filled at the pharmacy, took a handful of the first round of medications right away, and drove home, dubious of the medication's powerful magic. Within a couple of hours, I felt better! *Wow, I thought there actually was a possibility of going on the trip!*

The next morning at 5 a.m. I was fine! Armed with an unusually fat medicine bag, I departed for New Mexico. I was grateful that my new friend would be driving his four-wheel-drive vehicle and I could rest during the drive to Chaco. We were part of a caravan, all headed to the ancient archeological site in New Mexico.

It was pouring rain, and very early in the morning, when we departed from my home, but I didn't care. I felt good for the first time in many hours. We stopped for ice in town, at Wal-Mart, and I closed my eyes and waited while my travel buddy filled the ice chest with food stock and bags of ice. *It will be a long trip so best to rest now* was my thought.

Merrily we rolled along, until almost before reaching Gallup, New Mexico. It was then I began searching for my medications. They could not be found. I carefully searched through all our bags and boxes in the back of the vehicle, but to no avail! A feeling of panic enveloped me. I certainly didn't want the hives to reappear. But I couldn't find my medications anywhere!

I watched my energy go from that of elation to feelings of deflation and desperation in seconds. Then I remembered that there was a Wal-Mart also in Gallup.

When the group stopped in Gallup for lunch, I walked over to the Wal-Mart Pharmacy. I was pleased that, before leaving the hospital emergency room, I said to the attending physician, "I am going into a very remote canyon out of state for several days, without any cell phone reception. If I get into trouble, they will have to air-vac me out. Therefore, please give me a copy of your notes and prescribed medications so they will know what we did here."

He did so. I was surprised at the time, but later, in New Mexico, I was grateful. I showed the list of his prescribed medications to the pharmacist. He checked and found out that my insurance wouldn't pay for them as they had just been filled. I didn't hesitate to pay cash. It would be worth it to be armed with that which had just worked wonders for me!

Armed for the second time with the super drugs, I gratefully swallowed the arsenal of pills. And our caravan headed out again for Chaco Canyon.

We had rain periodically during the drive, and we arrived at Chaco in the late afternoon where each of us began setting up campsites around our assigned area.

Chaco Canyon and the Chaco archaeological site is an amazing monumental project. Situated in the Four Corners area of New Mexico are the remains of an ancient civilization. It was vast during the height of its reign, and for hundreds of years it was the hub of civilization. Even today, it leaves one breathless when visiting this archeological site—the largest in the southwest.

As I surveyed the site, I was intrigued by thoughts of this thriving culture that existed thousands of years before. It was the major center of an ancestral pueblo culture. The major civilization for hundreds of years. At its peak more than 100,000 people resided here, and roads perfectly laid out vastly in all four directions. It was a hub of activity and the major place for spiritual practices.

The landscape at Chaco, belies total understanding. Its many ruins hold stories yet to be discovered and archaeologists from all over the world come to visit and learn from this ancient civilization's ruins.

After visiting several ruins, we set out for the top of the mesa to visit another ruin of special interest. To climb to the upper most mesa above, we wedged our way through a small slot canyon, twisting, turning, and using our hands and upper body strength to pull ourselves up through the small openings. We goat-climbed along rock faced walls to the top of the mesa.

From atop the cliffs, lay dramatic views below of vast landscapes and many ruins. We walked past fossilized worms from millions of years ago, which still embedded in what was once an ocean's bottom.

The rock formations were startlingly ancient also. Each held a secret of the past. From millions of years ago. From the mesa top, we set an energetic pace to Pueblo Alto, another ancient settlement which is near the north road.

Only a few minutes into our trek, raindrops began falling- faster than our walking pace. Soon, it turned into a downpour along with thunderclaps shouting around us. With renewed determination, we plodded steadfastly onward. At one point, the pelting rain became stinging pea sized hail. The unrelenting hailstorm was fierce, blowing us about indifferently. We had difficulty in keeping our boots grounded, wavering about, as we did as a result of the pelting hail.

We looked about for any apparent refuge from the storm. We found ourselves huddled under the only visible small juniper tree which jutted out from the craggy rock face. It proved to provide no real shelter, however. The hailstorm continued to beat down on us. We were unable to see beyond our own boots. The foreboding storm was brutal.

A half hour seems longer when huddled together in a tiny space which provides no real shelter from a blustering storm. We tried to shield ourselves by turning our backs to the storm to diminish blowing rain turning into side wise pelting hail. The relentless howling wind forced us to remain huddle together as we waited out the worst of the storm.

When the storm eased up a little, onward we trudged, determinedly. sloshing through the rain-filled mud puddles, slip-sliding over clay ground that had become like slippery brown ice. Each step on the drenched ground was precarious. Rain and hail turned ground into slick mud. Our hike became much like skating on a frozen pond.

The thick terracotta mud clung to my hiking boots, making hiking a greater challenge, due to the added weight of clay on my boots. I was drenched to the bone. My rain suit provided little protection.

The hiker leading us down the mesa was over 80 years of age; spry and sprightly. He nearly danced down the mountain. His stamina and ease of fast-paced hiking, despite the conditions, was amazing to me.

I wondered how I would keep up with him, but I was determined to get out of the thrashing rains and pelting hailstorm.

I pulled my hood tightly around my face and watched intently his every step-slipping, sliding, and tromping—down we went, past footholds in the rock face that the ancient ones used. We passed noteworthy ruins that were barely visible beyond sheets of hail.

One step at a time, I told myself. *That is all you must do. Just one step at a time.* My feet became increasingly heavier with each step, as the slippery clay mud collected on my boots.

Eventually, we reached the slot canyon, where we descended, partly on all fours, partly by just seat sliding down each segment. Interestingly, when we arrived at the base of the mountain again, the sun came out to greet us! *Nice timing,* I thought ruefully.

When we returned to our campsites, piles of hail covered the ground. My tent's rain fly was torn off my tent and lay shredded on the ground beside it. As a result, the tent was filled with water. It was another reminder of the power and control of mother nature.

I considered that the experience was a powerful lesson from nature, which cleansed a part of me. I then felt renewed. I was pleased that I had found the inner strength to complete the hike despite all the weather-caused challenges of the weather we had endured along with my own health challenges.

Initially, when we were atop the mesa and as a group voting to continue the hike or turn back, I was not really looking forward to weathering the storm. But I was glad that I had done so. The experience reminded me there is an inner strength we can call upon when needed. Each of us has a wealth of inner strength that reveals itself when we find ourselves challenged with life's predicaments.

It was about then, when I recalled the emergency room physician's mandate, "rest, do nothing strenuous, and take your meds." *Oops*, I thought. *That went well.*

I looked down at my hiking boots, clotted with pounds of mud and mused, *hurrah for us human hikers who have the courage to accept the challenges that we face—even at the top of the mesa at Chaco.*

And hurrah for those ancient humans, who called this sacred place home long ago.

What about you?

When were you faced with a challenge, either physical or mental, in which you initially felt overwhelmed, yet you surprised yourself by rising to the challenge?

INSIGHT from your life:

Insight from *the Chaco Challenge*

HURRAH FOR YOU!

Chapter Twenty-six

THANKFUL FOR MY FALL

"It is during our darkest moments that we must focus to see the light."

Aristotle

When I unexpectedly had an accident by falling down a flight of stairs. As I was alone, I was faced with an incredible (to me) decision. Somehow, a glimmer of light, an option, occurred to me. It helped me deal with the painful injury. And as a result, it brought kind, caring and helpful people into my life.

Thankful for My Fall

It was pitch black that night, when my barking dog bolted from my bedside. Startled, I leaped up, in high gear, and raced after him, to discover the emergency that had alerted him.

In the pitch darkness, I tripped over the child gate that had been propped up in my bedroom doorway to keep my dog in the bedroom during the night. I fell headfirst, down many steps into the basement. Everything became black. When I had regained consciousness, I found myself outstretched at the bottom of the stairs, my body shaking uncontrollably, and teeth chattering loudly.

I thought, *Perhaps I won't live through this. I want to tell those I love that I care for them and want to spend precious time with them again.* But I was alone that night. No one would hear my plaintive calls. My cell phone was upstairs. It was a shocking thought to see how quickly one's day plans can change. I knew I had to fend for myself.

I tried to move. Each minor movement was agonizing. Gradually, I was able to upright myself, and then, I managed a slow agonizing crawl, dragging my right leg along.

I was in a dazed state, but I recognized that something was very wrong. I tried to think, but from a foggy state I couldn't determine why my leg wouldn't work. Also, my right hand didn't seem to function either.

By the time I crawled into the nearby bathroom on that floor level I was exhausted. I pulled myself up to the sink and looked into the mirror. I was aghast at the face that peered back at me. I saw a battered face and a wet blood-soaked nightgown. Swelling had already begun on my face. My eyes ached fiercely. My head was throbbing. I saw my right knee was swollen much like a large cantaloupe. Then I discovered my right-hand fingers. Two were stiffly locked in 90-degree angles and the middle finger had become turned completely backwards and was resting on the back of my hand.

At such moments in life, one has many odd thoughts. With a certain amount of disconnected calm, mine was, *Jeez, will I ever use it again*? Then came a second more sobering thought, *I may need help here.*

But with no means of contacting anyone,

I resorted to telling myself that if I were a cowboy riding alone on the open range and had such a problem, what would I do?

The answer was simple, but daunting. I would set my own finger! I took a deep and painful breath in, and then, I reached over and yanked my middle finger back into some proximity of normal position. I was surprised that I felt nothing, but likely due to my current state of shock.

Then I turned away from the disfigured image in the mirror and began a long and arduous trip upstairs. I crawled on one leg with my left hand and elbow supporting the painful upward movements, as I dragged the other lifeless, leg and hand with me.

I had intended to call for help when I reached my bedside, but as I lay down, I lost consciousness again.

It was daylight when I wakened with a throbbing headache, shooting pain in much of my body, and I found my teeth had chattered to such an extent, that one of them had become broken. Any movement involved tremendous effort and pain. As a result, I wanted to go to sleep again.

However, somehow, I forced myself to make a call, and I did receive help. Some friends took me to urgent care, and subsequently, I had x-rays and other medical tests to determine the extent of my injuries.

It took a long time to recover from the lingering effects of the accident, which involved a severe concussion, bloody nose, black eyes, bruised and battered rib cage, right leg, right knee; and right hand with disfigured fingers—one disjointed completely backwards. But, gradually, I graduated from lying in bed, completely helpless, to moving slowly around with a walker, then to a cane and then upright on my own.

I thought how amazing, and fortunate, that I didn't break a bone. When I became discouraged concerning my slow recovery progress, I reminded myself that I could have died in the headlong fall, down fourteen steep steps. It could have resulted in me being in a coma. I might not have had the presence of mind to jerk my finger back into place or to have stopped the bleeding. I was most fortunate.

I thought about those moments many times while recovering, and was grateful for my healing, and for the good medical professional care I received. But most of all, for the people in the tiny village of Pine where I resided. Their loving care was a nice reflection of the type of people living in our town.

After the fall, help came from many directions. I found some of the warmest, most caring, graciously giving human beings.

When I couldn't use my hand, or my leg, or my head for thinking straight and critically, these Earth Angels appeared from somewhere. And somehow, when I least expected it but most needed help, their helping hands were always there.

For a few examples, I didn't realize I wouldn't be able to drive my vehicle, walk correctly, open a jar or even a milk carton. I couldn't even turn doorknobs or write anything. I didn't think about the amount of energy it would take to find the right medical help using the phone, or who could help me with care of my dog.

It never entered my mind to be thankful for food that would come prepared in a container that one could open with one hand, for garbage that would suddenly disappear, so

I would not have to deal with it; for linens on my bed that would change themselves so that I might feel fresh, for groceries that could be purchased for me and put away in the refrigerator. And that other people would have to read mail and write checks for me. I never thought that being driven everywhere would feel like being "queen for the day" (once I got past that feeling of independence being sharply crimped.)

It never occurred to me when I had helped others for many years, that there is another side to the coin that is equally honoring to both parties. And that I would have the opportunity to experience that "receiving" side of the coin.

I didn't imagine that my handwriting, with my dominant good left hand, which was not injured, would appear shaky like a 90-year old woman's fragile fingers. It shocked me into realizing that the accident had impacted me more than I wanted to admit.

Good people become great when they arrive to help someone even when they are just acquaintances. I was most fortunate. I was blessed to be the recipient of such caring and kindness. From phone call messages voicing their care and concern to driving me even four-hour round trips to specialists, loan of a walker and cane, many people deserve to receive the Great Goodness People awards.

I suspect there are many of you reading this story that would have given me the same offerings of help. Here is my point here. It is rewarding to find that with many people the word "community" is a way of life.

As a result, in looking back, my head became clearer, my computer was repaired, my dogs were fed and groomed, my home was healthy, my refrigerator was stocked with nutritious and tasty food, my dishes were sparkling, my car tuned up, my television had new videos, my DVD now worked; I enjoyed free ice cream cone, my hair was clean, my outrageous cell phone bill was renegotiated, my storage room had been cleared out, and my backyard had no doggie leavings, my body and brain appreciated the healing treatments—due to both new and old friendships. And all that happened because of that one dark moment in the middle of the night.

Everyone who helped me directly and indirectly with their caring messages, their suggestions and their powerful prayers, deserved my heartfelt thanks.

In your life, you likely know some people like these caring, giving, real helpers of humanity. People who are caring, giving human beings without any thoughts of compensation for themselves. Most likely, you, too, are one of them.

Such givers of humanity represent a community that is not only special but strong and worthy of being a desired place to live.

Life is curious concerning the way in which we meet new friends and how we come to appreciate those already in our lives. Hurrah for friends, both new and old. Hurrah for humans who care!

What about you?

Can you recall a time when you or a loved one was injured, and you discovered good things came as a result of the incident?

INSIGHT from your life:

Insight from *Thankful For My Fall*

____

____

____

____

____

____

____

____

____

____

____

____

____

____

HURRAH FOR YOU!

Chapter Twenty-Seven

SPRINGTIME FLOWERS ADD MAGIC

"To see the world in a grain of sand, and a heaven in a wildflower, hold infinity in the palm of your hand and eternity in an hour."

William Blake

When I see children dancing and parents delighting in the magic of being outdoors in nature's wonder and beauty, I am happy to see their sharing with each other the magic that our world has created. This experience was pure joy to witness and to write about.

Springtime Flowers Add Magic

Springtime brought a colorful kaleidoscope of wildflowers. The early brittlebush with its bright, tiny, yellow flowers, the purples of lupine, the rich, golden, sunny desert poppies, the fire reds of paintbrush and many other colors pleasing to all eyes that bloom along Highway 87 that runs from our Arizona Rim Country down to Phoenix.

There were other breathtaking scenes, too. Stunning yellow-orange colors carpeted the hillsides and mountain valleys. Their dizzy splashes of brilliance left my eyes stunned with mountain magic. It was a powerful reminder to me that nature still has the best displays of grandeur and vibrant colors. It is hard to improve on such a feast for the eyes.

As I drove south to Phoenix, I saw people stopping by the roadsides, taking pictures or just standing and absorbing the stunning, magic carpet of blazing colors. Nature had brought out a dazzling variety of flowers almost in one springtime season. As I went along, I saw that a family had stopped by the roadside to enjoy the flowers. The young child had picked wildflowers and was handing them to her mother. I pulled over and stopped on the roadside to watch the tender interchange. With the help of her mother, the two began making a wreath for the child. The child's finishing touch for the wreath was a bright blue ribbon which the little girl removed from her hair.

Then with all the aplomb befitting such glorious surroundings, the child's mother ceremoniously placed the wreath of flowers on her little girl's head. The little girl began dancing around in the wildflowers. Her Father was busy with the camera, taking many shots of their flower child scene, certain to capture this fond memory. I still have this memory inside my head. I smiled at the sight of a simple joy of a family sharing a moment with nature.

A little farther down on my journey, I saw two young "elder teens." Their outlined forms were stretched out on the floral desert floor. Blue jean forms seem curiously intrusive in the patches of bedazzling orange flower-covered ground. I saw their entwined forms, sharing romantic touches, moving like the desert winds over the wildflowers. I smiled—romantic moments have real "flower power"!

Flowers have practical uses in our lives also. In the first part of springtime, I can be seen walking into the hillsides and wild crafting the first crops of the brittlebush.

It is the best springtime allergy relief that I have found. If gathered early, when the springtime allergies come in force, I have found many had good results to avert taking allergy medicines. Many people report it eliminates the severe sneezing or some have even abated their allergy symptoms all together. In preparing the tea, it is recommended to sip a few cups each day.

I remember studying wildflowers for desert herbology with highly respected teacher Peter Bigfoot of Reevis Mountain School in the Arizona Superstition Wilderness. Although rare, if he didn't know the exact remedy for a particular flower he would say, "It's good for the eyes." (Meaning the beauty of the flower is refreshing sight for us to see.)

I could see how this springtime brought such blankets of beauty for us to enjoy and indeed they were a remedy for our eyes. I thought to myself, "Enjoy them while they last, they are like all the seasons in our lives." These colorful flower fields dancing on the hillsides almost sang “We’re alive with music!”

Hurrah for the glory of springtime flowers and hurrah for the humans of all ages who love them!

What about you?

Can you recall a springtime that you delighted in nature's beauty? Or perhaps you saw children playing joyfully. What did you feel?

INSIGHT from your life:

Insight from *Springtime Flowers Add Magic*

____

____

____

____

____

____

____

____

____

____

____

____

____

HURRAH FOR YOU!

Chapter Twenty-eight

CRACKS OF LIGHT

"Every time you heal a dark part of yourself, you bring more light into the world."

Stephen C. Paul

Darkness can come into our lives in many ways. It can come from a feeling of loss of what we used to be and cannot reclaim. It may come as a blessing in disguise. At such times, the greater gift is to give ourselves kind compassion.

This is my story of remembering to give myself that compassion.

Cracks of Light

One moment in time can change a life dramatically. I experienced this impactful truth when I was broadsided by a young man driving a heavy Cadillac, while I was driving my little four-cylinder compact automobile. My little car was pushed down a side street for almost one block. I never knew it would impact my life so dramatically.

I wrote a poem at a much later date about the experience, which I include here as an introduction to my following story.

After I had been in rehabilitation long enough to be able to assess myself, I wrote the following words, which is my attempt to express what it was like to have a traumatic brain injury and live with it, on a daily basis.

Cracks of Light

"You'll be fine," they said.

Both strangers nodded in unison.

I knew it was a lie, even then.

I saw the fear in their eyes
As they turned away from me.

I tried to move but could not.
I felt myself floating upward
Somehow as though my body
No longer belonged to me.

Distant arriving sirens wailed,
Becoming increasingly louder.
Each moment ticked past,
As if waiting for a sentence.

Rain began falling on my face.
It was cool, somehow soothing.
But their faces still haunted me—
Something unspoken in their eyes.

I did not see my face until later,

When the doctors gave me
The walker I had said I didn't need.
I lied to myself, to remain sane.

Nothing seemed the same.
I felt like a menopausal teenager.
Erratic, unpredictable, unstable.
Unable to focus, function, think.

Then, with help of a walker,
I finally stood upright.
And, with each painful step,
Finally, I walked again!

It took a long time before
My brain injury was diagnosed.
Then began the longer process—
Rebuilding an unremembered self.

Can't go back, I told myself.
But how I longed for yesterday,
When I could float many projects
And delighted in daily challenges.

I struggled for familiar words
To form a simple sentence.
And hid from familiar faces
That had no meaning then.

Scars on my body healed faster
than my damaged brain and heart.
I held great sadness deep within,
For many unknown reasons.

But, finally, little cracks of light
Began to find their way within me.
When I took a deepening breath,
It set free some of my longings.

It didn't happen overnight, but
Came inch by inch, as I found myself
Building other nurturing skills
To help me create new parts of me.

I am very grateful for the progress.
Proud of help that I received.
Some of what was lost long ago
Recycled to me as different beauty.

Rebuilt through cracks of light,
My inner strength grew brighter.
I am grateful to those who helped me
Heal cracks from that moment in time.

###

The process of relearning the most basic

skills of human interaction was painful and laborious. I had a millisecond of attention ability. I could not find words nor stay focused long enough to construct a simple sentence. Everything seemed surreal, like a sci-fi movie. Nothing made sense any longer. My head pounded fiercely much of the time.

I had periods of blackouts, that I had no idea how they came about. I could not hold a thought for even a few moments. I searched in vain for words to express myself, and I felt as though I were in a bad time warp that held no meaning.

People came to my front door and acted friendly, until they realized that I had no memory of who they were—even long-term friends were wiped from my memory. When they realized that I didn't remember them, their disappointment turned into frustration and anger.

So, when I heard the doorbell ring, I would hide in our bedroom walk-in closet so that I didn't have to deal with the confusion and sadness, and the anger from people who at first acted friendly like they liked me.

I avoided all socializing. Fatigue,

frustration, intolerance, lethargy, depression, denial, lack of any motivation, were prevalent and inescapable daily.

I couldn't seem to communicate my thoughts, feelings, or produce any creative idea. My language was spotty and vague, and I couldn't find the right words, or even verbalize them when I thought of a word I wanted to use. My fragmented sentences only added to my disappointment of not being understood.

Sometimes whoever was listening to me would think that I had not heard their questions, so they raised their voices and shouted their question to me. They did not understand I did not have hearing loss, but an internal brain injury. When this occurred, I became silent and withdrawn. I felt that I didn't belong anywhere.

My executive functioning skills were diminished. With impaired memory and an attention deficit problem, my loss of judgment, organizational skills, and indecisiveness became daily challenges.

Sounds irritated my head like the nails scraping down a blackboard. The ringing in my ears was so loud I couldn't think properly. I was taken from audiologist to another and tried many different types of hearing devices. But none of them worked, since the prescribed apparatus was designed for an auditory solution, and not for a brain injury.

I was constantly afflicted by shooting and throbbing pains felt in my head. The headaches persisted, even with the heavy medications prescribed to alleviate them. They only dulled the pain somewhat.

After suffering with such headaches for many months, I went to my kitchen refrigerator freezer for something, and to my surprise, I placed my head in the freezer section and packed all the frozen foods on my head. I just stood there with the refrigerator door open. Soon, the painful throbbing in my head began to reduce in severity.

Wow, I thought. What is this about? But my head felt better. So, I made ice packs and packed my head nearly every day for a time. Later, I found learned that my brain matter was seriously injured to the extent that it was swelling and scraping against the inside of my hard skull, which was causing me the excruciating pain. No doctor had made that discovery!

I also found it hard to walk, as my balance was affected. It was impossible to carry on a conversation, so I kept quiet most of the time, for fear of being found to be "subnormal".

I couldn't read due to a short attention span and because my eyes ached much of the time. Too, my eyes lacked convergence and I had difficulty focusing. Things appeared blurry. I was supersensitive to light, and I wore dark glasses often. My sleep was erratic and unrestful, so my body was not restored for the next day.

When I looked outside, I felt as though I could have peeled away the picture of life in front of me and that nothing, but emptiness would remain. It felt as if I was nonexistent.

Time passed month after month, as I was driven to specialist after specialist, for treatment of my ears, eyes, and various internal organs. I also suffered a hip problem, injuries to my spine, my knee joint, my hand, head, and neck issues too.

No specialist diagnosed the traumatic brain injury until one day when I was getting a chiropractic adjustment in an attempt to alleviate a spinal problem, he said, "It appears to me that you have suffered a closed head injury also."

And he recommended that I see yet another specialist. His words about my having a brain injury made sense to me. I broke down in his office and sobbed. Intuitively I knew that it was true. We had been going about the "getting me fixed up" in the wrong way!

The doctors had felt that since I was an A+ type personality, if they fixed my body, I would be whole again. Their thinking was that I would be my old operational self again. That was their reasoning for my deep depression and my nonfunctionally penchant.

The neurological testing proved that indeed I had a severe traumatic brain injury. Until then, no one had addressed the subject of a brain injury. It was almost a half a year after the accident!

Then began the real work. At first, I was in denial concerning the severity of the brain injury, but finally I realized that avoiding and ignoring the reality was not going to fix the problem and bring about my healing.

I was in intense cognitive rehabilitation for more than a year, followed by less intensive cognitive rehabilitation. Finally, I was sent back to school to take English 101 class. It was a class I had taken many years ago when I was in college. But it seemed all new to me after the brain injury. A note taker was provided for me, as I couldn't listen and write at the same time.

There were many roadblocks and stops along the way, but a plan of action was finally in place.

Early on, I had difficulties functioning in daily life needs. As an example of my problems, frequently when I went to my dresser to get something to wear, I could not remember what was in the drawer. Even sticky notes were not helpful as I found it difficult to read them.

In our Brain Injury support group, most often we went around the room, tell who we were, what our injury was, and any other personal information that we wished to share.

One week, while at home in front of my dresser, it suddenly came to me, like a light shining through a crack in my head.

I was very excited to arrive at my support group that night and share my discovery. I told the group of my ongoing problem, and the way in which I had solved it.

I told them, as I stood at the dresser, I decided that everything in the top drawer, which was eye level, was for head wear. The next drawer at chest level, would have all my upper body apparel. From the waist up. The next drawer would have my lower body clothes, and the bottom drawer held all my leg and footwear. Wow! That was simple! And I would remember it because I would always have my own body with me! My fellow support group members were excited too.

So, it became a game for each of us to tell the group of a problem we might be struggling with, and during each week between our group meetings, we would all be working on solutions during the week.

We came up with some very helpful work-abouts for common everyday situations that traumatic brain injured (TBI) patients have which are unique to them. I came up with the idea that we should publish a book concerning our simple "work abouts" and I suggested that the title of the book be *Cracks of Light*.

Although we never followed through on the book, one day, my cognitive therapist invited me to take the challenge of learning the song signing to Whitney Houston's song *Greatest Love of All.* It was something I had planned to do prior to the accident.

At first, I hesitated, fearing I had not come far enough in rehab, but my therapist was very encouraging. So, I said yes. It was to be presented several months later at the National Head Injury Conference in our local city.

I arranged for a videotaping of the song by a professional signer. The video showed her signing from both front and side views.

Every day, for hours, I played the tape, frame by frame. Rewound it and played it repeatedly until I became too tired to remain focused.

I was not making the progress that I had hoped for and was becoming very discouraged. My brain of old would have easily learned that in a few days. But at that point in recovery, I labored over maintaining just a few of the signs.

I sighed heavily. Then left the house to go to the doctor's appointment. Somewhere along the way it dawned on me that the message I wanted to give to the conference attendees, was Whitney Houston's words, "The greatest love of all, lives inside of you." And I wasn't even giving that message to myself! How could I expect them to believe it?

I arrived home sobbing in relief. I had discovered what I needed for myself was compassion and to remember that love also lived inside me.

It still took me more than another month to learn the signing. But on the day of the presentation, I told the audience, "What I share with you today comes from my heart, and not my head."

Then I commented that we had spared no expense! We had Whitney Houston come and sing the song as I signed it. The audio-visual equipment worked just fine belting out Whitney Houston's powerful voice and my song signing went over well, too.

When I finished signing, everyone in the huge ballroom stood up, applauded and cheered me. When I think of that day, I feel chills down my arms. It was most definitely a red-letter day—one I will always recall with fondness.

And then, years later, I told my story at our Church service and then again signed the song, *The Greatest Love of All.* When I finished, the entire congregation stood and clapped supportively. I felt the same chills of appreciation and I felt twice blessed.

Today, when I am especially tired, I see some residuals of my brain injury limitations show up. But now I remember I am not my brain, nor am I my body, but a radiant being of love who cares greatly about our human race, my family and friends, and myself.

It is a good day, any day, to be alive and to be a loving human being.

Hurrah for *all* humans that overcome challenges and relearn to love themselves.

What about you?

Can you recall a time when you had an injury or lived with a limitation that prevented you from living life as you used to know it? What challenges did you face and how did you overcome them and learn to love yourself even more?

INSIGHT from your life:

Insight from *Cracks of Light*

____

____

____

____

____

____

____

____

____

____

____

____

HURRAH FOR YOU!

Chapter Twenty-nine

INDIAN MEDICINE MEN

"The greatest good you can do for another is not just to share your riches, but to reveal to him his own."

Benjamin Disraeli

I have learned healing methods from two native traditional Medicine Men who shared their healing ways and who influenced my life. This story is to honor their traditional ways of living and healing.

Indian Medicine Men

Two American Indian men who influenced my skills of healing were Mike Valenzuela, Aztec Medicine Man, and Willy Whitefeather, Cherokee Medicine Man.

I met Aztec Medicine Man Mike through my friend suggesting I get an appointment concerning a minor physical issue. I felt a strong connection with him as I felt his healing hands instantly correct my abdominal problem. As I got off the table, I felt as though I indeed experienced something very important.

He looked directly into my eyes and said, “You have the healing. Come follow me tomorrow.”

“Tomorrow” came and several of us shadowed Mike on his office visits. Each of his clients came in to see him with a variety of ailments.

Many people couldn’t explain what he did. Not even Mike could explain it. He said, “I can’t explain it, but my hands go into the body and people get better. I repair tissue and break up blockages. God gave me a special gift. As I keep me healthy, I can work on other people.”

The following day, a woman came in bent over with severe abdominal pain. Mike had all of us encircle the table on which she lay, and place our hands, stacked atop each other, on her abdomen. Mine were on the top of the pile. We all us sent healing thoughts to the woman and prayed for her.

Suddenly my hands began to tremble—first a shiver, then quite vigorously. I was surprised and concerned that I "wasn't doing it right." Mike came behind me and removed my hands from the stack.

Yep, probably not doing it right, I thought.

Then he had the others lift their hands and he placed mine directly on her. Still, I shook, but I felt comfort from the other hands now stacked on top of mine.

After a few minutes, the woman said, "The pain is gone! I can breathe easily."

When all our hands were removed, I felt rather woozy and weak.

I said to Mike in a worried tone, "What was I doing wrong? Why were my hands shaking as they were?"

He laughed, and he said, "You're a hand trembler. You have the gift, so you can come and apprentice with me, if you want. Her problem was that her soul was sick. Sometimes the pain goes away, but not the sickness. She needed a spiritual healing."

I considered that a high compliment. Unfortunately, I moved from the area, and I never followed Mike about. This Aztec Medicine Man is now in spirit. However, I still recall the simple ways he explained his gifted healings.

I recall that he said, "I am free to heal because I love myself and obey the universal laws. When I was three years old, I went to Guatemala to study from my revered grandfather, a medicine man, for fifteen years.

As a young boy, my mind was fresh and without fears. He showed me all the various organs and body parts, but it was like a movie and pictures were alive. They were in color and sound, and I could see the blood flowing and everything moving."

Another traditional American Indian with whom I studied was Whitefeather, a Cherokee Medicine Man. From him I learned how to read signs of the causes and effects upon our

Mother Earth, ceremonies that empowered us and healed others. His storytelling abilities were something I admired greatly. He gifted me with an eagle feather during a special naming ceremony and he bestowed upon me the Indian name “Keeshewa” meaning sunshine. I was also privileged to learn the Cherokee ways of healing and living in harmony with Mother Earth.

Typical of Whitefeather, was his devotion to helping people, no matter where he was. Each day he demonstrated how to be a kind and caring human being.

A simple example: I was having lunch with him in a restaurant. A disheveled, ragged man came in and sat in the booth next to us. It was clear he hadn’t eaten or bathed in a very long time, and his clothes clung to his body. His eyes remained downcast, as though to hide his feelings, or to avoid any other eyes looking at him. He ordered a cup of coffee and doused it with large quantity of sugar—for energy I thought.

Willy immediately got up and walked by his table, bent down, and pretended to pick up a five-dollar bill.

"Oh, sir, I'm sorry, but you must have dropped this, he said nodding his head in the affirmative.

The man's beaten, tired eyes looked up slowly. "No," he said sadly, "It isn't mine."

"It certainly isn't mine, said Willy. Don't know who lost it but looks like it is yours now!" He spoke in an encouraging tone, patted the guy on his back and added, "Have a good day, now, my friend."

No matter where Whitefeather went, he was always doing good for people. Besides learning the healing ways of the Indian from Mike and Whitefeather, my life was richly blessed from meeting them.

They were both truly a hurrah for humans.

What about you?

Have you ever been introduced to the Native Traditional ways of living? What were your thoughts about the value of such? And have you used any of their ways in your current life?

<u>INSIGHT from your life:</u>

Insight from *Indian Medicine Men*

____

____

____

____

____

____

____

____

____

____

____

____

HURRAH FOR YOU!

Chapter Thirty

TRUTH FROM GIANT REDWOOD TREES

"By choosing to live in Spirit, you entrust yourself to something greater than your life as a physical being."

Wayne Dyer

In life, we set out to experience one thing and very often, it brings us an unexpected lesson of a greater truth. I received this greater truth from a giant redwood tree.

Truth From Giant Redwood Trees

I rented a cabin deep in the Santa Cruz Mountains nestled among the coastal redwoods to escape my hectic business life in the city where I worked at Xerox Corporation. On weekends, I drove down from San Francisco to my little hermitage in the redwood forest.

Fresh smells of pine needles and rich earth smells always brought a smile for me. I breathed in deeply, sighed comfortably on the exhale, and walked to the back deck of my cabin.

I was thinking about my new friends, Kaylee and Justin, a young couple who had been married only about six months. They lived near me in the San Francisco Twin Peaks area.

They had been studying the predictions of Nostradamus and were convinced that they needed to live life to the fullest while they were still here on earth. They were spending all their money faster than they could make it, going deeper in debt and nonchalantly saying, "We only live once. Let's live it up! Everything will work out."

I must admit, I was a little incredulous and secretly critical about their momentary fun-life. I was raised with great emphasis on saving and preparing for the future. We were very judicious about using monies for practical needs, not “frivolous things”.

As I stood on my deck, I gazed out at “my redwood giants.” They had been spared from being cut down as the deck had been built around them. It was late afternoon, and the sunlight was streaming through the trees. *Magic, for sure,* I thought. I sat down on the deck and rested against a tree, picking up my current book, to read.

It wasn’t my personal choice, but I had promised my new couple-friends that I would read, cover to cover, the predictions of Nostradamus as soon as I arrived. And since I always try to keep my promises, I sighed, opened the book, and began to read about the catastrophic predictions of gloom and doom, and the destructive ways in which the world would shortly end.

Soon, I was engrossed in his lurking legacy. The cataclysmic upheavals of the world were graphically described: earthquakes, and the terror of fire and brimstone over our entire planet.

I closed my eyes and took a breath. It was too much to digest at once sitting. Suddenly, the ground began to shake and shudder. I was tossed back and forth with the undulating upheaval. The forest before me began weaving back and forth, in a blur.

I was stunned. At first moment, I could only guess it was *the* final earthquake that it would swallow this state up, breaking it off from the rest of the land mass. A second, more terrifying thought came, *perhaps it is true—perhaps this is the end of our world. The young couple may be right!*

Incredible, I thought, *that I am just reading about our world fate and here it started happening—at least a major earthquake for California!*

I felt panic racing through my head. My heart began racing faster. I heard the pounding inside my head. I could hardly breathe.

My first reaction was to run. Run to safety somewhere. But—where? I realized there was no way out. I couldn't get to any safe place.

In the next breath, something curious happened. Although my head was spinning in panic mode, my heart seemed to say, “The only safe place is within yourself.”

If there was no safe place to which I might run, no safety net, nothing I could do; then the best thing would be to accept “what was.” Silently I reassured myself that my safety was not outside myself, but deep inside, where my spirit would survive.

So, I breathed in deeply, and on the outbreath, I let go of all my struggling, and expectations that I would live through it.

In that moment, I experienced a profound, peaceful calm. I took another full easy breath, and I accepted as my fate, my death. I bowed my head and silent murmured, “Not my will but Yours be done.”

With that inside peacefulness, I noticed something peculiar. In my eagerness to find peace and safety, I had leaned forward to pray and now everything was still and silent.

It was then I discovered that my entire experience of the “big final earthquake in

California" was an illusion caused by my leaning against a redwood tree which was shaking vigorously, back and forth, in the gusts of the winds. As a result, I, too, shook.

I burst out laughing at the ridiculousness of my illusion. But instead of criticizing myself for being unaware, I decided to explore it further.

Then I saw deeper truth. I made my peace within myself, believing the great destruction of my world had come, and therefore even death was a place of peace for me. I was not afraid to die.

And now, "resurrected" from my own illusion, I could laugh at myself, but I could be thankful for knowing that it was my *belief* of what was happening that helped me deal with an issue that is very real for all of us humans—our fear of death.

I thought about my friends—the young couple and promised myself to add a little more balance to my life. I would be more spontaneous and frivolous, as though it was *my* last day to enjoy earth.

I sighed deeply with relief and hugged my

teacher, my redwood tree, as it continued to dance with me.

And I thought, Hurrah for our friends, these wise ancient trees. And hurrah for my young couple who could live in the now moments, and who had given me the opportunity to discover my own inner peace, on a deeper scale.

What about you?

Sometimes our great learnings come in the form of an illusion. Were you kind to yourself when you looked at your illusion and found a deeper truth of greater value?

INSIGHT from your life

from *Truth from Giant Redwood Trees*

HURRAH FOR YOU!

Chapter Thirty-one

A PITY PARTY

"Doing what you like is freedom. Liking what you do is happiness!"

Author Unknown

There may be times in our lives when we are so focused upon our specific issues that we lose sight of the bigger picture of life around us. This story shows how a little humor from a friend can help us gain perspective.

A Pity Party

I found someone who was an excellent example of a "pity poor me" person. She constantly complained about what seemed to me to be small, insignificant inconveniences in her day. From the person who zoomed ahead of her in traffic to breaking a newly polished fire-engine-red, long nail. I was amazed and a bit frustrated with the way in which she filled her days with complaining over such seemingly insignificant matters.

Since the woman was involved in my life for a while, which seemed much too long for my peace and serenity, I decided I must do something to maintain my sanity and peace. I thought of several things, but this is the one that I decided to try.

When I saw Jennifer coming towards me one morning, and she began her liturgy of complaints, I listened intently and then exclaimed in a most ardent and compelling tone in my voice, "Jennifer, HOW DO YOU DO IT?"

She was perplexed and her words stopped short. "What do you mean?" she asked in a baffled tone.

"Well, I don't believe *I* could bear up under all those things you have to deal with every day!" I exclaimed in a tone of urgency and explosiveness. "It would be waaaaay too much for me to handle," I added, to frost the first sentence.

Clearly, she stood there in a state of shock and perplexity. Finally, she countered reassuringly, "Oh, it isn't *THAT* bad!"

That was the day, an amazing thing happened to Jennifer and for me. She stopped incessantly complaining every day. Yes, there were times when she still whined and complained, but it was much less than previously, and on those occasions, I managed to slip in a comment when she did so, such as, "Is it *THAT* BAD?"

Jennifer then would catch herself, smile and chortle, "Well, I guess not."

That turning point was the day I also realized that in my own life, when I have felt overwhelmed or over-reacting to life situations, I would say to myself, "Well, is it THAT bad?"

Most of the times, I would chuckle within myself and think of Jennifer and her turnaround attitude. The gift she gave herself that day is the same gift that I continue to give myself.

Hurrah for us humans who are evolving and growing because we are willing to see ourselves and make a change to better ourselves and those people around us.

What about you?

Can you recall a time when you heard a friend complaining about many things and you wished you had a magic wand to calm and quiet them down? How about yourself? Have you caught yourself complaining unnecessarily too? Can you think of a humorous way to change that around into a positive outlook?

INSIGHT from your life:

Insight from *A Pity Party*

____

____

____

____

____

____

____

____

____

____

HURRAH FOR YOU!

Chapter Thirty-two

CANCER BRINGS HEALING

"One of the secrets of life is that all that is really worth the doing is what we do for others."

Lewis Carroll

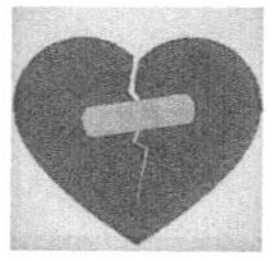

Because of a traumatic pronouncement to me about my advanced illness, I began to search for some way to heal my body without the standard methods currently used. My search took me on a new journey of discovery into health and healing.

Cancer Brings Healing

"You have serious advanced metastasized melanoma cancer," the doctor pronounced. His face was emotionless, as though he had made such pronouncements many times before. But this was the first time I had heard it. I sat in his office chair, in a stunned condition, staring with disbelief through him and into the distant vacant scene outside his window.

"Do you understand the seriousness of your situation? We must begin intensive cancer treatments immediately!" he added emphatically. He sounded very authoritative.

"No," I said, adding, "and I don't want to hear any more about it from you."

My hands were shaking as I stood up, turned, and stumbled blindly out of the office. The hallway was a blur, and sunlight seeped into the walkway making it impossible to see where I was going.

Most of that day I do not remember. I only remember not feeling anything and sitting motionless for hours without even thinking. It was as though I was in a war zone and was suffering from shell shock. I couldn't respond to friends that called. Finally, one friend came over to my home and told me something that felt real. Her words gave me hope that all was not lost, and she took me to a bookstore to get a book on natural healing.

She showed me Edgar Cayce's book concerning healing. As I exited the bookstore with my purchase, I began voraciously reading the book. Another friend told me about a healing program that Dr. Gladys McGarey created. It was a special retreat available for people with cancer. It was called Temple Beautiful. I decided to go there, longing for a place that felt safe, even if only for my feelings and my mental health.

At the program, the facilitator spoke of the body, mind, and spirit connection and how they were all connected. Heal one, heal the others. That sounded real to me. A great connection.

Throughout the healing program, we lived together, ate together, learned together, held each other, and allowed our tears to be shed, whenever they needed. Unburdening my heart fears felt like a key to recovery.

One night while at the retreat, I had a dream. It was a dark and stormy night, both outside and inside my dreaming head. Out of the stormy darkness, a flash of light came and then came a hand with golden light emanating from it. The hand touched my face where the melanoma was and instantly, I knew it was the hand of Christ that was touching me. I did not question its realness. I was certain. Upon awakening, I still felt the light tingling on the side of my face.

Later that day, one of the facilitators lectured on castor oil and its use. "It is called the Palma de Christo," we were told.

With some excitement stirring within me, I asked, "What does it mean, the "Palma de Christo?" "Palm of Christ" came the answer. And inside of me a huge feeling of tingling went up my spine, verifying that which I already knew. Immediately, I began using the castor oil packs on my body, without questioning. I had already felt the healing power of the hand of Christ. The oil packs felt like an anointing of that which was already happening.

At one point in the retreat, I said through my tears, "I don't want to die!" Dr. Gladys, (as she was called), with utmost compassion and, somehow, with the power that besets those quality people who have gone beyond such visions we possess, simply replied with soft, immutable power, "You, don't *have* to die, Ann."

Somehow when she spoke to me, her words felt like I was being given a powerful blessing to heal myself.

The healing surroundings that were created by Dr. Gladys McGarey and staff was something I will not forget—and it has helped sustain me in other medical crises also throughout the years. I went on to choose an intense natural healing therapy for my cancer treatment which lasted almost two years.

Many years later, I recognized that as a turning point in my life—a point at which I could begin to realize that we have our own inside intrinsic power of life force, where our natural state of being is health, happiness, and incredible unconditional love for ourselves.

In that elevated state of health, we cannot help but touch the lives of all those we come in contact. Dr. Gladys' way of touching and inspiring people was through her profession as a doctor, writer, public speaker, mother, grandmother, and many more roles.

But I believe the best way a person can help others is by living his or her life in such a manner that he or she is an example of that which all humans desire to attain when they are at their very best.

Dr. Gladys' authentic, dignified, honest, and healing ways of living her personal and professional life have inspired me through many personal challenges. She exemplified a true hurrah for humans.

What about you?

Have you been guided somehow to reach out to the right professional person, who helped you through a tough time who inspired you to be better than you were before meeting them? How has that person influenced your life today?

<u>INSIGHT from your life:</u>

Insight from *Cancer Brings A Healing*

____

____

____

____

____

____

____

____

____

____

____

____

HURRAH FOR YOU!

Chapter Thirty-three

CHIPS FALL AT CAMPBELL RIVER

"The magic in our minds is made real through the labor of love in our hands."

A.M. Eveland

I admire artists and creative craftsmen. Their ability to have an idea, laced with inspiration, and make it manifest in a tangible medium that we can all enjoy. I was surprised by the chainsaw artists in Canada and their amazing skills that created bigger-than-life-size art.

Chips Fall at Campbell River

The seaside town of Campbell River on Vancouver Island in British Columbia, Canada, is the salmon capital of the world. It is usually a tranquil, serene, and gentle village scene, much like our mountain village in Arizona.

However, things change quickly with the summertime event of the woodcarving contest. The last day of June, Campbell River becomes a bursting and bustling place. Woodcarvers and tourists alike pour into this little seaside town on the pacific coast.

Stout massive logs are hauled into the oceanfront park near the Sea Walk (a walkway that extends the length of town along the Pacific Ocean) all in preparation for their freedom celebration July First.

This event's enthusiasm quickly piques the curiosity of visitors as well as the residents themselves. Any Canadian can enter the contest. Some woodcarvers arrive early, eager to put their artistic skills to the frontier carving test. Some travel clear across the country to enter this world watched event.

When chainsaws begin to buzz loudly, crowds gather to watch these once giant trees transformed into art. As the cutting begins, chips fall wherever they may!

Deliberate and determined, artists donned in protective head and body gear whittle away at the massive logs. Chainsaws do the rough cutting; electric grinders, sanders and Dremel tools finish their pieces off. There is a prize, of $70,000 or more with several sections of entries.

With only a few days to finish their pieces, each artist chooses a design ahead. They work eagerly, cheered on by the growing number of onlookers.

This event creates a special type of community. Casual visitors mingle and chat with residents and artists. The spirit of the community is infused with many cultures and ages, but all of the people are cheering the cutters on.

The carvers help each other when one needs to move or lift the large heavy massive logs, fostering a feeling of comradeship in the competition itself. It has been a tradition there each summer for many years. And when the cutting is over, there is the silent bidding for the pieces.

Some carvers withhold bids on their pieces and donate them in devotion or recognition of special people or events. One year a carving was created for the victims of a disaster; another sold for $30,000. Sometimes the massive selections are left in the park for visitors to enjoy. The larger than life size carving that becomes part of the park display offers insights to the hearts and messages of the carvers. Each carving is their personal story, and they become the Sea Walk Park Beings.

When I planned my trip to Vancouver Island one summer, around the end of June, I extended my visit to beyond the first of July and enjoyed their traditional festival. They celebrate their Independence Day on July 1st, as we celebrate ours on July 4th. I sat up on top of a cliff that evening with friends and watched a magnificent display of fireworks. The magic of this island captivated my heart as I met some of the most genuine and caring folks. I was impressed with the cleanliness of this Island. The towns were spanking clean, without litter.

If you go to Campbell River, you will see the blues, greens, browns, natural colors of the earth which breathe easier, as Canada is very conscious of being GREEN. They have specific ways they reforest and plan for the future. They plant immediately and let other areas of the mountains rest to grow future wood. Frequent public awareness television shows and talk shows educate citizens of the importance of taking care of the earth for their heritage.

I was encouraged with the many ways they recycle and conserve, instead of glutting and over selling, making the consumer rush into stores to buy more things with disposable containers that fill our landfills.

I found the Canadian people to be well-mannered, some think to a fault. Respectful of laws, quieter by nature, and the children seem to have a respectful way of growing up; whining and yelling I did not see at all. They are civil in their social events.

And driving behind or in front of a Canadian? Well, road rage or even impatient honking just isn't experienced. They are patient if you don't start up quickly after the lights turn green. In their conversations, they tend to be considerate and polite. Boisterous and bawdy are quietly avoided.

I think their country is becoming stronger and their financial system healthier and they are good neighbors for us.

I enjoyed visiting our neighbors to the north, and seeing the trees transformed into massive, bigger than life statues with incredible details.

I was glad to return home to my Arizona mountain village with other pine trees and pleasant people.

I felt an enthusiastic hurrah for witnessing Canada's wooden giant carvings, for meeting our neighbors to our north and give my hurrah for the beauty in our Country too.

What about you?

When you have seen some magnificent art piece created by an artist's hands that was bigger than life, did it strike you with feeling of awe, appreciation, and wonder?

<u>INSIGHT from your life:</u>

Insight from *Chips Fall at Campbell River*

HURRAH FOR YOU!

Chapter Thirty-four

WINTER JOYS

"Through the eyes of a child, I see the world beautiful again."

A.M. Eveland

We can refresh the way we look at life at times when we see children with their excitement and wonder at things. This helped me look at my surroundings with fresh eyes and a bit of playfulness that winter morning.

Winter Joys

Winter snowstorms came in like a lion that winter, quickly dumping almost six inches and turning our townscape into a white wilderness of silence. Suddenly, everything was still and silent.

Some neighbors said the storm was dangerous. It caused accidents. Others sighed heavily when they had to shovel snow off their walkways. Some people avoided it completely and nestled inside their warmed homes.

There were some, however, who found delight in the weather. They were the children, who made us aware of how to enjoy the simple and free things of life. They delighted in the snow and in everything it covered.

It transformed all that it touched. The fire hydrants wore thick, white stocking snow caps. Rooftops groaned under the frozen blankets of white. The streets were silent, except for the soft whispers of the falling snow flecks that gently floated down from the equally white-covered skies.

There were no walkers around the lake where I live. No autos moving in the early morning, in which my breath sent clouds of mist into the air.

The only sound I heard when I took my morning walk was an occasional thump as a clump of snow fell from heavily laden tree branches. To be truthful, it was my faithful friend, my doggie, that got me to dress up like a stuffed penguin and take him outdoors for our early morning walk. Dogs are very smart, you know.

I was glad he did so. The morning had not melted any snow, but the streetlights shone brightly, revealing scintillating, and twinkling little silver-white specks falling to the ground.

My canine companion and I walked in silence, not wanting to shatter the breathtaking view with any unnecessary sound. I looked down at my black doggie as he pranced through the drifts and became spattered with quiet snowflakes. He shook them off from time to time, and I noticed his short legs caused his belly to skim on the snow. But they disappeared with each step he took. Neither of us objected.

Our feet crunched on the snow as we passed the boat dock, with one lone boat tied to post. Launching was impossible that day with a snowpack and ice forming on the water's surface.

I thought of my scientific-minded friend and of the fact, that if he had been on our walk, he perhaps would have said, "You realize, do you not, that snow is really small water vapors that freeze into tiny crystals high in the sky, in the cloud cover, and they then attach to each other and descend, turning into snowflakes. Even though snow and ice are made of the same elements, snow is composed of crystals of regular shapes, and the ice forms as solid chunks, or sheets of ice. It relates to the way that the water freezes into its final form."

He would have added, "Snow isn't white, even though it appears so to our eyes. It is colorless and it appears to be white as a result of minute reflections from the sun."

Well, that would be enough to tune me out. I like the appreciation that came to me concerning children and their fresh, nonanalytical way of experiencing snow.

We continued our walk, and observed many families, as they arrived, with their children dragging new toboggans uphill. Then, with respectful turns, they slid downhill, giggling and squealing with delight. The onlookers cheered, as though they were party to the planning of the activity.

I then paused and noticed a family introducing their toddler son to magical snow. In front of our town's Christmas-scene lights, they had helped their child erect his very first snowman. Certainly, it was moment to remember. With an approving nod from his parents, I snapped his photo. He then giggled with delight. I thought this to be a precious moment. It was a moment of frivolity.

In some way, this child's snowman creation had brought back memories for me, of snowball fights, larger snowmen (and snowwomen, yes, appropriately proportioned) along with nostalgic Christmas carols and bedtime stories.

I admit that I had become curious about the nature of snow and concerning the amounts of falling snow.

Later, from the internet, I learned that the most snowfall recorded in one year was 2,334 inches on Mount Rainier, in Washington state. And the world's largest snowflake was measured at Fort Keogh, Montana on January 28, 1887. It was measured at 15 inches across and was 8 inches thick. It did indeed make the Guinness Book of Records. *And that was enough research for one day*, I thought.

As I left the snowbound lake to the active, energetic, young ones, I ruminated, *the walk was well worth the time devoted to it.*

I scooped up a fist full of snow and let it fly. How good it felt to be a child again.

Hurrah for all of us humans who can still play like children again!

What about you?

When have you been touched by watching little children play in delightful innocence? Did that inspire you to do something spontaneous and a little childlike too? How did that feel for you?

<u>INSIGHT from your life:</u>

Insight from *Simple Joys*

____

____

____

____

____

____

____

____

____

____

____

____

____

HURRAH FOR YOU!

Chapter Thirty-five

MY MOTHER'S MESSAGE

"Clouds come floating into my life, no longer to carry rain or usher storm, but to add color to my sunset sky."

Rabindranath Tagore

My Mother's death impacted me greatly. I was overcome with sadness. As I drove back home, I wished the dark clouds in my heart would pass. Somehow, my prayers were answered through an unusual way.

My Mother's Message

My mother's funeral was on an October day in Tucson, Arizona. Mom's body was placed in the mausoleum beside my Dad.

It was an incredibly sad day, in which relatives and friends attended the service. Gathered were many relatives of our Green family. In some way, we felt a measure of solace and a lingering of her presence by being together with one another.

Each of the surviving adult children spoke, as a part of the service, honoring her. We then left her there with him—the man with whom she had celebrated more than 50 anniversaries—the man she had long ago chose to marry. Many things had happened since the exchange of the words, "I do."

Now, they lay peacefully in highest spaces in the mausoleum. She had once said, "I didn't let anyone walk over me in life, and I am not going to let them walk over me when I am dead." So, there they were looking down upon all their descendants, and high enough up to place their earthly remains a bit closer to heaven.

They had lived their lives with true, essential values and were rare salt-of-the-earth people. They had taught such values to their children. With their deaths, we were reminded of the values they had instilled upon us.

As I left Tucson, I drove the old back road to Phoenix. It was the one Dad always insisted on taking when he came up to see us. He didn't like the bustling, congested freeways.

The day of the service was bright and sunny, a sharp contrast to the heavy, gray sadness I felt. There was not a car in sight, coming or going, on the two-lane asphalt highway as I journeyed home to Phoenix.

I felt grateful to be alone—very alone. Being alone in my sadness, I allowed myself to sob freely. I sobbed and loudly cried out to my mother, "Mom, I feel lost without you. What do you want me to do now? Please tell me what you want now. Please!" I was rather startled by my cries. I sounded like a child. I sounded as though nothing would ease my pain unless I could talk to her again about all the feelings present in my heart and mind.

I was so fully immersed in my feelings, I did not notice that a small car suddenly came up behind me, closer than was comfortable, which startled me to full alertness. Then the car passed me, zipped over right in front of me, and then slowed down, causing me to have to de-accelerate also.

I felt a bit irritated by the sudden intrusion., and said out loud, “You’re so much in a hurry to pass me, then you slow down and stay right in front of me!” I growled my lament.

I was forced to go slower and with a solid yellow line, I could not pass, so I continued to follow the little car. Then I noticed the license plate. It read: “LivGrn.” What? I was startled. Since my family surname name was Green, it shocked me. And here, after my plaintiff pleading for a sign from my Mom as to what she wanted me to do next, came her message reading “Live Green.” Live GREEN! Was she saying, “Go on now and live the way I have taught you? You already know how. Go on and live as a real Green member of this family would do and carry on our family values throughout life.

As I reread the “message” out loud I laughed with glee. And then another surprise. The moment when I received the message and laughed out loud, the car ahead of me sped away and was soon far ahead of me, disappearing in the distance. Again, I repeated Mom’s message to me, ‘Live *Green*!’ Again, the highway was deserted and the awakening message from my mother still echoed loudly in my mind the entire drive back to Phoenix.

I shouted out, “Okay, Mom, I got it! Thanks!” I felt the message had instructed me to be a living example of the way in which she had lived and taught us the same values.

Hurrah for our human mothers who give us so much to carry forward in our lives, even after they have passed on. Hurrah for all of us humans that struggle to find new meaning in our lives after our mothers have gone.

What about you?

Have you experienced a connection with someone close who has passed on and somehow felt they have sent you a message? How did you feel when that happened?

INSIGHT from your life:

Insight from *My Mother's Message*

____

____

____

____

____

____

____

____

____

____

____

____

____

HURRAH FOR YOU!

ABOUT THE AUTHOR

Author Annemarie Eveland lives in a small town in the mountains of Central Arizona. She travels for both work and pleasure.

Her professional background is varied: Social Director at a five-star resort, created and operated her Le Picnic catering business, realtor, national speaker, presenter, ordained minister, certified in natural healing therapies, two advanced University degrees and is a certified consultant in personality profiling for corporate businesses and for individuals.

Since 1980, she has specialized in the science of reading people through their physical structure. Annemarie is certified as presenter, trainer, consultant, and personal counselor. Her trainings concerning *Reading People Before They Speak* have been presented in Canada, Mexico, Western Europe, and throughout the United States. Her audiences are varied, from trainings on cruise ships, Dale Carnegie Corporation in Mexico, schools, churches, private homes, businesses, organizations, and philanthropic presentations.

Annemarie has written numerous articles for newspapers, business journals, newsletters, and training manuals. Her children's storybook, *Keesha and the Rainbow Parrot Guide* and the *Guidebook* (a companion book for parents and teachers) teaches children how to appreciate themselves and understand other children who are different from them.

In addition, Annemarie designed and taught required graduate coursework at an accredited private college in Arizona. She is certified to teach all levels of the science she utilizes in reading people—before they speak. Trial attorneys have hired Annemarie as a professional consultant for jury selection and client preparation for trials.

Annemarie's passion lies in working privately with individuals who desire to master their minds, open their hearts, and appreciate their natural gifts and talents. Her insightful compassionate nature empowers people to appreciate who they are, teaches them how to deal with people different than themselves and helps them deepen connections with family and friends. A useful tool for dealing with people face-to-face.

She designed and facilitated many weekend retreats and enjoys creating private retreats for individuals who are intent on expanding their awareness and connecting to the deeper spiritual side of themselves.

Her featured guest appearances on TV, radio, talk shows, and keynote speaker at universities and business conferences have had wide appeal. For several years, she wrote inspiring human-interest columns for two newspapers in several states. Currently, she writes for an outdoor adventure magazine and freelances for other publications.

Annemarie is available for public speaking engagements, workshops, retreats, educational programs, consultations for organizations or for private sessions.

On the personal side:

Annemarie enjoys all forms of nature, traveling, writing, photography, watercolors, hiking, kayaking, natural healing, quiet contemplation and connecting meaningfully with people.

She cherishes family, good friends and is an active community supporter wherever she travels. Annemarie volunteers with Search and Rescue in the Arizona Rim Country as well as other humanitarian organizations.

She wholeheartedly believes, "We are one in spirit, but express ourselves as unique, individual human beings.

Hurrah for Humans!"

Made in the USA
Middletown, DE
27 July 2024

58042602R00166